Messing About in Quotes

Messing About in
Quotes

A Little Oxford Dictionary
of Humorous Quotations

Edited by

Gyles Brandreth

OXFORD
UNIVERSITY PRESS

OXFORD
UNIVERSITY PRESS

Great Clarendon Street, Oxford, OX2 6DP,
United Kingdom

Oxford University Press is a department of the University of Oxford.
It furthers the University's objective of excellence in research, scholarship,
and education by publishing worldwide. Oxford is a registered trade mark of
Oxford University Press in the UK and in certain other countries

© Oxford University Press 2018

The moral rights of the author have been asserted

First edition 2018

Impression: 1

All rights reserved. No part of this publication may be reproduced, stored in
a retrieval system, or transmitted, in any form or by any means, without the
prior permission in writing of Oxford University Press, or as expressly permitted
by law, by licence or under terms agreed with the appropriate reprographics
rights organization. Enquiries concerning reproduction outside the scope of the
above should be sent to the Rights Department, Oxford University Press, at the
address above

You must not circulate this work in any other form
and you must impose this same condition on any acquirer

Published in the United States of America by Oxford University Press
198 Madison Avenue, New York, NY 10016, United States of America

British Library Cataloguing in Publication Data
Data available

Library of Congress Control Number: 2018943464

ISBN 978-0-19-881318-7

Printed in Italy by L.E.G.O. S.p.A.

Links to third party websites are provided by Oxford in good faith and
for information only. Oxford disclaims any responsibility for the materials
contained in any third party website referenced in this work.

Contents

Foreword   *vii*

List of Subjects   *xi*

Quotations   1

Foreword

Believe me, there is *nothing*–absolutely nothing–half so much worth doing as simply messing about in quotes.

I know. I have been doing it for years–since I was eleven, in fact. I can be precise about the date because it was when I was eleven that I started to keep a diary and in my diary, as well as listing my favourite sweets (Spangles), my favourite television programme (*Billy Bunter*) and my favourite book (*The Wind in the Willows* by Kenneth Grahame), on a regular basis I made a note of memorably amusing quotations. The first one that I recorded was a line that I was introduced to by my father. It came from a short story by Saki (the pen name of H. H. Munro):

> *The cook was a good cook, as cooks go; and as cooks go, she went.*

I knew nothing about Saki and his mordantly witty work at the time, but I loved the line. It was the brilliance of the word-play that delighted me. Sixty years on, it still does. Saki, you will be pleased to know, features in this little Oxford dictionary of humorous quotations, alongside several more of my father's favourite quotable authors, including Mark Twain, Jerome K. Jerome, Dorothy Parker and, of course, P. G. Wodehouse:

> *The Right Hon. was a tubby little chap who looked as if he had been poured into his clothes and had forgotten to say 'When!'*

This may be a little book, but it isn't lacking in ambition. It aims to provide you with the best from the classic repertoire of pithy, witty observers of the human condition (from Woody Allen to Oscar Wilde) and to introduce you to plenty of surprises and contemporary *bon mots*. There are a good number of quotations here that have never been anthologized before.

'If you steal from one author,' according to the American playwright Wilson Mizner, 'it's plagiarism; if you steal from many, it's research.' Happily, we are not stealing from anyone. We are borrowing, with acknowledgement. But there has been research. All our quotations come from verifiable sources and the fact that this collection has the authority it does is thanks to Susan Ratcliffe, Associate Editor, Quotations, at Oxford University Press. I also want to acknowledge my debt to my wife, Michele Brown, who is responsible for finding many of the more unexpected and illuminating gems in the collection–such as this from the American comedian, Elayne Boosler:

> *You never see a man walking down the street with a woman who has a little pot belly and a bald spot.*

As well as wit, wisdom and sound advice ('Always buy a good pair of shoes and a good bed–if you're not in one you're in the other' Gloria Hunniford), there is a nice selection of unintended humour in the pages that follow, including contributions from the master of the genre, George W. Bush, forty-third President of the United States:

> *Our enemies are innovative and resourceful, and so are we. They never stop thinking about new ways to harm our country and our people, and neither do we.*

In the hope that you will find this a useful as well as an entertaining volume, the quotations are arranged by theme. Whether you are making a presentation or giving a wedding speech or addressing a political rally for the first time, I trust you will find something here to assist you as you prepare what you are planning to say. At school and university I regularly used quotations to give my essays a lift ('I always have a quotation for everything–it saves original thinking' Dorothy L. Sayers). In my working life–as a journalist, as an author, as a member of parliament, and as a professional after-dinner speaker–I have never been entirely lost for words, thanks to the quantity of quotations I have squirrelled away over the years. These, I reckon, are the best of them.

Enjoy.

Gyles Brandreth
2018

List of Subjects

Academic Life
Acting
Actors
Advertising
Advice
Ageing
Ambition
America
Anger and Argument
Animals and Birds
Apology and Excuses
Appearance
Architecture
Argument *see Anger and Argument*
The Aristocracy
The Armed Forces
Art
Audiences
Australia
Autobiography
Awards and Honours

Baseball
Beauty
Betting and Gambling
The Bible
Biography
Birds *see Animals and Birds*

Birth and Pregnancy
The Body
Books
Bores
Boxing
The British
Bureaucracy
Business

Canada
Catchphrases *see Comedy Routines and Catchphrases*
Cats and Dogs
Censorship
Certainty and Doubt
Challenges *see Life and its Challenges*
Champagne
Character
Children
Choice
Christmas
The Cinema
Cities *see Towns and Cities*
Class
The Clergy
Colours
Comebacks

List of Subjects

Comedy Routines and
    Catchphrases
Computers and the Internet
Conversation
Cookery
Countries and Peoples
The Country *see Nature
    and the Country*
Cricket
Crime and Punishment
Critics and Criticism

Dance
Dating
Death
Debt
Definitions
Democracy
Depression
Description
Despair *see Hope and
    Despair*
Diaries
Dictionaries
Diets
Diplomacy
Discontent *see Satisfaction
    and Discontent*
Divorce
Dogs *see Cats and Dogs*
Doubt *see Certainty and
    Doubt*
Dreams *see Sleep and Dreams*
Dress
Drink

Driving
Drugs
Drunkenness and
    Hangovers

Eating
Economics
Education
Enemies
England
Epitaphs
Examinations
Excuses *see Apology and
    Excuses*
Exercise

Faces
Failure
Fame
The Family
Family Life
Fashion
Feminism
Film Producers and
    Directors
Film Stars
Fishing
Flattery *see Praise and
    Flattery*
Flying
Food
Foolishness
Football
France
Friends

Funerals
The Future *see Past, Present, and Future*

Gambling *see Betting and Gambling*
Games *see Sports and Games*
Gardens
The Generation Gap
Gifts
God
Golf
Gossip
Government

Hair
Handwriting
Hangovers *see Drunkenness and Hangovers*
Happiness
Headlines
Health *see Sickness and Health*
Heroes
History
Holidays
Hollywood
Honours *see Awards and Honours*
Hope and Despair
Hospitality *see Parties and Hospitality*
Housework
The Human Race
Humour

Husbands
Hypocrisy

Ideas
Idleness
Ignorance
Insults
Intelligence and Intellectuals
The Internet *see Computers and the Internet*
Ireland and the Irish

Jewellery
Journalism
Judges

Kissing

Language
Languages
Last Words
The Law
Lawyers
Letters
Libraries
Lies
Life and its Challenges
Lifestyle
Literature
Love

Management
Manners
Marriage

List of Subjects

Medicine
Memory
Men
Men and Women
Mental Health
Middle Age
The Mind
Mistakes and Misfortunes
Modern Life
Money
Morality
Mothers
Movies *see The Cinema*
Murder
Music
Musicians

Names
Nature and the Country
Newspapers

Office Life
Old Age
Opera
Optimism and Pessimism

The Paranormal
Parents
Parliament
Parties and Hospitality
Past, Present, and Future
People and Personalities
Peoples *see Countries and Peoples*

Personalities *see People and Personalities*
Pessimism *see Optimism and Pessimism*
Philosophy
Poetry
Poets
Political Parties
Politicians
Politics
Poverty
Power
Praise and Flattery
Pregnancy *see Birth and Pregnancy*
Prejudice
Present *see Past, Present, and Future*
Presidents
Prime Ministers
Progress
Publishing
Punishment *see Crime and Punishment*
Puns

Quotations

Reading
Relationships
Religion
Restaurants
Retirement
Royalty

Satisfaction and Discontent
Science
Scotland
Secrecy
Self-Knowledge and
    Self-Deception
Sex
Sickness and Health
Singing *see Songs and
    Singing*
Sleep and Dreams
Snobbery
Society and Social Life
Songs and Singing
Speeches
Sports and Games
Statistics
Success

Taxes
Technology
Telegrams
Television
Tennis
The Theatre
Time
Towns and Cities

Transport
Travel
Trust and Treachery
Truth

Unintended Humour
The Universe

Virtue and Vice

Wales
War
Wealth
The Weather
Weddings
Wine
Wit and Wordplay
Wives
Women and Woman's Role
Wordplay *see Wit and
    Wordplay*
Words
Work
Writers
Writing

Youth

Academic Life

see also EDUCATION

You can always tell a Harvard man, but you can't tell him much.

James Barnes 1866-1936 American writer

No academic person is ever voted into the chair until he has reached an age at which he has forgotten the meaning of the word 'irrelevant'.

Francis M. Cornford 1874-1943 English academic

Old professors never die, they merely lose their faculties.

Stephen Fry 1957- English comedian, actor, and writer

I find that the three major administrative problems on campus are sex for the students, athletics for the alumni, and parking for the faculty.

Clark Kerr 1911-2003 American academic

In university they don't tell you that the greater part of the law is learning to tolerate fools.

Doris Lessing 1919-2013 English writer

of writer friends with degrees in English:

University seems to have turned them into Conan the Grammarians, who fret over perfect sentence construction.

Kathy Lette 1958- Australian writer

The Socratic method is a game at which only one (the professor) can play.

Ralph Nader 1934- American consumer protectionist

1

replying to Woodrow Wilson's 'And what in your opinion is the trend of the modern English undergraduate?':

Steadily towards drink and women, Mr President.

F. E. Smith 1872–1930 British Conservative politician and lawyer

Acting

see also ACTORS, FILM STARS, THEATRE

METHOD ACTOR: What is my motivation?
ABBOTT: Your job.

George Abbott 1887–1995 American director, producer, and dramatist

CLAUDETTE COLBERT: I knew these lines backwards last night.
NOËL COWARD: And that's just the way you're saying them this morning.

Noël Coward 1899–1973 English dramatist, actor, and composer

when asked to say something terrifying during rehearsals:

We open in two weeks.

John Gielgud 1904–2000 English actor

when asked by Michael Hordern for advice before playing Lear for the first time:

All I can tell you is, get a light Cordelia.

John Gielgud 1904–2000 English actor

An actor is a kind of a guy who if you ain't talking about him ain't listening.

George Glass 1910–84 American film producer

JOSEPHINE HULL: Shakespeare is so tiring. You never get a chance to sit down unless you're a king.

George S. Kaufman 1889-1961 and **Howard Teichmann** 1916-87 American dramatists, *in the film* The Solid Gold Cadillac

on nudity:

The part never calls for it. And I've never ever used that excuse. The box office calls for it.

Helen Mirren 1945- English actress

I used to work for a living, then I became an actor.

Roger Moore 1927-2017 English actor

Acting is merely the art of keeping a large group of people from coughing.

Ralph Richardson 1902-83 English actor

I wish sir, you would practise this without me. I can't stay dying here all night.

Richard Brinsley Sheridan 1751-1816 Irish dramatist and Whig politician

I told Mad Frankie Fraser 'I'm doing Hamlet'—he said, 'I'll do him for you.'

Arthur Smith 1954- English comedian

definition of acting:

Shouting in the evenings.

Patrick Troughton 1920-87 British actor

Talk low, talk slow, and don't say much.

John Wayne 1907-79 American actor

They say an actor is only as good as his parts. Well, my parts have done me pretty well, darling.

Barbara Windsor 1937- English actress

 # Actors

see also ACTING, FILM STARS

My only regret in the theatre is that I could never sit out front and watch me.

John Barrymore 1882-1942 American actor

This Thane of Cawdor would be unnerved by Banquo's valet, never mind Banquo's ghost.

Alan Brien 1925-2008 English journalist, *of Michael Hordern in* Macbeth

Tallulah Bankhead barged down the Nile last night as Cleopatra—and sank.

John Mason Brown 1900-69 American critic

You were the first person I thought of to play a chimpanzee.

Tim Burton 1958- American film director, *asking Helena Bonham Carter to star in* Planet of the Apes

She [Edith Evans] took her curtain calls as though she had just been un-nailed from the cross.

Noël Coward 1899-1973 English dramatist, actor, and composer

seeing a poster for Michael Redgrave and Dirk Bogarde in The Sea Shall Not Have Them:

I fail to see why not; everyone else has.

Noël Coward 1899-1973 English dramatist, actor, and composer

of Creston Clarke as King Lear:

He played the King as though under momentary apprehension that someone else was about to play the ace.

Eugene Field 1850-95 American writer

Dear Ingrid—speaks five languages and can't act in any of them.

John Gielgud 1904-2000 English actor, *of Ingrid Bergman*

She was good at playing abstract confusion in the same way that a midget is good at being short.

Clive James 1939- Australian critic and writer,
on Marilyn Monroe

There were three things that Chico was always on—a phone, a horse or a broad.

Groucho Marx 1890-1977 American film comedian

watching Spencer Tracy on the set of Dr Jekyll and Mr Hyde:

Which is he playing now?

W. Somerset Maugham 1874-1965 English novelist

Left eyebrow raised, right eyebrow raised.

Roger Moore 1927-2017 English actor, *summary of his acting range*

of Katharine Hepburn at the first night of The Lake:

She ran the whole gamut of the emotions from A to B.

Dorothy Parker 1893-1967 American critic

Any man who hates dogs and babies can't be all bad.

Leo Rosten 1908-97 American writer and social scientist,
of W. C. Fields, and often attributed to him

It is greatly to Mrs Patrick Campbell's credit that, bad as the play was, her acting was worse.
George Bernard Shaw 1856-1950 Irish dramatist

Forty years ago he was Slightly in *Peter Pan*, and you might say that he has been wholly in *Peter Pan* ever since.
Kenneth Tynan 1927-80 English theatre critic, *of Noël Coward*

on the Burton-Taylor Private Lives:
He's miscast and she's Miss Taylor.
Emlyn Williams 1905-87 Welsh dramatist

 Advertising

Doing business without advertising is like winking at a girl in the dark. You know what you are doing but nobody else does.
Stewart Henderson Britt 1907-79 American advertising consultant

Advertising may be described as the science of arresting human intelligence long enough to get money from it.
Stephen Leacock 1869-1944 Canadian humorist

The consumer isn't a moron; she is your wife.
David Ogilvy 1911-99 British-born advertising executive

asked why he had made a commercial for American Express:
To pay for my American Express.
Peter Ustinov 1921-2004 British actor

Don't sell the steak, sell the sizzle.
Elmer Wheeler American salesman

Advice

Never play cards with a man called Doc. Never eat at a place called Mom's. Never sleep with a woman whose troubles are worse than your own.

Nelson Algren 1909-81 American novelist

Consult, *v.* To seek another's approval of a course already decided on.

Ambrose Bierce 1842-c.1914 American writer

Be yourself. That's the worst advice you could give an impressionist.

Rory Bremner 1961- British impressionist and comedian

Start every day with a smile and get it over with.

W. C. Fields 1880-1946 American humorist

appearing as an agony aunt:

QUESTION: My fiancé gave me a car, a mink coat, and a stove. Is it proper for me to accept these gifts?
GABOR: Of course not! Send back the stove.

Zsa Zsa Gabor 1917-2016 Hungarian-born actress

Always buy a good pair of shoes and a good bed—if you're not in one you're in the other.

Gloria Hunniford 1941- British broadcaster, *advice from her mother*

It's useless to hold a person to anything he says while he's in love, drunk or running for office.

Shirley MacLaine 1934- American actress

Don't accept rides from strange men, and remember that all men are strange as hell.

    Robin Morgan 1941- American feminist

When in doubt buy shoes.

    Marcelle D'Argy Smith British journalist

Dr Ruth says we women should tell our lovers how to make love to us. My boyfriend goes nuts if I tell him how to drive.

    Pam Stone 1959- American comedian

Above all, gentlemen, not the slightest zeal.

    Charles-Maurice de Talleyrand 1754-1838 French statesman

Always be sincere, even if you don't mean it.

    Harry S. Truman 1884-1972 American Democratic statesman

 # Ageing

see also MIDDLE AGE, OLD AGE

It's sad to grow old—but nice to ripen.

    Brigitte Bardot 1934- French actress

I can remember when the air was clean and sex was dirty.

    George Burns 1896-1996 American comedian

Grandchildren don't make a man feel old; it's the knowledge that he's married to a grandmother.

    G. Norman Collie

The years that a woman subtracts from her age are not lost. They are added to the ages of other women.

    Diane de Poitiers 1499-1566 French mistress of Henri II

Life begins at 40—but so do fallen arches, rheumatism, faulty eyesight, and the tendency to tell the same story to the same person three or four times.

William Feather 1889-1981 American writer

I'm over the hill, but nobody prepared me for what was going to be on the other side.

Jane Fonda 1937- American actress, *on being 70*

QUESTIONER: Which of the Gabors is the oldest?
ZSA ZSA: She vould never admit it, but it's Mama.

Zsa Zsa Gabor 1917-2016 Hungarian-born actress

You know you're getting old when the candles cost more than the cake.

Bob Hope 1903-2003 American comedian

the new five ages of man:
Lager, Aga, Saga, Viagra, Gaga.

Virginia Ironside 1945- English journalist

A woman telling her true age is like a buyer confiding his final price to an Armenian rug dealer.

Mignon McLaughlin 1913-83 American writer

When you've reached a certain age and think that a face-lift or a trendy way of dressing will make you feel twenty years younger, remember—nothing can fool a flight of stairs.

Denis Norden 1922- English humorist

George, you're too old to get married again. Not only can't you cut the mustard, honey, you're too old to open the jar.

LaWanda Page 1920-2002 American comedienne, *at a dinner to honour George Burns*

9

Age is a question of mind over matter. If you don't mind, it doesn't matter.

Leroy ('Satchel') Paige 1906-82 American baseball player

I said to my husband, my boobs have gone, my stomach's gone, say something nice about my legs. He said, 'Blue goes with everything'.

Joan Rivers 1933-2014 American comedienne

Just remember, once you're over the hill you begin to pick up speed.

Charles Monroe Schulz 1922-2000 American cartoonist

One should never trust a woman who tells one her real age. A woman who would tell one that, would tell one anything.

Oscar Wilde 1854-1900 Irish dramatist and poet

😄 Ambition

seeing a commemorative stone engraved 'Laid by the Poet Laureate' (John Masefield):

Every nice girl's ambition.

John Betjeman 1906-84 English poet

At the age of six I wanted to be a cook. At seven I wanted to be Napoleon. And my ambition has been growing steadily ever since.

Salvador Dali 1904-89 Spanish painter

The average Hollywood film star's ambition is to be admired by an American, courted by an Italian, married to an Englishman, and have a French boyfriend.

Katharine Hepburn 1907-2003 American actress

For years politicians have promised the moon, I'm the first one to be able to deliver it.

Richard Milhous Nixon 1913-94 American Republican statesman

Everybody wants to save the earth; nobody wants to help Mom do the dishes.

P. J. O'Rourke 1947- American humorous writer

When I was a child, my mother said to me 'If you become a soldier, you'll be a general. If you become a monk, you'll end up as the Pope.' Instead, I became a painter and wound up as Picasso.

Pablo Picasso 1881-1973 Spanish painter

I always wanted to be somebody, but now I realise I should have been more specific.

Lily Tomlin 1939- American comedienne and actress

on being advised against joining the overcrowded legal profession:
There is always room at the top.

Daniel Webster 1782-1852 American politician

America

see also TOWNS

California is a fine place to live—if you happen to be an orange.

Fred Allen 1894-1956 American humorist

I had forgotten just how flat and empty it [middle America] is. Stand on two phone books almost anywhere in Iowa and you get a view.

Bill Bryson 1951- American travel writer

When you're born, you get a ticket to the freak show.
If you're born in America, you get a front row seat.
   George Carlin 1937-2008 American comedian

When I was a boy I was told that anybody could become
President. I'm beginning to believe it.
   Clarence Darrow 1857-1938 American lawyer

The thing that impresses me most about America is the
way parents obey their children.
   Edward VIII 1894-1972 British king

Never criticize Americans. They have the best taste that
money can buy.
   Miles Kington 1941-2008 English humorist

So I really think that American gentlemen are the best after
all, because kissing your hand may make you feel very very
good but a diamond and safire bracelet lasts forever.
   Anita Loos 1893-1981 American writer

The continental United States slopes gently from east to
west, with the result that everything with a screw loose
rolls into California.
   John Naughton 1946- Irish academic

Wherever there is suffering, injustice and oppression, the
Americans will show up, six months late, and bomb the
country next to where it's happening.
   P. J. O'Rourke 1947- American humorous writer

In America any boy may become President and I suppose
it's just one of the risks he takes!
   Adlai Stevenson 1900-65 American Democratic politician

In Europe, when a rich woman has an affair with a conductor, they have a baby. In America, she endows an orchestra for him.

Edgard Varèse 1885-1965 French-born American composer

The land of the dull and the home of the literal.

Gore Vidal 1925-2012 American writer

The youth of America is their oldest tradition. It has been going on now for three hundred years.

Oscar Wilde 1854-1900 Irish dramatist and poet

Anger and Argument

Anger makes dull men witty, but it keeps them poor.

Francis Bacon 1561-1626 English courtier

Violence is the repartee of the illiterate.

Alan Brien 1925-2008 English journalist

The time for action is past. Now is the time for senseless bickering!

Ashleigh Brilliant 1933- American writer and cartoonist

I've never won an argument with her; and the only times I thought I had I found out the argument wasn't over yet.

Jimmy Carter 1924- American Democratic statesman, *of his wife Rosalynn*

What counts is not necessarily the size of the dog in the fight—it's the size of the fight in the dog.

Dwight D. Eisenhower 1890-1969 American Republican statesman

I'll not listen to reason...Reason always means what
someone else has got to say.
   Elizabeth Gaskell 1810-65 English novelist

There is no arguing with Johnson; for when his pistol
misses fire, he knocks you down with the butt end of it.
   Oliver Goldsmith 1730-74 Irish writer

Any stigma, as the old saying is, will serve to beat a dogma.
   Philip Guedalla 1889-1944 British historian

The only person who listens to both sides of a husband
and wife argument is the woman in the next apartment.
   Sam Levenson 1911-80 American humorist

John Major's self-control in cabinet was rigid. The most
angry thing he would ever do was to throw down his
pencil.
   Gillian Shephard 1940- English Conservative politician

*on seeing two Edinburgh women hurling insults at one another across
an alleyway:*
Those two women will never agree; they are arguing from
different premises.
   Sydney Smith 1771-1845 English essayist

Animals and Birds
see also CATS

The lion and the calf shall lie down together but the calf
won't get much sleep.
   Woody Allen 1935- American film director, writer, and actor

A hen is only an egg's way of making other eggs.
Samuel Butler 1835-1902 English novelist

I am fond of pigs. Dogs look up to us. Cats look down on us. Pigs treat us as equal.
Winston Churchill 1874-1965 British Conservative statesman

Animals generally return the love you lavish on them by a swift bite in passing—not unlike friends and wives.
Gerald Durrell 1925-95 English zoologist and writer

after an operation to remove a fishbone stuck in her throat:
After all these years of fishing, the fish are having their revenge.
Queen Elizabeth, the Queen Mother 1900-2002

Honey bees are amazing creatures. I mean, think about it, do earwigs make chutney?
Eddie Izzard 1962- British comedian

No animal should ever jump up on the dining room furniture unless absolutely certain that he can hold his own in the conversation.
Fran Lebowitz 1950- American writer

One disadvantage of being a hog is that at any moment some blundering fool may try to make a silk purse out of your wife's ear.
J. B. Morton 1893-1975 British journalist

My mother made me ride horses when I was young. I didn't like it. They're too difficult to steer.
Stirling Moss 1929- British motor-racing driver

God in His wisdom made the fly
And then forgot to tell us why.
   Ogden Nash 1902-71 American humorist

I live in a city. I know sparrows from starlings. After that
everything's a duck as far as I'm concerned.
   Terry Pratchett 1948-2015 English fantasy writer

I know two things about the horse
And one of them is rather coarse.
   Naomi Royde-Smith c.1875-1964 English novelist and dramatist

😄 Apology and Excuses

VERY SORRY CAN'T COME. LIE FOLLOWS BY POST.
   Lord Charles Beresford 1846-1919 British politician, *message to
   the Prince of Wales, on being summoned to dine at the eleventh hour*

Go ahead and do it. It is much easier to apologize than it is
to get permission.
   Grace Hopper 1906-92 American naval officer and computer
   scientist

Several excuses are always less convincing than one.
   Aldous Huxley 1894-1963 English novelist

on being asked to apologize for calling a fellow MP a liar:
Mr Speaker, I said the honourable member was a liar it is
true and I am sorry for it. The honourable member may
place the punctuation where he pleases.
   Richard Brinsley Sheridan 1751-1816 Irish dramatist and
   Whig politician

JOHN MCGINLEY: Excuses are like assholes, Taylor—everybody's got one.

Oliver Stone 1946- American film director, *in the film* Platoon

It is a good rule in life never to apologize. The right sort of people do not want apologies, and the wrong sort take a mean advantage of them.

P. G. Wodehouse 1881-1975 English-born writer

I nearly missed the show tonight. I got to the Underground and saw this sign: 'Dogs must be carried on the escalators.' Took me forty minutes to find one.

Harry Worth 1917-89 English comedian

Appearance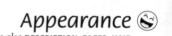

see also DESCRIPTION, FACES, HAIR

to her former lover Lord Alington as he dined with another woman in a restaurant:

Don't you recognize me with my clothes on?

Tallulah Bankhead 1903-68 American actress

I refuse to think of them as chin hairs. I think of them as stray eyebrows.

Janette Barber 1953- American comedian and producer

She is not so much dressed as richly upholstered.

J. M. Barrie 1860-1937 Scottish writer and dramatist

I know I looked awful because my mother phoned and said I looked lovely.

Jo Brand 1957- English comedian, *after getting a makeover on television*

Appearance

After forty a woman has to choose between losing her figure or her face. My advice is to keep your face, and stay sitting down.

Barbara Cartland 1901-2000 English writer

Sunburn is very becoming—but only when it is even—one must be careful not to look like a mixed grill.

Noël Coward 1899-1973 English dramatist, actor, and composer

Even I don't wake up looking like Cindy Crawford.

Cindy Crawford 1966- American model

The most delightful advantage of being bald—one can hear snowflakes.

R. G. Daniels 1916-93 British magistrate

A drag queen's like an oil painting: You gotta stand back from it to get the full effect.

Harvey Fierstein 1954- American dramatist and actor

In Los Angeles everyone has perfect teeth. It's crocodile land.

Gwyneth Paltrow 1972- American actress

It costs a lot of money to look this cheap.

Dolly Parton 1946- American singer and songwriter

Prince Charles' ears are so big he could hang-glide over the Falklands.

Joan Rivers 1933-2014 American comedienne

My body is a temple, and my temple needs redecorating.

Joan Rivers 1933-2014 American comedienne, *explaining why she's having more plastic surgery at the age of 78*

EDINA: What you don't realize is that inside, inside of me there is a thin person screaming to get out.
MOTHER: Just the one, dear?

Jennifer Saunders 1958- English actress and writer

It is only shallow people who do not judge by appearances.

Oscar Wilde 1854-1900 Irish dramatist and poet

The Right Hon. was a tubby little chap who looked as if he had been poured into his clothes and had forgotten to say 'When!'

P. G. Wodehouse 1881-1975 English-born writer

Architecture

In my experience, if you have to keep the lavatory door shut by extending your left leg, it's modern architecture.

Nancy Banks-Smith 1929- British journalist

They said it was split-level and open-plan. But then again so is an NCP car park.

Alan Carr 1976- English comedian

on the proposed extension to the National Gallery, London:
Like a monstrous carbuncle on the face of a much-loved and elegant friend.

Charles, Prince of Wales 1948- heir apparent to the British throne

The National Theatre seems like a clever way of building a nuclear power station in the middle of London without anyone objecting.

Charles, Prince of Wales 1948- heir apparent to the British throne

You have to give this much to the Luftwaffe: when it knocked down our buildings it didn't replace them with anything more offensive than rubble.

Charles, Prince of Wales 1948- heir apparent to the British throne

My client—God—is in no hurry.

Antonio Gaudí 1853-1926 Spanish architect, *of the church of the Sagrada Familia in Barcelona (begun 1884)*

Why is it only Tudor that we mock?

Harry Hill 1964- English comedian

A lot of nuns in a rugger scrum.

George Molnar 1910-98 Hungarian-born Australian cartoonist, *on the exterior of the Sydney Opera House*

The green belt was a Labour idea and we are determined to build on it.

John Prescott 1938- British Labour politician

on Brighton Pavilion:
As if St Paul's had come down and pupped.

Sydney Smith 1771-1845 English clergyman and essayist

The physician can bury his mistakes, but the architect can only advise his client to plant vines.

Frank Lloyd Wright 1867-1959 American architect

 # Argument
see ANGER *and* Argument

The Aristocracy 😎

see also CLASS

The Stately Homes of England,
How beautiful they stand,
To prove the upper classes
Have still the upper hand.

   Noël Coward 1899-1973 English dramatist, actor, and composer

I can trace my ancestry back to a protoplasmal
primordial atomic globule. Consequently, my family
pride is something in-conceivable. I can't help it. I was
born sneering.

   W. S. Gilbert 1836-1911 English writer

I am an ancestor.

   Marshal Junot 1771-1813 French general, *reply when taunted on*
   his lack of ancestry, having been made Duke of Abrantes

A duchess will be a duchess in a bath towel. It's all a matter
of style.

   Carol Lawrence 1932- American actress

An aristocracy in a republic is like a chicken whose head
has been cut off: it may run about in a lively way, but in
fact it is dead.

   Nancy Mitford 1904-73 English writer

Those comfortably padded lunatic asylums which
are known, euphemistically, as the stately homes
of England.

   Virginia Woolf 1882-1941 English novelist

21

😃 The Armed Forces

see also WAR

My home at my uncle's brought me acquainted with a circle of admirals. Of *Rears* and *Vices*, I saw enough. No, do not be suspecting me of a pun, I entreat.

    Jane Austen 1775-1817 English novelist

We joined the Navy to see the world,
And what did we see? We saw the sea.

    Irving Berlin 1888-1989 American songwriter

Don't talk to me about naval tradition. It's nothing but rum, sodomy, and the lash.

    Winston Churchill 1874-1965 British Conservative statesman

to the Duke of Newcastle, who had complained that General Wolfe was a madman:

Mad, is he? Then I hope he will *bite* some of my other generals.

    George II 1683-1760 British king

on a regimental march:

GENERAL: Isn't it a little fast, Korngold? The men can't march to that.

KORNGOLD: Ah yes, well, you see Sir, this was composed for the retreat!

    Erich Korngold 1897-1957 Austrian-born American composer

of a general who sent his dispatches from 'Headquarters in the Saddle':

The trouble with Hooker is that he's got his headquarters where his hindquarters ought to be.

    Abraham Lincoln 1809-65 American statesman

Join a Highland regiment, me boy. The kilt is an unrivalled garment for fornication and diarrhoea.
John Masters 1914-83 British writer

Napoleon's armies always used to march on their stomachs shouting: 'Vive l'Intérieur!'
W. C. Sellar 1898-1951 and **R. J. Yeatman** 1898-1968 British writers

When the military man approaches, the world locks up its spoons and packs off its womankind.
George Bernard Shaw 1856-1950 Irish dramatist

As for being a General, well at the age of four with paper hats and wooden swords we're all Generals. Only some of us never grow out of it.
Peter Ustinov 1921-2004 British actor, director, and writer

Art

Oh, I wish I could draw. I've always wanted to draw. I'd give my right arm to be able to draw. It must be very relaxing.
Alan Ayckbourn 1939- English dramatist

Of course he [William Morris] was a wonderful all-round man, but the act of walking round him has always tired me.
Max Beerbohm 1872-1956 English critic, essayist, and caricaturist

The joy of conceptual art is that the description is everything. Oh yes, there is real artistry at work here. It just isn't on the walls but in the catalogue descriptions.
Benet Brandreth 1975- English lawyer

The thing what makes you know that Vernon Ward is a good painter is if you look at his ducks, you can see the eyes follow you around the room.

Peter Cook 1937-95 English comedian and actor

If I were alive in Rubens's time, I'd be celebrated as a model. Kate Moss would be used as a paint brush.

Dawn French 1957- British comedy actress

on attempting to paint two actors, David Garrick and Samuel Foote:

Rot them for a couple of rogues, they have everybody's faces but their own.

Thomas Gainsborough 1727-88 English painter

It's amazing what you can do with an E in A-level art, twisted imagination and a chainsaw

Damien Hirst 1965- English artist

I don't want justice, I want mercy.

William Morris 'Billy' Hughes 1862-1952 British-born Australian statesman, *on having his portrait painted*

when Carl André's Equivalent VIII *consisting of 120 bricks was exhibited at the Tate Gallery :*

I think the fellow needs to have his hod examined.

Osbert Lancaster 1908-86 English writer and cartoonist

'What are you painting?' I said. 'Is it the Heavenly Child?' 'No' he said, 'It is a cow.'

Stephen Leacock 1869-1944 Canadian humorist

Dali is the only painter of LSD without LSD.

Timothy Leary 1920-96 American psychologist

Monet began by imitating Manet, and Manet ended by imitating Monet.

George Moore 1852–1933 Irish novelist

To me, the *Mona Lisa* just looks like she's chewing a toffee.

Justin Moorhouse 1970– English comedian

Epstein is a great sculptor. I wish he would wash, but I believe Michelangelo *never* did, so I suppose it is part of the tradition.

Ezra Pound 1885–1972 American poet

I don't think rock'n'roll songwriters should worry about Art…As far as I'm concerned, Art is just short for Arthur.

Keith Richards 1943– English rock musician

on the probable reaction to the painting of the subjects of Turner's Girls Surprised while Bathing*:*

I should think devilish surprised to see what Turner has made of them.

Dante Gabriel Rossetti 1828–82 English poet and painter

The photographer is like the cod which produces a million eggs in order that one may reach maturity.

George Bernard Shaw 1856–1950 Irish dramatist

I always ask the sitter if they want truth or flattery. They always ask for truth, and I always give them flattery.

Ruskin Spear 1911–90 British painter

I doubt that art needed Ruskin any more than a moving train needs one of its passengers to shove it.

Tom Stoppard 1937– British dramatist

the ingredients for a successful exhibition:

You've got to have two out of death, sex and jewels.

Roy Strong 1935- English art historian

There is only one position for an artist anywhere: and that is, upright.

Dylan Thomas 1914-53 Welsh poet

Painters are so bitchy. Magritte told Miró that Kandinsky had feet of Klee.

Dick Vosburgh 1929-2007 American writer

advice on how to become an artist:

All you need to know is which end of the brush to put in your mouth.

James McNeill Whistler 1834-1903 American-born painter

Yes—one does like to make one's mummy just as nice as possible!

James McNeill Whistler 1834-1903 American-born painter, *on his portrait of his mother*

in his case against Ruskin, replying to the question: 'For two days' labour, you ask two hundred guineas?':

No, I ask it for the knowledge of a lifetime.

James McNeill Whistler 1834-1903 American-born painter

on the 'Old Masters':

They are all old but they are not all masters.

James McNeill Whistler 1834-1903 American-born painter

All that I desire to point out is the general principle that Life imitates Art far more than Art imitates Life.

Oscar Wilde 1854-1900 Irish dramatist and poet

Audiences

The best audience is intelligent, well educated, and a little drunk.

    Alben W. Barkley 1877-1956 American politician

How can I tell the age of the audience out there? I stand in the wings and count the HEAVY SIGHS as they take their seats.

    Gyles Brandreth 1948- English writer and broadcaster

They were really tough—they used to tie their tomatoes on the end of a yo-yo, so they could hit you twice.

    Bob Hope 1903-2003 American comedian

There was laughter in the back of the theatre, leading to the belief that someone was telling jokes back there.

    George S. Kaufman 1889-1961 American dramatist

I know two kinds of audiences only—one coughing, and one not coughing.

    Artur Schnabel 1882-1951 Austrian-born pianist

The play was a great success, but the audience was a total failure.

    Oscar Wilde 1854-1900 Irish dramatist and poet

Australia

Australia is a huge rest home, where no unwelcome news is ever wafted on to the pages of the worst newspapers in the world.

    Germaine Greer 1939- Australian feminist

When New Zealanders emigrate to Australia, it raises the average IQ of both countries.

Robert Muldoon 1921-92 New Zealand statesman

In Australia,
Inter alia,
Mediocrities
Think they're Socrates.

Peter Porter 1929- Australian poet

By God what a site! By man what a mess!

Clough Williams-Ellis 1883-1978 British architect, *of Sydney*

☺ Autobiography
see also BIOGRAPHY

An autobiography is an obituary in serial form with the last instalment missing.

Quentin Crisp 1908-99 English writer

Autobiography—that unrivalled vehicle for telling the truth about other people.

Philip Guedalla 1889-1944 British historian and biographer

Next to the writer of real estate advertisements, the autobiographer is the most suspect of prose artists.

Donal Henahan 1921-2012 American music critic

reviewing James D. Watson The Double Helix:

Like all good memoirs it has not been emasculated by considerations of good taste.

Peter Medawar 1915-87 English immunologist and writer

Every autobiography...becomes an absorbing work of fiction, with something of the charm of a cryptogram.

H. L. Mencken 1880-1956 American journalist and literary critic

To write one's memoirs is to speak ill of everybody except oneself.

Henri Philippe Pétain 1856-1951 French soldier and statesman

Of all forms of fiction autobiography is the most gratuitous.

Tom Stoppard 1937- British dramatist

Only when one has lost all curiosity about the future has one reached the age to write an autobiography.

Evelyn Waugh 1903-66 English novelist

I shall not say why and how I became, at the age of fifteen, the mistress of the Earl of Craven.

Harriette Wilson 1789-1846 English courtesan, *opening words of her* Memoirs

Awards and Honours

You should always accept because of the pain it brings to your enemies.

Maurice Bowra 1898-1971 English scholar and literary critic

My career must be slipping. This is the first time I've been available to pick up an award.

Michael Caine 1933- English film actor

Oscar night at my house is called Passover.

Bob Hope 1903-2003 American comedian

on the Order of the Garter:

A very useful institution. It fosters a wholesome taste for bright colours, and gives old men who have good legs an excuse for showing them.

Lord Salisbury 1830-1903 British Conservative statesman

congratulated on being awarded a baronetcy:

Thanks—but more importantly than that, I have just been elected a member of Sunningdale Golf Club.

Denis Thatcher 1915-2003 English businessman

I had another convulsion of pleasure when Yale made me a Doctor of Literature, because I was not competent to doctor anybody's literature but my own.

Mark Twain 1835-1910 American writer

Medals, they're like haemorrhoids. Sooner or later every asshole gets one.

Billy Wilder 1906-2002 American screenwriter and director

 # Baseball

see also **SPORTS**

Think! How the hell are you gonna think and hit at the same time?

Yogi Berra 1925-2015 American baseball player

If people don't want to come out to the ball park, nobody's going to stop 'em.

Yogi Berra 1925-2015 American baseball player

Baseball is very big with my people. It figures. It's the only way we can get to shake a bat at a white man without starting a riot.

Dick Gregory 1932-2017 American comedian and civil rights activist

Don't look back. Something may be gaining on you.

Leroy ('Satchel') Paige 1906-82 American baseball player, *a baseball pitcher's advice*

I don't think I can be expected to take seriously any game which takes less than three days to reach its conclusion.

Tom Stoppard 1937- British dramatist, *a cricket enthusiast on baseball*

Baseball, it is said, is only a game. True. And the Grand Canyon is only a hole in Arizona. Not all holes, or games, are created equal.

George F. Will 1941- American columnist

Beauty ☺

It has been said that a pretty face is a passport. But it's not, it's a visa and it runs out fast.

Julie Burchill 1960- English journalist and writer

Youth and beauty are not accomplishments. They're the temporary happy by-products of time and/or DNA.

Carrie Fisher 1956-2017 American actress and writer

I have a left shoulder-blade that is a miracle of loveliness. People come miles to see it. My right elbow has a fascination that few can resist.

W. S. Gilbert 1836-1911 English writer

I'm tired of all this nonsense about beauty being only skin-deep. That's deep enough. What do you want—an adorable pancreas?

Jean Kerr 1923-2003 American writer

A beautiful young lady is an act of nature. A beautiful old lady is a work of art.

Louis Nizer 1902-94 British-born American lawyer

I always say beauty is only sin deep.

Saki 1870-1916 Scottish writer

If beauty is truth, why don't women go to the library to have their hair done?

Lily Tomlin 1939- American comedienne and actress

Betting and Gambling

Rowe's Rule: the odds are five to six that the light at the end of the tunnel is the headlight of an oncoming train.

Paul Dickson 1939- American writer

Never give a sucker an even break.

W. C. Fields 1880-1946 American humorist

Horse sense is a good judgement which keeps horses from betting on people.

W. C. Fields 1880-1946 American humorist

asked how his bridge-partner should have played a hand:

Under an assumed name.

George S. Kaufman 1889-1961 American dramatist

I long ago come to the conclusion that all life is 6 to 5 against.

Damon Runyon 1884–1946 American writer

It may be that the race is not always to the swift, nor the battle to the strong—but that's the way to bet.

Damon Runyon 1884–1946 American writer

The Bible 🦢

An apology for the Devil: It must be remembered that we have only heard one side of the case. God has written all the books.

Samuel Butler 1835–1902 English novelist

The number one book of the ages was written by a committee, and it was called the Bible.

Louis B. Mayer 1885–1957 Russian-born American film executive

The Ten Commandments should be treated like an examination. Only six need to be attempted.

Bertrand Russell 1872–1970 British philosopher and mathematician

LORD ILLINGWORTH: The Book of Life begins with a man and a woman in a garden.
MRS ALLONBY: It ends with Revelations.

Oscar Wilde 1854–1900 Irish dramatist and poet

I read the book of Job last night. I don't think God comes well out of it.

Virginia Woolf 1882–1941 English novelist

 Biography

see also **AUTOBIOGRAPHY**

Biography, like big game hunting, is one of the recognized forms of sport, and it is as unfair as only sport can be.

Philip Guedalla 1889–1944 British historian and biographer

Biography is the mesh through which our real life escapes.

Tom Stoppard 1937– British dramatist

Discretion is not the better part of biography.

Lytton Strachey 1880–1932 English biographer

Then there is my noble and biographical friend who has added a new terror to death.

Charles Wetherell 1770–1846 English lawyer and politician, *on Lord Campbell's* Lives of the Lord Chancellors *being written without the consent of heirs or executors*

Every great man nowadays has his disciples, and it is always Judas who writes the biography.

Oscar Wilde 1854–1900 Irish dramatist and poet

Birds

see **ANIMALS** *and* Birds

Birth and Pregnancy

If men had to have babies, they would only ever have one each.

Diana, Princess of Wales 1961–97 British princess, *while in late pregnancy*

Having a baby is like getting a tattoo on your face. You really need to be certain it's what you want before you commit.

Elizabeth Gilbert 1969- American writer

If men could get pregnant, abortion would be a sacrament.

Florynce Kennedy 1916-2001 American lawyer

I didn't 'fall' pregnant! I was bloody well pushed.

Kathy Lette 1958- Australian writer

Having a baby is like trying to push a grand piano through a transom.

Alice Roosevelt Longworth 1884-1980 American daughter of Theodore Roosevelt

I fear the seventh granddaughter and fourteenth grandchild becomes a very uninteresting thing—for it seems to me to go on like the rabbits in Windsor Park!

Victoria 1819-1901 British queen

I was caesarean born, but not so you'd notice. It's just that when I leave a house I go out through the window.

Steven Wright 1955- American comedian

The Body

see also **APPEARANCE, FACES**

I'm the female equivalent of a counterfeit $20 bill. Half of what you see is a pretty good reproduction, the rest is a fraud.

Cher 1946- American singer and actress

Imprisoned in every fat man a thin one is wildly signalling to be let out.

Cyril Connolly 1903-74 English writer

He's so small, he's the only man I know who has turn-ups on his underpants.

Jerry Dennis American writer

If you could see my legs when I take my boots off, you'd form some idea of what unrequited affection is.

Charles Dickens 1812-70 English novelist

What is man, when you come to think upon him, but a minutely set, ingenious machine for turning, with infinite artfulness, the red wine of Shiraz into urine?

Isak Dinesen 1885-1962 Danish novelist and short-story writer

to William Cecil, who suffered from gout:
My lord, we make use of you, not for your bad legs, but for your good head.

Elizabeth I 1533-1603 English queen

Oh, how I regret not having worn a bikini for the entire year I was twenty-six.

Nora Ephron 1941-2012 American screenwriter

My body, on the move, resembles in sight and sound nothing so much as a bin-liner full of yoghurt.

Stephen Fry 1957- English comedian, actor, and writer

Mr Richards was a tall man with what must have been a magnificent build before his stomach went in for a career of its own.

Margaret Halsey 1910-97 American writer

[Alfred Hitchcock] thought of himself as looking like Cary Grant. That's tough, to think of yourself one way and look another.

Tippi Hedren 1930- American actress

seaside postcard showing a very fat man whose stomach obscures the small boy at his feet:

Can't see my little Willy.

Donald McGill 1875-1962 English cartoonist

If I see something sagging, dragging or bagging, I'm going to have the stuff tucked or plucked.

Dolly Parton 1946- American singer and songwriter

Cuddling up to a piece of gristle.

Guy Ritchie 1968- English film director, *on Madonna*

My body is so bad, a Peeping Tom looked in my window and pulled down the shade.

Joan Rivers 1933-2014 American comedienne

Thou seest I have more flesh than another man, and therefore more frailty.

William Shakespeare 1564-1616 English dramatist

Let's forget the six feet and talk about the seven inches.

Mae West 1892-1980 American film actress

JACK LEMMON: Look how she moves! It's like Jell-O on springs!

Billy Wilder 1906-2002 and **I. A. L. Diamond** 1915-88 American screenwriters, *watching Marilyn Monroe, in the film* Some Like It Hot

The lunches of fifty-seven years had caused his chest to slip down into the mezzanine floor.

P. G. Wodehouse 1881–1975 English-born writer

Books

see also DICTIONARIES, LIBRARIES, PUBLISHING, READING

The covers of this book are too far apart.

Ambrose Bierce 1842–c.1914 American writer

on Fanny Hill:

The two most fascinating subjects in the universe are sex and the eighteenth century.

Brigid Brophy 1929–95 Irish novelist

on hearing that a fellow guest was 'writing a book':

Neither am I.

Peter Cook 1937–95 English comedian and actor

PETER BOGDANOVICH: I'm giving John Wayne a book as a birthday present.
JOHN FORD: He's *got* a book.

John Ford 1895–1973 American film director

When the [Supreme] Court moved to Washington in 1800, it was provided with no books, which probably accounts for the high quality of early opinions.

Robert H. Jackson 1892–1954 American lawyer

Book—what they make a movie out of for television.

Leonard Louis Levinson 1904–74

I opened it at page 96—the secret page on which I write my name to catch out borrowers and book-sharks.

Flann O'Brien 1911-66 Irish novelist and journalist

This is not a novel to be tossed aside lightly. It should be thrown with great force.

Dorothy Parker 1893-1967 American critic and humorist

A best-seller is the gilded tomb of a mediocre talent.

Logan Pearsall Smith 1865-1946 American-born man of letters

No furniture so charming as books.

Sydney Smith 1771-1845 English clergyman and essayist

title of her bestseller on punctuation taken from a badly punctuated wildlife manual:

Eats, shoots and leaves.

Lynne Truss 1955- English writer

A thick, old-fashioned heavy book with a clasp is the finest thing in the world to throw at a noisy cat.

Mark Twain 1835-1910 American writer

Should not the Society of Indexers be known as Indexers, Society of, The?

Keith Waterhouse 1929-2009 English writer

In every first novel the hero is the author as Christ or Faust.

Oscar Wilde 1854-1900 Irish dramatist and poet

The good ended happily, and the bad unhappily. That is what fiction means.

Oscar Wilde 1854-1900 Irish dramatist and poet

The trouble with a book is that you never know what's in it until it's too late.

Jeanette Winterson 1959- English novelist and critic

 # Bores

definition of a bore:

A person who talks when you wish him to listen.

Ambrose Bierce 1842-c.1914 American writer

What's wrong with being a boring kind of guy?

George Bush 1924- American Republican statesman

VISITOR TO ETON: I hope that I am not boring you.
PROVOST: Not yet.

Lord Hugh Cecil 1869-1956 British Conservative politician and educationist

He is not only dull in himself, but the cause of dullness in others.

Samuel Foote 1720-77 English actor and dramatist, *on a dull law lord*

A bore is a fellow who opens his mouth and puts his feats in it.

Henry Ford 1863-1947 American car manufacturer

Under pressure, people admit to murder, setting fire to the village church, or robbing a bank, but never to being bores.

Elsa Maxwell 1883-1963 American columnist and hostess

Life is too short, and the time we waste in yawning never can be regained.
Stendhal 1783–1842 French novelist

A bore is a man who, when you ask him how he is, tells you.
Bert Leston Taylor 1866–1901 American writer

He is an old bore. Even the grave yawns for him.
Herbert Beerbohm Tree 1852–1917 English actor-manager, *of the actor Israel Zangwill*

Boxing
see also SPORTS

It's gonna be a thrilla, a chilla, and a killa,
When I get the gorilla in Manila.
Muhammad Ali 1942–2016 American boxer

It's just a job. Grass grows, birds fly, waves pound the sand. I beat people up.
Muhammad Ali 1942–2016 American boxer

Boxing is show-business with blood.
David Belasco 1853–1931 American theatrical producer

Tall men come down to my height when I hit 'em in the body.
Jack Dempsey 1895–1983 American boxer

I want to keep fighting because it is the only thing that keeps me out of the hamburger joints. If I don't fight, I'll eat this planet.
George Foreman 1948– American boxer

We're all endowed with God-given talents. Mine happens to be hitting people in the head.

Sugar Ray Leonard 1956- American boxer

In boxing the right cross-counter is distinctly one of those things it is more blessed to give than to receive.

P. G. Wodehouse 1881-1975 English-born writer

 The British

see also ENGLAND, SCOTLAND, WALES

on British men:

Grubby and distinctly grey around the underwear region.

Germaine Greer 1939- Australian feminist

Modest about our national pride—and inordinately proud of our national modesty.

Ian Hislop 1960- English satirical journalist

British Beatitudes!...Beer, beef, business, bibles, bulldogs, battleships, buggery and bishops.

James Joyce 1882-1941 Irish novelist

What two ideas are more inseparable than Beer and Britannia?

Sydney Smith 1771-1845 English clergyman and essayist

Other nations use 'force'; we Britons alone use 'Might'.

Evelyn Waugh 1903-66 English novelist

Bureaucracy

see also MANAGEMENT

A memorandum is written not to inform the reader but to protect the writer.

Dean Acheson 1893–1971 American politician

Give a civil servant a good case and he'll wreck it with clichés, bad punctuation, double negatives and convoluted apology.

Alan Clark 1928–99 British Conservative politician

Whatever was required to be done, the Circumlocution Office was beforehand with all the public departments in the art of perceiving—HOW NOT TO DO IT.

Charles Dickens 1812–70 English novelist

when his secretary suggested throwing away out-of-date files:

A good idea, only be sure to make a copy of everything before getting rid of it.

Sam Goldwyn 1882–1974 American film producer

Official dignity tends to increase in inverse ratio to the importance of the country in which the office is held.

Aldous Huxley 1894–1963 English novelist

on his dislike of working in teams:

A camel is a horse designed by a committee.

Alec Issigonis 1906–88 British engineer

I think it will be a clash between the political will and the administrative won't.

Jonathan Lynn 1943– and **Antony Jay** 1930–2016 English writers

By the time the civil service has finished drafting a document to give effect to a principle, there may be little of the principle left.

Lord Reith 1889-1971 British administrator and politician

Here lies a civil servant. He was civil
To everyone, and servant to the devil.

C. H. Sisson 1914-2003 English poet

A committee should consist of three men, two of whom are absent.

Herbert Beerbohm Tree 1852-1917 English actor-manager

 Business

see also MANAGEMENT

Focus groups are people who are selected on the basis of their inexplicable free time and their common love of free sandwiches.

Scott Adams 1957- American cartoonist

Some are born great, some achieve greatness and some hire public relations officers.

Daniel Boorstin 1914-2004 American historian

Price is what you pay. Value is what you get.

Warren Buffett 1930- American businessman

I always invest in companies an idiot could run, because one day one will.

Warren Buffett 1930- American businessman

I find it rather easy to portray a businessman. Being bland, rather cruel and incompetent comes naturally to me.
John Cleese 1939- English comic actor and writer

A verbal contract isn't worth the paper it is written on.
Sam Goldwyn 1882-1974 American film producer

I'm not a businessman, I'm a business, man.
Jay-Z 1969- American rapper and businessman

Never invest in any idea you can't illustrate with a crayon.
Peter Lynch 1944- American investor

The longer the title, the less important the job.
George McGovern 1922-2012 American Democratic politician

Skill is fine and genius is splendid, but the right contacts are more valuable than either.
Archibald Hector McIndoe 1900-60 New Zealand
plastic surgeon

Running a company on market research is like driving while looking in the rear view mirror.
Anita Roddick 1942-2007 English businesswoman

Never invest your money in anything that eats or needs repainting.
Billy Rose 1899-1966 American producer and songwriter

It's a recession when your neighbour loses his job; it's a depression when you lose yours.
Harry S. Truman 1884-1972 American Democratic statesman

Put all your eggs in one basket—and WATCH THAT BASKET.

Mark Twain 1835-1910 American writer

The public be damned! I'm working for my stockholders.

William H. Vanderbilt 1821-85 American railway magnate

Nothing is illegal if one hundred well-placed business men decide to do it.

Andrew Young 1932- American politician

Canada

definition of a Canadian:

Somebody who knows how to make love in a canoe.

Pierre Berton 1920-2004 Canadian writer

Americans are benevolently ignorant about Canada, while Canadians are malevolently well-informed about the United States.

John Bartlet Brebner 1895-1957 Canadian historian

I don't even know what street Canada is on.

Al Capone 1899-1947 American gangster

I see Canada as a country torn between a very northern, rather extraordinary, mystical spirit which it fears and its desire to present itself to the world as a Scotch banker.

Robertson Davies 1913-95 Canadian novelist

In any world menu, Canada must be considered the vichyssoise of nations—it's cold, half-French, and difficult to stir.

Stuart Keate 1913-87 Canadian journalist

asked about Canadian sovereignty over the Arctic:
That's ours—lock, stock and iceberg.
> **Brian Mulroney** 1939- Canadian Conservative statesman

I'm world famous, Dr Parks said, all over Canada.
> **Mordecai Richler** 1931-2001 Canadian writer

Catchphrases
see **COMEDY ROUTINES** *and Catchphrases*

Cats and Dogs
see also **ANIMALS**

Cats, I always think, only jump into your lap to check if you are cold enough, yet, to eat.
> **Anne Enright** 1962- Irish novelist and short-story writer

To his dog, every man is Napoleon: hence the constant popularity of dogs.
> **Aldous Huxley** 1894-1963 English novelist

Outside of a dog, a book is a man's best friend. Inside of a dog, it's too dark to read.
> **Groucho Marx** 1890-1977 American film comedian

A door is what a dog is perpetually on the wrong side of.
> **Ogden Nash** 1902-71 American humorist

That indefatigable and unsavoury engine of pollution, the dog.
> **John Sparrow** 1906-92 English academic

The more one gets to know of men, the more one values dogs.

A. Toussenel 1803-85 French writer

If man could be crossed with a cat it would improve man, but it would deteriorate the cat.

Mark Twain 1835-1910 American writer

If a dog jumps up into your lap, it is because he is fond of you; but if a cat does the same thing, it is because your lap is warmer.

Alfred North Whitehead 1861-1947 English philosopher and mathematician

 Censorship

Will Hays is my shepherd, I shall not want, He maketh me to lie down in clean postures.

Gene Fowler 1890-1960 American writer, *on the establishment of the 'Hays Office' to monitor the Hollywood film industry*

TONY HANCOCK: It's red hot, mate. I hate to think of this sort of book getting into the wrong hands. As soon as I've finished this, I shall recommend they ban it.

Ray Galton 1930- and **Alan Simpson** 1929-2017 English writers

Freedom of the press is guaranteed only to those who own one.

A. J. Liebling 1904-63 American writer

She sits among the cabbages and leeks.

Marie Lloyd 1870-1922 English music-hall artist, *substitution for 'she sits among the cabbages and peas', which was supposedly forbidden by a local watch committee*

on being appointed Irish film censor:

I am between the devil and the Holy See.

James Montgomery 1870–1943 Irish businessman and
film censor

A censor is a man who knows more than he thinks you
ought to.

Laurence J. Peter 1919–90 Canadian writer

We are paid to have dirty minds.

John Trevelyan 1903–86 British film censor

Certainty and Doubt

see also RELIGION

He used to be fairly indecisive, but now he's not so certain.

Peter Alliss 1931– English golfer

I've never had a humble opinion. If you've got an opinion,
why be humble about it?

Joan Baez 1941– American singer and songwriter

Often undecided whether to desert a sinking ship for one
that might not float, he would make up his mind to sit on
the wharf for a day.

Lord Beaverbrook 1879–1964 Canadian-born British newspaper
proprietor and Conservative politician, *of Lord Curzon*

Oh! let us never, never doubt
What nobody is sure about!

Hilaire Belloc 1870–1953 British writer and Liberal politician

when asked whether he really believed a horseshoe hanging over his door would bring him luck:

Of course not, but I am told it works even if you don't believe in it.

Niels Bohr 1885-1962 Danish physicist

I'll give you a definite maybe.

Sam Goldwyn 1882-1974 American film producer

CHICO MARX: Well, who you gonna believe, me or your own eyes?

Bert Kalmar 1884-1947 and **others** screenwriters, *in the film* Duck Soup

I wish I was as cocksure of anything as Tom Macaulay is of everything.

Lord Melbourne 1779-1848 British Whig statesman

I am not denying anything I did not say.

Brian Mulroney 1939- Canadian Conservative statesman

To convince Cézanne of anything is like teaching the towers of Notre Dame to dance.

Émile Zola 1840-1902 French novelist

 Challenges
see LIFE *and Its Challenges*

Champagne

I could not live without champagne. In victory I deserve it. In defeat I need it.

Winston Churchill 1874-1965 British Conservative statesman

Remember gentlemen, it's not just France we are fighting for, it's Champagne!

  Winston Churchill 1874-1965 British Conservative statesman

Gentlemen, in the little moment that remains to us between the crisis and the catastrophe, we may as well take a glass of champagne.

  Paul Claudel 1868-1955 French poet and diplomat, *during the Depression of the early 1930s*

Champagne, if you are seeking the truth, is better than a lie-detector.

  Graham Greene 1904-91 English novelist

Three be the things I shall never attain:
Envy, content, and sufficient champagne.

  Dorothy Parker 1893-1967 American critic and humorist

Character

see also SELF-KNOWLEDGE

A gentleman is someone who can play the accordion, but doesn't.

  Anonymous

When people are on their best behaviour they aren't always at their best.

  Alan Bennett 1934- English dramatist and actor

The best measure of a man's honesty isn't his tax return. It's the zero adjust on his bathroom scale.

  Arthur C. Clarke 1917-2008 English science fiction writer

I am so sorry. We have to stop there. I have just come to the end of my personality.

Quentin Crisp 1908-99 English writer, *closing down an interview*

Those who stand for nothing fall for anything.

Alex Hamilton 1936- British writer and broadcaster

Shyness is egotism out of its depth.

Hugh Kingsmill 1889-1949 English man of letters

He wanted to be the bride at every wedding and the corpse at every funeral.

Alice Roosevelt Longworth 1884-1980 American socialite, *on her father Theodore Roosevelt*

SIR HUMPHREY APPLEBY: A cynic is what an idealist calls a realist.

Jonathan Lynn 1943- and **Antony Jay** 1930-2016 English writers, *in* Yes Minister

He was a bit like a corkscrew. Twisted, cold and sharp.

Kate Cruise O'Brien 1948-98 Irish writer

He's so wet you could shoot snipe off him.

Anthony Powell 1905-2000 English novelist

You can tell a lot about a fellow's character by his way of eating jellybeans.

Ronald Reagan 1911-2004 American Republican statesman

He was so crooked, you could have used his spine for a safety-pin.

Dorothy L. Sayers 1893-1957 English writer

A man does not have to be an angel in order to be a saint.

Albert Schweitzer 1875–1965 Franco-German missionary

Few things are harder to put up with than the annoyance of a good example.

Mark Twain 1835–1910 American writer

CECIL GRAHAM: What is a cynic?
LORD DARLINGTON: A man who knows the price of everything and the value of nothing.

Oscar Wilde 1854–1900 Irish dramatist and poet

Slice him where you like, a hellhound is always a hellhound.

P. G. Wodehouse 1881–1975 English-born writer

Children

see also BIRTH, FAMILY, YOUTH

And always keep a-hold of Nurse
For fear of finding something worse.

Hilaire Belloc 1870–1953 British writer and Liberal politician

The place is very well and quiet and the children only scream in a low voice.

Lord Byron 1788–1824 English poet

on being asked what sort of child he was:

When paid constant attention, extremely lovable. When not, a pig.

Noël Coward 1899–1973 English dramatist, actor, and composer

There was never child so lovely but his mother was glad to get him asleep.

Ralph Waldo Emerson 1803-82 American philosopher and poet

HOMER SIMPSON: Kids are the best, Apu. You can teach them to hate the things you hate. And they practically raise themselves, what with the Internet and all.

Matt Groening 1954- American humorist and satirist

at the first night of J. M. Barrie's Peter Pan:
Oh, for an hour of Herod!

Anthony Hope 1863-1933 English novelist

The real menace in dealing with a five-year-old is that in no time at all you begin to sound like a five-year-old.

Jean Kerr 1923-2003 American writer

definition of a baby:
A loud noise at one end and no sense of responsibility at the other.

Ronald Knox 1888-1957 English writer and Roman Catholic priest

The parent who could see his boy as he really is, would shake his head and say: 'Willie is no good; I'll sell him.'

Stephen Leacock 1869-1944 Canadian humorist

Ask your child what he wants for dinner only if he's buying.

Fran Lebowitz 1950- American writer

Parents—especially step-parents—are sometimes a bit of a disappointment to their children. They don't fulfil the promise of their early years.

Anthony Powell 1905-2000 English novelist

Go directly—see what she's doing, and tell her she mustn't.
  Punch 1841-1992 English humorous weekly periodical

I'm in that benign form of house arrest that is looking
after a baby.
  J. K. Rowling 1965- English novelist

I have found the best way to give advice to your children is
to find out what they want and then advise them to do it.
  Harry S. Truman 1884-1972 American Democratic statesman

If you want your children to turn out well, spend twice as
much time with them, and half as much money.
  Abigail Van Buren 1918-2013 American journalist

I love my children…I'm delighted to see them come and
delighted to see them go.
  Mary Wesley 1912-2002 English novelist

The main purpose of children's parties is to remind you
that there are children more awful than your own.
  Katharine Whitehorn 1928- English journalist

Children begin by loving their parents; after a time they
judge them; rarely, if ever, do they forgive them.
  Oscar Wilde 1854-1900 Irish dramatist and poet

Choice ☺

That's a bit like asking a man crawling across the Sahara
whether he would prefer Perrier or Malvern Water.
  Alan Bennett 1934- English dramatist and actor, *replying to a
  question by Ian McKellen on his sexual orientation*

woman to waiter, seeing Sally acting an orgasm:

I'll have what she's having.

Nora Ephron 1941–2012 American writer and journalist, *in the film* When Harry Met Sally

George V was asked which film he would like to see while convalescing:

Anything except that damned Mouse.

George V 1865–1936 British king

A compromise in the sense that being bitten in half by a shark is a compromise with being swallowed whole.

P. J. O'Rourke 1947– American humorous writer

Do I believe in free will? Of course, I have no choice.

Isaac Bashevis Singer 1904–91 Polish-born American novelist and short-story writer

in the post office, pointing at the centre of a sheet of stamps:

I'll take that one.

Herbert Beerbohm Tree 1852–1917 English actor-manager

Christmas

on her husband:

Fang is the cheapest man alive. On Christmas Eve, he puts the kids to bed, fires one shot, and tells them Santa has committed suicide.

Phyllis Diller 1917–2012 American actress

A Merry Christmas to all my friends except two.

W. C. Fields 1880–1946 American humorist

GROUCHO MARX: It's all right. That's—that's in every contract. That's—that's what they call a sanity clause. CHICO MARX: You can't fool me. There ain't no Sanity Claus.

George S. Kaufman 1889-1961 and **Morrie Ryskind** 1895-1985 screenwriters, *in the film* A Night at the Opera

A lovely thing about Christmas is that it's compulsory, like a thunderstorm, and we all go through it together.

Garrison Keillor 1942- American humorous writer and broadcaster

Christmas begins about the first of December with an office party and ends when you finally realize what you spent, around April fifteenth of the next year.

P. J. O'Rourke 1947- American humorous writer

I stopped believing in Santa Claus when I was six. Mother took me to see him in a department store and he asked for my autograph.

Shirley Temple 1928-2014 American film actress

The Cinema

see also FILM PRODUCERS, FILM STARS, HOLLYWOOD

This film wasn't released—it escaped.

Robert Altman 1922-2006 American film director, *on* M.A.S.H.

Adolph Zukor had protested at the escalating costs of The Ten Commandments:

What do you want me to do? Stop shooting now and release it as *The Five Commandments*?

Cecil B. De Mille 1881-1959 American film producer

GEORGES FRANJU: Movies should have a beginning, a middle and an end.
JEAN-LUC GODARD: Certainly. But not necessarily in that order.

Jean-Luc Godard 1930- French film director

of one of his own films:

It's more than magnificent, it's mediocre.

Sam Goldwyn 1882-1974 American film producer

told that he could not film Radclyffe Hall's The Well of Loneliness *as it dealt with lesbians:*

So, make them Latvians.

Sam Goldwyn 1882-1974 American film producer

Our comedies are not to be laughed at.

Sam Goldwyn 1882-1974 American film producer

It would have been cheaper to lower the Atlantic!

Lew Grade 1906-98 British television producer and executive, *of the disaster movie* Raise the Titanic

'Do you have a leading lady for your film?'
'We're trying for the Queen, she sells.'

George Harrison 1943-2001 English singer and songwriter

The length of a film should be directly related to the endurance of the human bladder.

Alfred Hitchcock 1899-1980 British-born film director

on directing Elizabeth Taylor in Cleopatra:

I'm not [biting my fingernails]. I'm biting my knuckles. I finished the fingernails months ago.

Joseph L. Mankiewicz 1909-93 American screenwriter, producer, and director

The trouble, Mr Goldwyn, is that you are only interested in art and I am only interested in money.

George Bernard Shaw 1856-1950 Irish dramatist, *telegraphed version of the outcome of a conversation between Shaw and Sam Goldwyn*

Anything but Beethoven. Nobody wants to see a movie about a blind composer.

Jack Warner 1892-1978 Canadian-born American film producer

Cities

see TOWNS *and Cities*

Class

see also ARISTOCRACY, SNOBBERY

His lordship may compel us to be equal upstairs, but there will never be equality in the servants' hall.

J. M. Barrie 1860-1937 Scottish writer and dramatist

You know you're working class when your TV is bigger than your bookcase.

Rob Beckett English comedian

When every one is somebodee,
Then no one's anybody.

W. S. Gilbert 1836-1911 English writer

when William Douglas Home, son of the 13th Earl of Home, was sent to prison in 1944, his mother told him:

Be sure to pack your evening clothes. The governor is bound to ask you to dine.

Lady Douglas Home 1909-90

Will the people in the cheaper seats clap your hands? All the rest of you, if you'll just rattle your jewellery.

John Lennon 1940-80 English pop singer and songwriter

definition of a gentleman:
Someone who can make a grouse do for six.

Nigel Nicolson 1917-2004 English writer

The upper middle classes like anything ecological: it assuages their guilt. Give your posh friends a bag of muddy parsnips. They'll love it.

Grayson Perry 1960- English ceramic artist

I don't want to talk grammar, I want to talk like a lady.

George Bernard Shaw 1856-1950 Irish dramatist

Nothing is more bourgeois than to be afraid to look bourgeois.

Andy Warhol 1927-87 American artist

Really, if the lower orders don't set us a good example, what on earth is the use of them?

Oscar Wilde 1854-1900 Irish dramatist and poet

 The Clergy
see also RELIGION

Don't like bishops...Blessed are the meek my foot! They're all on the climb. Ever heard of meekness stopping a bishop from becoming a bishop? Nor have I.

Maurice Bowra 1898-1971 English scholar and literary critic

Mr Doctor, that loose gown becomes you so well I wonder
your notions should be so narrow.

Elizabeth I 1533-1603 English queen, *to the Puritan Dr
Humphreys*

I remember the average curate at home as something
between a eunuch and a snigger.

Ronald Firbank 1886-1926 English novelist

Evangelical vicar, in want of a portable, second-hand font,
would dispose, for the same, of a portrait, in frame, of the
Bishop, elect, of Vermont.

Ronald Knox 1888-1957 English writer and Roman Catholic
priest

to a clergyman who thanked him for the enjoyment he'd given the world:

And I want to thank you for all the enjoyment you've
taken out of it.

Groucho Marx 1890-1977 American film comedian

As the French say, there are three sexes—men, women,
and clergymen.

Sydney Smith 1771-1845 English clergyman and essayist

Merit, indeed! ... We are come to a pretty pass if they talk
of *merit* for a bishopric.

Lord Westmorland 1759-1841, Tory statesman

The Bishop ... was talking to the local Master of Hounds
about the difficulty he had in keeping his vicars off the
incense.

P. G. Wodehouse 1881-1975 English-born writer

 Colours

I cannot pretend to feel impartial about the colours. I rejoice with the brilliant ones, and am genuinely sorry for the poor browns.

Winston Churchill 1874-1965 British Conservative statesman

on the choice of colour for the Model T Ford:

Any colour—so long as it's black.

Henry Ford 1863-1947 American car manufacturer and businessman

It's just my colour: it's *beige*!

Elsie Mendl 1865-1950 American socialite and interior decorator, *on her first view of the Parthenon*

If I could find anything blacker than black, I'd use it.

J. M. W. Turner 1775-1851 English landscape painter

Pink is the navy blue of India.

Diana Vreeland 1903-89 American fashion editor

I think it pisses God off if you walk by the colour purple in a field somewhere and don't notice it.

Alice Walker 1944- American poet

 Comebacks

NANCY ASTOR: If I were your wife I would put poison in your coffee!

WINSTON CHURCHILL: And if I were your husband I would drink it.

Nancy Astor 1879-1964 American-born British Conservative politician

on finishing Bill of Divorcement:

KATHARINE HEPBURN: Thank God, I don't have to act with you any more.
BARRYMORE:I didn't know you ever had, darling.

John Barrymore 1882-1942 American actor

PLAYER: I can see your tits from here.
BRADY: Well, when I sell you to Crewe, you won't be able to see from there.

Karren Brady 1969- British businesswoman, *as managing director of Birmingham City Football Club*

BESSIE BRADDOCK: Winston, you're drunk.
CHURCHILL: Bessie, you're ugly. But tomorrow I shall be sober.

Winston Churchill 1874-1965 British Conservative statesman

Joan Rivers interviewing Joan Collins about her marriages:

JOAN RIVERS: Which husband was the best lover?
JOAN COLLINS: Yours.

Joan Collins 1933- British actress

to Clare Boothe Luce, who had stood aside for her saying, 'Age before Beauty':

Pearls before swine.

Dorothy Parker 1893-1967 American critic and humorist

ESTHER MUIR: I've never been so insulted in my life.

GROUCHO MARX: Well, it's early yet.

Robert Pirosh 1910-89, **George Seaton** 1911-79, and **George Oppenheimer** screenwriters, *in the film* A Day at the Races

responding to a savage review by Rudolph Louis:

I am sitting in the smallest room of my house. I have your review before me. In a moment it will be behind me.

Max Reger 1873-1916 German composer

SMITH (TO THE COURT): At the time, my client was as drunk as a judge.

JUDGE (INTERJECTING): Mr Smith, I think you'll find the phrase is 'as drunk as a lord'.

SMITH: As your Lordship pleases.

F. E. Smith 1872-1930 British Conservative politician and lawyer

to Richard Adams, who had described Vidal's novel on Lincoln as 'meretricious'

Really? Well, meretricious and a happy New Year to you too!

Gore Vidal 1925-2012 American novelist and critic

EARL OF SANDWICH: 'Pon my soul, Wilkes, I don't know whether you'll die upon the gallows or of the pox.

WILKES: That depends, my Lord, whether I first embrace your Lordship's principles, or your Lordship's mistresses.

John Wilkes 1727-97 English parliamentary reformer

😆 Comedy Routines and Catchphrases

Shome mishtake, shurely?

Anonymous, *catchphrase in* Private Eye *magazine*

CORBETT: It's goodnight from me.
BARKER: And it's goodnight from him.
> **Ronnie Barker** 1929-2005 and **Ronnie Corbett** 1930-2016
> British comedians

GEORGE BURNS: Say goodnight, Gracie.
GRACIE ALLEN: Goodnight, Gracie.
> **George Burns** 1896-1996 American comedian

I have a cunning plan.
> **Richard Curtis** 1956- and **Ben Elton** 1959- screenwriters,
> *Baldrick's habitual overoptimistic promise*

You might very well think that. I couldn't possibly
comment.
> **Michael Dobbs** 1948- British novelist and broadcaster, *the*
> *Chief Whip's habitual response to questioning*

KENNETH WILLIAMS: Stop messing about!
> **Ray Galton** 1930- and **Alan Simpson** 1929-2017 English writers

George—don't do that.
> **Joyce Grenfell** 1910-79 English comedy actress and writer

No sex, please—we're British.
> **Anthony Marriott** 1931-2014 and **Alistair Foot**

What do you think of the show so far? Rubbish!
> **Eric Morecambe** 1926-84 English comedian

I didn't get where I am today without—.
> **David Nobbs** 1935-2015 British comedy writer, *habitual boast*
> *of Reggie Perrin's boss CJ*

LANCE-CORPORAL JONES [CLIVE DUNN]: They don't like it up 'em!
> **Jimmy Perry** 1923-2016 and **David Croft** 1922-2011 screenwriters, *in* Dad's Army

Ohhh, I don't *believe* it!
> **David Renwick** 1951- British television writer, *said by Victor Meldrew (Richard Wilson)*

Art thou his father?
Ay, sir, so his mother says, if I may believe her.
> **William Shakespeare** 1564-1616 English dramatist

 # Computers and the Internet

see also SCIENCE, TECHNOLOGY

Now we have the World Wide Web (the only thing I know of whose shortened form—www—takes three times longer to say than what it's short for).
> **Douglas Adams** 1952-2001 English science fiction writer

To err is human but to really foul things up requires a computer.
> **Anonymous**

Programming today is a race between software engineers striving to build bigger and better idiot-proof programs and the Universe trying to produce bigger and better idiots. So far, the Universe is winning.
> **Rick Cook** 1944- American fantasy writer

You can't retrieve your life (unless you're on Wikipedia, in which case you can retrieve an inaccurate version of it).
> **Nora Ephron** 1941-2012 American screenwriter and director

The email of the species is deadlier than the mail.
Stephen Fry 1957- English comedian, actor, and writer

DAVID WALLIAMS: Computer says No.
Matt Lucas 1974- and **David Walliams** 1971- British
comedians

Whenever I'm on my computer, I don't type 'lol'. I type 'lqtm': 'laugh quietly to myself'. It's more honest.
Demetri Martin 1973- American comedian

Computers make it easier to do a lot of things, but most of the things they make it easier to do don't need to be done.
Andy Rooney 1919-2011 American broadcaster

Conjunctivitus.com—now there's a site for sore eyes.
Tim Vine 1967- English comedian

We've all heard that a million monkeys banging on a million typewriters will eventually reproduce the entire works of Shakespeare. Now, thanks to the Internet, we know this is not true.
Robert Wilensky 1951- American academic

Conversation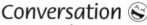

see also SPEECHES

Although there exist many thousand subjects for elegant conversation, there are persons who cannot meet a cripple without talking about feet.
Ernest Bramah 1868-1942 English writer

Too much agreement kills a chat.
> **Eldridge Cleaver** 1935- American civil rights activist

Blessed is the man who, having nothing to say, abstains from giving us wordy evidence of the fact.
> **George Eliot** 1819-80 English novelist

How time flies when you's doin' all the talking.
> **Harvey Fierstein** 1954- American dramatist and actor

If you are ever at a loss to support a flagging conversation, introduce the subject of eating.
> **Leigh Hunt** 1784-1859 English poet and essayist

The opposite of talking isn't listening. The opposite of talking is waiting.
> **Fran Lebowitz** 1950- American writer

No-one really listens to anyone else, and if you try it for a while you'll see why.
> **Mignon McLaughlin** 1913-83 American writer

commenting that George Bernard Shaw's wife was a good listener:
God knows she had plenty of practice.
> **J. B. Priestley** 1894-1984 English novelist, dramatist, and critic

Faith, that's as well said, as if I had said it myself.
> **Jonathan Swift** 1667-1745 Irish poet and satirist

She never lets ideas interrupt the easy flow of her conversation.
> **Jean Webster** 1876-1916 American novelist

If one plays good music, people don't listen and if one plays bad music people don't talk.

Oscar Wilde 1854–1900 Irish dramatist and poet

Cookery

see also DIETS, FOOD

Anyone who tells a lie has not a pure heart, and cannot make a good soup.

Ludwig van Beethoven 1770–1827 German composer

Be content to remember that those who can make omelettes properly can do nothing else.

Hilaire Belloc 1870–1953 British writer and Liberal politician

[My] standard position in regard to cooking is on the sofa with my feet up.

Peg Bracken 1918–2007 American writer

The discovery of a new dish does more for the happiness of mankind than the discovery of a new star.

Anthelme Brillat-Savarin 1755–1826 French jurist and gourmet

I always give my bird a generous butter massage before I put it in the oven. Why? Because I think the chicken likes it—and, more importantly, I like it.

Julia Child 1912–2004 American cook

You cannot trust people who have such bad cuisine. It is the country with the worst food after Finland.

Jacques Chirac 1932– French statesman, *on the British*

Cookery

I have made a *consommé* devoutly to be wished.
Noël Coward 1899-1973 English dramatist, actor, and composer

We approached our new microwave oven with the trepidation of two people returning to a reactor station after a leak.
Fanny Cradock 1909-94 English cook

An unwatched pot boils *immediately*.
H. F. Ellis 1907-2000 English writer

Old Italian chefs never die—they're just put out to pasta.
Shelby Friedman

Heaven sends us good meat, but the Devil sends cooks.
David Garrick 1717-79 English actor-manager

A cucumber should be well sliced, and dressed with pepper and vinegar, and then thrown out, as good for nothing.
Samuel Johnson 1709-84 English poet, critic, and lexicographer

Sorry, I don't do offal.
Jamie Oliver 1975- English chef and broadcaster, *invited to help improve the food in the Westminster kitchens*

A woman always has half an onion left over, no matter what the size of the onion, the dish or the woman.
Terry Pratchett 1948-2015 English fantasy writer

I read recipes the same way I read science fiction. I get to the end and I think, 'Well, that's not going to happen'.
Rita Rudner 1953- American comedienne and writer

The cook was a good cook, as cooks go; and as cooks go, she went.

Saki 1870–1916 Scottish writer

The most remarkable thing about my mother is that for 30 years she served nothing but leftovers. The original meal was never found.

Tracey Ullman 1959– English-born actress

Countries and Peoples

see also AMERICA, AUSTRALIA, BRITISH,
CANADA, FRANCE, IRELAND

It's where they commit suicide and the king rides a bicycle, Sweden.

Alan Bennett 1934– English dramatist and actor

They're Germans. Don't mention the war.

John Cleese 1939– and **Connie Booth** 1944– English and American-born comic actors

When it comes to clichés, the Germans are extremely diligent, efficient and disciplined about living up to them.

Rainer Erlinger 1965– German physician and lawyer

I'm not Jewish. I only look intelligent.

Werner Finck 1902–78 German comedian, *to Nazis in his cabaret audience*

on being asked his opinion of New Zealand:

I find it hard to say, because when I was there it seemed to be shut.

Clement Freud 1924–2009 English politician, broadcaster, and writer

Holland...lies so low they're only saved by being dammed.
Thomas Hood 1799-1845 English poet and humorist

And we will all go together when we go—
Every Hottentot and every Eskimo.
Tom Lehrer 1928- American humorist

In fact, I'm not really a *Jew*. Just Jew-*ish*. Not the whole hog, you know.
Jonathan Miller 1934- English writer and director

Frogs...are slightly better than Huns or Wops, but abroad is unutterably bloody and foreigners are fiends.
Nancy Mitford 1904-73 English writer

New Zealand was colonised initially by those Australians who had the initiative to escape.
Robert Muldoon 1921-92 New Zealand statesman

MICHAEL CAINE: There's only two things I hate in this world. People who are intolerant of other people's cultures and the Dutch.
Mike Myers 1963- Canadian actor, *in the film* Goldmember

The people of Crete unfortunately make more history than they can consume locally.
Saki 1870-1916 Scottish writer

England and America are two countries divided by a common language.
George Bernard Shaw 1856-1950 Irish dramatist

I look upon Switzerland as an inferior sort of Scotland.
Sydney Smith 1771-1845 English clergyman and essayist

Lump the whole thing! say that the Creator made Italy from designs by Michael Angelo!

Mark Twain 1835-1910 American writer

I don't like Norwegians at all. The sun never sets, the bar never opens, and the whole country smells of kippers.

Evelyn Waugh 1903-66 English novelist

The Country
see NATURE *and the Country*

Cricket
see also SPORTS

the umpire to the bowler, after 'not out' was called when W. G. Grace was unexpectedly bowled first ball:

They have paid to see Dr Grace bat, not to see you bowl.

Anonymous

after South Africa's 'Tufty' Mann had baffled George Mann of Middlesex with three successive deliveries:

It is a clear case of Mann's inhumanity to Mann.

John Arlott 1914-91 English journalist and broadcaster

on being seen looking at a newspaper while fielding in the deep:

I just wanted to find out who we were playing.

Warwick Armstrong 1879-1947 Australian cricketer

on being approached for a contribution to W. G. Grace's testimonial:

It's not in support of cricket but as an earnest protest against golf.

Max Beerbohm 1872-1956 English critic, essayist, and caricaturist

Never read print, it spoils one's eye for the ball.

W. G. Grace 1848-1915 English cricketer, *habitual advice to his players*

Cricket—a game which the English, not being a spiritual people, have invented in order to give themselves some conception of eternity.

Lord Mancroft 1914-87 British Conservative politician

having watched a match at Lord's for several hours:
MICHAEL DAVIE: Are you enjoying it?
GROUCHO MARX: It's great. When does it start?

Groucho Marx 1890-1977 American film comedian

I need nine wickets from this match, and you buggers had better start drawing straws to see who I don't get.

Freddie Trueman 1931-2006 English cricketer, *to an opposing team*

To the spectator, cricket is more a therapy than a sport. It is like watching fish dart about a pool.

Michael Wale English journalist

It's a well-known fact that, when I'm on 99, I'm the best judge of a run in all the bloody world.

Alan Wharton 1923-93 English cricketer

Cricket is basically baseball on valium.

Robin Williams 1951-2014 American actor

 Crime and Punishment

see also LAW, MURDER

*to the prison chaplain who asked if he were sewing (mailbags), when
imprisoned for fraud:*

No, reaping.

> **Horatio Bottomley** 1860–1933 British newspaper proprietor
> and financier

What is robbing a bank compared with founding a bank?

> **Bertolt Brecht** 1898–1956 German dramatist

Thieves respect property. They merely wish the property
to become their property that they may more perfectly
respect it.

> **G. K. Chesterton** 1874–1936 English essayist, novelist, and poet

Thou shalt not steal; an empty feat,
When it's so lucrative to cheat.

> **Arthur Hugh Clough** 1819–61 English poet

of a burglar:

He found it inconvenient to be poor.

> **William Cowper** 1731–1800 English poet

CLAUDE RAINS: Major Strasser has been shot. Round up
the usual suspects.

> **Julius J. Epstein** 1909–2001 and **others** American screenwriters,
> *in the film* Casablanca

Hanging is too good for him. He must be posted to the
infantry.

> **Frederick the Great** 1712–86 Prussian monarch, *on being asked
> to endorse the execution of a cavalryman who sodomized his horse*

Awaiting the sensation of a short, sharp shock,

From a cheap and chippy chopper on a big black block.

W. S. Gilbert 1836-1911 English writer

It was beautiful and simple as all truly great swindles are.

O. Henry 1862-1910 American short-story writer

If I ever hear you accuse the police of using violence on a prisoner in custody again, I'll take you down to the station and beat the eyes out of your head.

Joe Orton 1933-67 English dramatist

Critics and Criticism

A bad review may spoil your breakfast but you shouldn't allow it to spoil your lunch.

Kingsley Amis 1922-95 English novelist and poet

There is less in this than meets the eye.

Tallulah Bankhead 1903-68 American actress, *of a revival of Maeterlinck's play 'Aglavaine and Selysette'*

apparent reassurance to a leading lady after a particularly bad first night:

My dear, good is not the word.

Max Beerbohm 1872-1956 English critic, essayist, and caricaturist

Critics are like eunuchs in a harem; they know how it's done, they've seen it done every day, but they're unable to do it themselves.

Brendan Behan 1923-64 Irish dramatist

summing up the long-running 1920s Broadway hit Abie's Irish Rose:

Hebrews 13.8. [Jesus Christ, the same yesterday, and today, and forever.]

Robert Benchley 1889-1945 American humorist

to a Hollywood writer who had criticized Alan Bennett's 'An Englishman Abroad':

Listen, dear, you couldn't write 'fuck' in the dust on a Venetian blind.

Coral Browne 1913-91 Australian actress

on book reviewing:

The thankless task of drowning other people's kittens.

Cyril Connolly 1903-74 English writer

on leaving halfway through an especially cloying screening:

My family has a history of diabetes.

Judith Crist 1922-2012 American film critic

I have knocked everything but the knees of the chorus girls, and nature has anticipated me there.

Percy Hammond 1873-1936 American critic

Asking a working writer what he thinks about critics is like asking a lamp-post how it feels about dogs.

Christopher Hampton 1946- English dramatist

When I read something saying I've not done anything as good as *Catch-22* I'm tempted to reply, `Who has?'

Joseph Heller 1923-99 American novelist

I didn't like the play, but then I saw it under adverse conditions—the curtain was up.

Groucho Marx 1890-1977 American film comedian

And it is that word 'hummy', my darlings, that marks the first place in 'The House at Pooh Corner' at which Tonstant Weader fwowed up.

Dorothy Parker 1893-1967 American critic and humorist

House Beautiful is play lousy.

Dorothy Parker 1893-1967 American critic and humorist

Let my people go!

Mort Sahl 1926- Canadian-born American comedian, *at a viewing of* Exodus

Never pay any attention to what critics say...A statue has never been set up in honour of a critic!

Jean Sibelius 1865-1957 Finnish composer

I never read a book before reviewing it; it prejudices a man so.

Sydney Smith 1771-1845 English clergyman and essayist

As learned commentators view
In Homer more than Homer knew.

Jonathan Swift 1667-1745 Irish poet and satirist

My dear Sir: I have read your play. Oh, my dear Sir! Yours faithfully.

Herbert Beerbohm Tree 1852-1917 English actor-manager, *rejecting a play*

A critic is a man who knows the way but can't drive the car.

Kenneth Tynan 1927-80 English theatre critic

The original Greek is of great use in elucidating Browning's translation of the *Agamemnon*.

Robert Yelverton Tyrrell 1844-1914 Irish classicist

Critics search for ages for the wrong word which, to give them credit, they eventually find.

Peter Ustinov 1921-2004 British actor, director, and writer

Norman Mailer, annoyed at Vidal's literary style of criticism, hit him over the head with a glass tumbler:

Ah, Mailer is, as usual, lost for words.

Gore Vidal 1925-2012 American novelist and critic

One must have a heart of stone to read the death of Little Nell without laughing.

Oscar Wilde 1854-1900 Irish dramatist and poet

Dance

I made the little buggers hop.

Thomas Beecham 1879-1961 English conductor, *on conducting the Diaghilev Ballet*

on being asked whether the fashion for nudity would extend to dance:

No. You see there are portions of the human anatomy which would keep swinging after the music had finished.

Robert Helpmann 1909-86 Australian dancer

GROUCHO MARX: I could dance with you till the cows come home. On second thoughts, I'd rather dance with the cows till you came home.

Bert Kalmar 1884-1947 and **others** screenwriters, *in the film* Duck Soup

Dancing is wonderful training for girls, it's the first way you learn to guess what a man is going to do before he does it.

Christopher Morley 1890-1957 American writer

[Dancing is] a perpendicular expression of a horizontal desire.

George Bernard Shaw 1856-1950 Irish dramatist

 # Dating

see also RELATIONSHIPS

'Mrs Merton' to Debbie McGee:

But what first, Debbie, attracted you to millionaire Paul Daniels?

Caroline Aherne 1963-2016 English comedian

Tell me about yourself—your struggles, your dreams, your telephone number.

Peter Arno 1904-68 American cartoonist

I will not...sulk about having no boyfriend, but develop inner poise and authority and sense of self as woman of substance, complete *without* boyfriend, as best way to obtain boyfriend.

Helen Fielding 1958- British writer as Bridget Jones

On a plane...you can pick up more and better people than on any other public conveyance since the stagecoach.

Anita Loos 1893-1981 American writer

In European countries, there are more princes than dentists.

Tara Palmer-Tomkinson 1971-2017 English socialite, *on finding a suitable man*

A man on a date wonders if he'll get lucky. The woman already knows.

Monica Piper

When a girl marries she exchanges the attentions of many men for the inattention of one.

Helen Rowland 1875-1950 American writer

Whenever I date a guy, I think: Is this the man I want my children to spend their weekends with?

Rita Rudner 1953- American comedienne and writer

Won't you come into the garden? I would like my roses to see you.

Richard Brinsley Sheridan 1751-1816 Irish dramatist and Whig politician

when courting his future wife:

I would worship the ground you walk on, Audrey, if you only lived in a better neighbourhood.

Billy Wilder 1906-2002 American screenwriter and director

All my friends started getting boyfriends. But I didn't want a boyfriend, I wanted a thirteen colour biro.

Victoria Wood 1953-2016 British writer and comedienne

Death

see also EPITAPHS, FUNERALS, LAST WORDS

It's not that I'm afraid to die. I just don't want to be there when it happens.

Woody Allen 1935- American film director, writer, and actor

Death

I don't want to achieve immortality through my work...
I want to achieve it through not dying.

Woody Allen 1935- American film director, writer, and actor

Even death is unreliable: instead of zero it may be some
ghastly hallucination, such as the square root of minus one.

Samuel Beckett 1906-89 Irish dramatist, novelist, and poet

When I came back to Dublin, I was courtmartialled in my
absence and sentenced to death in my absence, so I said
they could shoot me in my absence.

Brendan Behan 1923-64 Irish dramatist

When I am dead, I hope it may be said:
'His sins were scarlet, but his books were read.'

Hilaire Belloc 1870-1953 British writer and Liberal politician

If you live to be one hundred you've got it made. Very few
people die past that age.

George Burns 1896-1996 American comedian

I saw that show 'Fifty Things To Do Before You Die'. I
would have thought the obvious one was 'Shout For Help'.

Jimmy Carr 1972- Irish comedian

I read the *Times* and if my name is not in the obits I proceed
to enjoy the day.

Noël Coward 1899-1973 English dramatist, actor, and composer

When I die I want to decompose in a barrel of porter and
have it served in all the pubs in Dublin. I wonder would
they know it was me?

J. P. Donleavy 1926-2017 Irish-American novelist

In this world nothing can be said to be certain, except death and taxes.

Benjamin Franklin 1706–90 American politician, inventor, and scientist

Once you're dead, you're made for life.

Jimi Hendrix 1942–70 American rock musician

I had an interest in death from an early age. It fascinated me. When I heard 'Humpty Dumpty sat on a wall,' I thought, 'Did he fall or was he pushed?'

P. D. James 1920–2014 English writer

But there, everything has its drawbacks, as the man said when his mother-in-law died, and they came down upon him for the funeral expenses.

Jerome K. Jerome 1859–1927 English writer

Depend upon it, Sir, when a man knows he is to be hanged in a fortnight, it concentrates his mind wonderfully.

Samuel Johnson 1709–84 English poet, critic, and lexicographer

ex-President Eisenhower's death prevented her photograph appearing on the cover of Newsweek:

Fourteen heart attacks and he had to die in my week. In MY week.

Janis Joplin 1943–70 American singer

on how he would kill himself:

With kindness.

George S. Kaufman 1889–1961 American dramatist

Death is the most convenient time to tax rich people.

David Lloyd George 1863–1945 British Liberal statesman

Either he's dead, or my watch has stopped.
Groucho Marx 1890-1977 American film comedian

Death and taxes and childbirth! There's never any convenient time for any of them.
Margaret Mitchell 1900-49 American novelist

One dies only once, and it's for such a long time!
Molière 1622-73 French comic dramatist

on being told by Robert Benchley that Calvin Coolidge had died:
How can they tell?
Dorothy Parker 1893-1967 American critic and humorist

Waldo is one of those people who would be enormously improved by death.
Saki 1870-1916 Scottish writer

Death is always a great pity of course but it's not as though the alternative were immortality.
Tom Stoppard 1937- British dramatist

Early to rise and early to bed makes a male healthy and wealthy and dead.
James Thurber 1894-1961 American humorist

after his obituary appeared prematurely:
The report of my death was an exaggeration.
Mark Twain 1835-1910 American writer, *usually quoted as, 'Reports of my death have been greatly exaggerated'*

Death is very sophisticated. It's like a Noel Coward comedy. You light a cigarette and wait for it in the library.
Theadora Van Runkle 1928-2011 American costume designer

of Truman Capote's death:

Good career move.

Gore Vidal 1925-2012 American novelist and critic

Just think who we'd have been seen dead with!

Rebecca West 1892-1983 English novelist and journalist, *on discovering that her name, with Noël Coward's, had been on the Nazi blacklist for arrest and probable execution*

at the mention of a huge fee for a surgical operation:

Ah, well, then, I suppose that I shall have to die beyond my means.

Oscar Wilde 1854-1900 Irish dramatist and poet

of the wallpaper in the room where he was dying:

One of us must go.

Oscar Wilde 1854-1900 Irish dramatist and poet

Debt

see also MONEY, POVERTY

Annual income twenty pounds, annual expenditure nineteen nineteen six, result happiness. Annual income twenty pounds, annual expenditure twenty pounds ought and six, result misery.

Charles Dickens 1812-70 English novelist

Good news rarely comes in a brown envelope.

Henry D'Avigdor-Goldsmid 1909-76 British businessman and Conservative politician

In the midst of life we are in debt.

Ethel Watts Mumford 1878-1940 American humorist

I feel these days like a very large flamingo. No matter what way I turn, there is always a very large bill.

Joseph O'Connor 1963- Irish novelist

The National Debt is a very Good Thing and it would be dangerous to pay it off, for fear of Political Economy.

W. C. Sellar 1898–1951 and **R. J. Yeatman** 1898–1968 British writers

If I hadn't my debts I shouldn't have anything to think about.

Oscar Wilde 1854–1900 Irish dramatist and poet

Definitions

definition of an acquaintance:

A person whom we know well enough to borrow from, but not well enough to lend to.

Ambrose Bierce 1842-c.1914 American writer

What is originality? Undetected plagiarism.

William Ralph Inge 1860–1954 English writer

Doorman: a genius who can open the door of your car with one hand, help you in with the other and still have one left for the tip.

Dorothy Kilgallen 1913–65 American journalist

Knowledge is knowing a tomato is a fruit; Wisdom is not putting it in a fruit salad.

Miles Kington 1941–2008 English humorist

A gossip is one who talks to you about others; a bore is one who talks to you about himself; and a brilliant conversationalist is one who talks to you about yourself.

Lisa Kirk 1925-90 American actress and singer

Do you know the difference between involvement and commitment? Think of ham and eggs. The chicken is involved. The pig is committed.

Martina Navratilova 1956- Czech-born American tennis player

Being powerful is like being a lady—if you have to tell people you are, you aren't.

Margaret Thatcher 1925-2013 British Conservative stateswoman, *originally said by American trade unionist Jesse Carr*

Democracy
see also GOVERNMENT, POLITICS

Democracy means government by discussion, but it is only effective if you can stop people talking.

Clement Attlee 1883-1967 British Labour statesman

Democracy must be something more than two wolves and a sheep voting on what to have for dinner.

James Bovard 1956- American writer

Hell, I never vote *for* anybody. I always vote *against*.

W. C. Fields 1880-1946 American humorist

on John F. Kennedy's electoral victory in Wisconsin:

A triumph for democracy. It proves that a millionaire has just as good a chance as anybody else.

Bob Hope 1903-2003 American comedian

Under democracy one party always devotes its energies to trying to prove that the other party is unfit to rule—and both commonly succeed and are right.

H. L. Mencken 1880-1956 American journalist and literary critic

All animals are equal but some animals are more equal than others.

George Orwell 1903-50 English novelist

on the death of a supporter of Proportional Representation:

He has joined what even he would admit to be the majority.

John Sparrow 1906-92 English academic

It's not the voting that's democracy, it's the counting.

Tom Stoppard 1937- British dramatist

Democracy means simply the bludgeoning of the people by the people for the people.

Oscar Wilde 1854-1900 Irish dramatist and poet

a voter canvassed by Wilkes had declared that he would sooner vote for the devil:

And if your friend is not standing?

John Wilkes 1727-97 English parliamentary reformer

 Depression

He's really turned his life around. He used to be depressed and miserable. Now he's miserable and depressed.

David Frost 1939-2013 English broadcaster and writer

Noble deeds and hot baths are the best cures for depression.
    Dodie Smith 1896-1990 English novelist and dramatist

Depression is melancholy minus its charms.
    Susan Sontag 1933-2004 American writer

Depression is merely anger without enthusiasm.
    Steven Wright 1955- American comedian

Description
see also APPEARANCE

About as cuddly as a cornered ferret.
    Lynn Barber 1944- English journalist, *of Anne Robinson*

His smile bathed us like warm custard.
    Basil Boothroyd 1910-88 English writer

What can you do with a man who looks like a female llama surprised when bathing?
    Winston Churchill 1874-1965 British Conservative statesman, *of Charles de Gaulle*

of Arnold Schwarzenegger:
I once described him as looking like a brown condom full of walnuts.
    Clive James 1939- Australian critic and writer

A man who so much resembled a Baked Alaska—sweet, warm and gungy on the outside, hard and cold within.
    Francis King 1923-2011 British writer, *of C. P. Snow*

[He looks like] an explosion in a pubic hair factory.
Jonathan Miller 1934- English writer and director, *of Paul Johnson*

She fitted into my biggest armchair as if it had been built round her by someone who knew they were wearing armchairs tight about the hips that season.
P. G. Wodehouse 1881–1975 English writer

 # Despair
see HOPE *and Despair*

 # Diaries

What is more dull than a discreet diary? One might just as well have a discreet soul.
Chips Channon 1897-1958 American-born British Conservative politician

I have decided to keep a full journal, in the hope that my life will perhaps seem more interesting when it is written down.
Sue Townsend 1946-2014 English writer, as Adrian Mole

I always say, keep a diary and some day it'll keep you.
Mae West 1892–1980 American film actress

I never travel without my diary. One should always have something sensational to read in the train.
Oscar Wilde 1854–1900 Irish dramatist and poet

Dictionaries 😄

Like Webster's Dictionary, we're Morocco bound.

Johnny Burke 1908-64 American songwriter

The greatest masterpiece in literature is only a dictionary out of order.

Jean Cocteau 1889-1963 French dramatist and film director

Lexicographer. A writer of dictionaries, a harmless drudge.

Samuel Johnson 1709-84 English poet, critic, and lexicographer

on dictionaries:

Defining what is unknown in terms of something equally unknown.

Flann O'Brien 1911-66 Irish novelist and journalist

I've been in *Who's Who*, and I know what's what, but it'll be the first time I ever made the dictionary.

Mae West 1892-1980 American actress, *on having an inflatable life jacket named after her*

Diets 😄

The only time to eat diet food is while you're waiting for the steak to cook.

Julia Child 1912-2004 American cook

I'm on a whisky diet. I've lost three days already.

Tommy Cooper 1921-84 British comedian

You die of a heart attack but so what? You die thin.

Bob Geldof 1954- Irish rock musician, *on the Atkins diet*

I'm of the pie-eaters' liberation front. I'm fat and proud to be fat.

Boris Johnson 1964- British Conservative politician

Diets are like boyfriends—it never works to go back to them.

Nigella Lawson 1960- British journalist and cookery writer

Life, if you're fat, is a minefield—you have to pick your way, otherwise you blow up.

Miriam Margolyes 1941- British-born actress

Is Elizabeth Taylor fat? Her favourite food is seconds.

Joan Rivers 1933-2014 American comedienne

EDINA: You are what you eat remember, darling.
SAFFY: Which would make you a large vegetarian tart.

Jennifer Saunders 1958- English actress and writer

Little snax,
Bigger slax.

Ruth S. Schenley American writer

Free your mind, and your bottom will follow.

Sarah, Duchess of York 1959- , *slimming advice*

 Diplomacy

see also POLITICS

American *diplomacy*. It's like watching somebody trying to do joinery with a chainsaw.

James Hamilton-Paterson 1941- English writer

Kissinger brought peace to Vietnam the same way
Napoleon brought peace to Europe: by losing.

Joseph Heller 1923-99 American novelist

Diplomacy—lying in state.

Oliver Herford 1863-1935 English-born American humorist

There cannot be a crisis next week. My schedule is already
full.

Henry Kissinger 1923- American politician

on the life of a Foreign Secretary:
Forever poised between a cliché and an indiscretion.

Harold Macmillan 1894-1986 British Conservative
statesman

The French are masters of 'the dog ate my homework'
school of diplomatic relations.

P. J. O'Rourke 1947- American humorous writer

The chief distinction of a diplomat is that he can say no in
such a way that it sounds like yes.

Lester Bowles Pearson 1897-1972 Canadian statesman

There is a story that when Mrs Thatcher first met
Gorbachev he gave her a ball-point and she offered him
Labour-voting Scotland.

Nicholas Shakespeare 1957- British writer

A diplomat . . . is a person who can tell you to go to hell in
such a way that you actually look forward to the trip.

Caskie Stinnett 1911-98 American writer

An ambassador is an honest man sent to lie abroad for the good of his country.

Henry Wotton 1568–1639 English poet and diplomat

 Discontent

see SATISFACTION *and Discontent*

Divorce

see also MARRIAGE

It was partially my fault that we got divorced…I tended to place my wife under a pedestal.

Woody Allen 1935- American film director, writer, and actor

He taught me housekeeping; when I divorce I keep the house.

Zsa Zsa Gabor 1917–2016 Hungarian-born film actress

A TV host asked my wife, 'Have you ever considered divorce?' She replied: 'Divorce never, murder often.'

Charlton Heston 1924–2008 American actor

on how he and his wife managed to stay married for 33 years:

Well, we never wanted to get divorced at the same time.

Bruce Paltrow 1943–2002 American film producer

Love the quest; marriage the conquest; divorce the inquest.

Helen Rowland 1875–1950 American writer

advice to wronged wives:

Don't get mad, get everything.

Ivana Trump 1949- Czech former wife of Donald Trump

Dogs
see CATS *and Dogs*

Doubt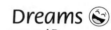
see CERTAINTY *and Doubt*

Dreams
see SLEEP *and Dreams*

Dress

If my jeans could talk they'd plead for mercy.

Phyllis Diller 1917-2012 American actress

You should never have your best trousers on when you go
out to fight for freedom and truth.

Henrik Ibsen 1828-1906 Norwegian dramatist

when a waiter at Buckingham Palace spilled soup on her dress:

Never darken my Dior again!

Beatrice Lillie 1894-1989 Canadian-born comedienne

A woman's dress should be like a barbed wire fence:
serving its purpose without obstructing the view.

Sophia Loren 1934- Italian actress

There is something silly about a man who wears a white suit all the time, especially in New York.

Norman Mailer 1923-2007 American novelist and essayist, *of Tom Wolfe*

on being asked what she wore in bed:

Chanel No. 5.

Marilyn Monroe 1926-62 American actress

The only really firm rule of taste about cross dressing is that neither sex should ever wear anything they haven't yet figured out how to go to the bathroom in.

P. J. O'Rourke 1947- American humorous writer

A dress has no meaning unless it makes a man want to take it off.

Françoise Sagan 1935-2004 French novelist

We know Jesus can't have been English. He is always wearing sandals, but never with socks.

Linda Smith 1958-2006 British comedian

She wore far too much rouge last night, and not quite enough clothes. That is always a sign of despair in a woman.

Oscar Wilde 1854-1900 Irish dramatist and poet

Drink

see also DRUNKENNESS, WINE

One reason why I don't drink is because I wish to know when I am having a good time.

Nancy Astor 1879-1964 American-born British Conservative politician

I saw a notice which said 'Drink Canada Dry' and I've just started.

Brendan Behan 1923-64 Irish dramatist

on being told that the particular drink he was consuming was slow poison:

So who's in a hurry?

Robert Benchley 1889-1945 American humorist

I have taken more out of alcohol than alcohol has taken out of me.

Winston Churchill 1874-1965 British Conservative statesman

on being invited by a friend to dine at a Middle Eastern restaurant:

The aftertaste of foreign food spoils the clean, pure flavour of gin for hours.

Eddie Condon 1905-73 American jazz musician

when seriously ill and given a blood transfusion:

This must be Fats Waller's blood. I'm getting high.

Eddie Condon 1905-73 American jazz musician

Sure I eat what I advertise. Sure I eat Wheaties for breakfast. A good bowl of Wheaties with Bourbon can't be beat.

Dizzy Dean 1910-74 American baseball player

I understand that absinthe makes the tart grow fonder.

Ernest Dowson 1867-1900 English poet

A man shouldn't fool with booze until he's fifty; then he's a damn fool if he doesn't.

William Faulkner 1897-1962 American novelist

Some weasel took the cork out of my lunch.
>   **W. C. Fields** 1880–1946 American humorist

I always keep a supply of stimulant handy in case I see a snake—which I also keep handy.
>   **W. C. Fields** 1880–1946 American humorist

There is no such thing as a small whisky.
>   **Oliver St John Gogarty** 1878–1957 Irish writer and surgeon

HOMER SIMPSON: To alcohol! The cause of…and solution to…all of life's problems.
>   **Matt Groening** 1954– American humorist and satirist

I went out with a guy who once told me I didn't need to drink to make myself more fun to be around. I told him, I'm drinking so that you're more fun to be around.
>   **Chelsea Handler** 1975– American comedienne and writer

We drink one another's healths, and spoil our own.
>   **Jerome K. Jerome** 1859–1927 English writer

Claret is the liquor for boys; port, for men; but he who aspires to be a hero (smiling) must drink brandy.
>   **Samuel Johnson** 1709–84 English poet, critic, and lexicographer

I distrust camels, and anyone else who can go a week without a drink.
>   **Joe E. Lewis** 1902–71 American comedian

Love makes the world go round? Not at all. Whisky makes it go round twice as fast.
>   **Compton Mackenzie** 1883–1972 English novelist

Prohibition makes you want to cry into your beer and denies you the beer to cry into.

Don Marquis 1878-1937 American poet and journalist

I'd hate to be a teetotaller. Imagine getting up in the morning and knowing that's as good as you're going to feel all day.

Dean Martin 1917-95 American singer and actor

I'm only a beer teetotaller, not a champagne teetotaller.

George Bernard Shaw 1856-1950 Irish dramatist

Alcohol...enables Parliament to do things at eleven at night that no sane person would do at eleven in the morning.

George Bernard Shaw 1856-1950 Irish dramatist

when told that drinking would ruin the coat of his stomach:

Then my stomach must digest its waistcoat.

Richard Brinsley Sheridan 1751-1816 Irish dramatist and Whig politician

I have a rare intolerance to herbs which means I can only drink fermented liquids, such as gin.

Julie Walters 1950- British actress

Driving 🚗

of Annie's parking:

WOODY ALLEN: That's OK, we can walk to the kerb from here.

Woody Allen 1935- American film director, writer, and actor, *in the film* Annie Hall

Have you ever noticed that anybody driving slower than you is an idiot, and anyone going faster than you is a maniac?

George Carlin 1937-2008 American comedian

Speed has never killed anyone. Suddenly becoming stationary, that's what gets you.

Jeremy Clarkson 1960- English broadcaster

Somebody actually complimented me on my driving today. They left a little note on the windscreen. It said: 'Parking fine'.

Tommy Cooper 1921-84 British comedian

[There are] only two classes of pedestrians in these days of reckless motor traffic—the quick, and the dead.

Lord Dewar 1864-1930 British industrialist

In Milan, traffic lights are instructions. In Rome, they are suggestions. In Naples, they are Christmas decorations.

Antonio Martino 1942- Italian politician

Drugs

LSD? Nothing much happened, but I did get the distinct impression that some birds were trying to communicate with me.

W. H. Auden 1907-73 English poet

Cocaine habit-forming? Of course not. I ought to know. I've been using it for years.

Tallulah Bankhead 1903-68 American actress

You start out playing rock 'n' roll so you can have sex and do drugs. But you end up doing drugs so you can still play rock 'n' roll and have sex.

Mick Jagger 1943- English rock musician

Sure thing, man. I used to be a laboratory myself once.

Keith Richards 1943- English rock musician, *on being asked to autograph a fan's school chemistry book*

Reality is a crutch for people who can't cope with drugs.

Lily Tomlin 1939- American comedienne and actress

Cocaine is God's way of saying you're making too much money.

Robin Williams 1951-2014 American actor

Drunkenness and Hangovers

see also DRINK

Take the juice of two quarts of whisky.

Eddie Condon 1905-73 American jazz musician, *recommended hangover cure*

I often sit back and think 'I wish I'd done that' and find out later that I already have.

Richard Harris 1930-2002 Irish actor

I don't get hangovers. You have to stop drinking to get a hangover.

Lemmy 1945-2015 English rock musician

You're not drunk if you can lie on the floor without holding on.

Dean Martin 1917-95 American singer and actor

One more drink and I'd have been under the host.

Dorothy Parker 1893-1967 American critic and humorist

But I'm not so think as you drunk I am.

J. C. Squire 1884-1958 English man of letters

[An alcoholic:] A man you don't like who drinks as much as you do.

Dylan Thomas 1914-53 Welsh poet

on being given aspirin from a small tin box by Jeeves:
Thank you, Jeeves. Don't slam the lid.

P. G. Wodehouse 1881-1975 English-born writer

My dad was the town drunk. Usually that's not so bad, but New York City?

Henny Youngman 1906-98 American comedian

Eating
see also FOOD

I believe that if ever I had to practise cannibalism, I might manage if there were enough tarragon around.

James Beard 1903-85 American chef

Good to eat, and wholesome to digest, as a worm to a toad, a toad to a snake, a snake to a pig, a pig to a man, and a man to a worm.

Ambrose Bierce 1842-c.1914 American writer

In general they [my children] refused to eat anything that hadn't danced on TV.

Erma Bombeck 1927-96 American humorist

The healthy stomach is nothing if not conservative. Few radicals have good digestions.

Samuel Butler 1835-1902 English novelist

MISS PIGGY: Never eat more than you can lift.

Jim Henson 1936-90 American puppeteer

The trouble with eating Italian food is that five or six days later you're hungry again.

George Miller

Chopsticks are one of the reasons the Chinese never invented custard.

Spike Milligan 1918-2002 Irish comedian

He found that a fork in his inexperienced hand was an instrument of chase rather than capture.

H. G. Wells 1866-1946 English novelist

Economics

see also MONEY

A man explained inflation to his wife thus: 'When we married you measured 36-24-36. Now you're 42-42-42. There's more of you, but you're not worth as much.'

Joel Barnett 1923-2014 British Labour politician

It's the economy, stupid.

James Carville 1944- American political consultant, *slogan on a sign put up at the Clinton presidential campaign headquarters*

I never could make out what those damned dots meant.

Lord Randolph Churchill 1849-94 British Conservative politician, *on decimal points*

Not all Germans believe in God, but they all believe in the Bundesbank.

Jacques Delors 1925- French socialist politician

Balancing the budget is like going to heaven. Everybody wants to do it, but nobody wants to do what you have to do to get there.

Phil Gramm 1942- American Republican politician

The safest way to double your money is to fold it over and put it in your pocket.

Frank McKinney Hubbard 1868-1930 American humorist

claiming to have been the first person to explain monetarism to Margaret Thatcher:

It makes one feel like the geography teacher who showed a map of the world to Genghis Khan.

Peter Jay 1937- British economist

An economist is an expert who will know tomorrow why the things he predicted yesterday didn't happen today

Laurence J. Peter 1919-90 Canadian writer

The only function of economic forecasting is to make astrology look respectable.

Ezra Solomon 1920-2002 Burmese-born American economist

Education

see also ACADEMIC, EXAMINATIONS

I read Shakespeare and the Bible and I can shoot dice.
That's what I call a liberal education.

Tallulah Bankhead 1903-68 American actress

I won't say ours was a tough school, but we had our own
coroner. We used to write essays like: What I'm going to
be if I grow up.

Lenny Bruce 1925-66 American comedian

Life isn't like coursework, baby. It's one damn essay crisis
after another.

Boris Johnson 1964- British Conservative politician

Take up car maintenance and find the class is full of other
thirty-something women like me, looking for a fella.

Marian Keyes 1963- Irish writer

Stand firm in your refusal to remain conscious during
algebra. In real life, I assure you, there is no such thing as
algebra.

Fran Lebowitz 1950- American writer

At school I never minded the lessons. I just resented
having to work terribly hard at playing.

John Mortimer 1923-2009 English writer and barrister

GROUCHO MARX: With a little study you'll go a long way,
and I wish you'd start now.

S. J. Perelman 1904-79 American humorist, *in the film* Monkey
Business

You can't expect a boy to be vicious till he's been to a good school.

Saki 1870–1916 Scottish writer

For every person who wants to teach there are approximately thirty who don't want to learn—much.

W. C. Sellar 1898–1951 and **R. J. Yeatman** 1898–1968 British writers

Me havin' no education, I had to use my brains.

Bill Shankly 1913–81 Scottish footballer and football manager

He who can, does. He who cannot, teaches.

George Bernard Shaw 1856–1950 Irish dramatist

Educ: during the holidays from Eton.

Osbert Sitwell 1892–1969 English writer

Soap and education are not as sudden as a massacre, but they are more deadly in the long run.

Mark Twain 1835–1910 American writer

 Enemies

The Bible tells us to love our neighbours and also to love our enemies; probably because they are generally the same people.

G. K. Chesterton 1874–1936 English essayist, novelist, and poet

What are parties given for in London but that enemies may meet?

Henry James 1843–1916 American novelist

People wish their enemies dead—but I do not; I say give them the gout, give them the stone!

Lady Mary Wortley Montagu 1689-1762 English writer

asked on his deathbed if he forgave his enemies:

I have none. I had them all shot.

Ramón María Narváez 1800-68 Spanish general

I find that forgiving one's enemies is a most curious morbid pleasure; perhaps I should check it.

Oscar Wilde 1854-1900 Irish dramatist and poet

A man cannot be too careful in the choice of his enemies.

Oscar Wilde 1854-1900 Irish dramatist and poet

England

see also **BRITISH, TOWNS**

The North, where England tucks its shirt in its underpants.

Simon Armitage 1963- English poet

I'm English and as such crave disappointment.

Bill Bailey 1964- English comedian

I only said the English weren't famous for sex, that's all. Like the Boat Race, in out, in out, in out, then everyone collapsed over their oars.

Julian Barnes 1946- English novelist

The English may not like music, but they absolutely love the noise it makes.

Thomas Beecham 1879-1961 English conductor

The English like eccentrics. They just don't like them living next door.

Julian Clary 1959- English comedian

Mad dogs and Englishmen
Go out in the midday sun.

Noël Coward 1899-1973 English dramatist, actor, and composer

Very flat, Norfolk.

Noël Coward 1899-1973 English dramatist, actor, and composer

Even crushed against his brother in the Tube, the average Englishman pretends desperately that he is alone.

Germaine Greer 1939- Australian feminist

The English never smash in a face. They merely refrain from asking it to dinner.

Margaret Halsey 1910-97 American writer

My parents were English. We were too poor to be British.

Bob Hope 1903-2003 American comedian, *on his British origins*

If an Englishman gets run down by a truck he apologizes to the truck.

Jackie Mason 1931- American comedian

An Englishman, even if he is alone, forms an orderly queue of one.

George Mikes 1912-87 Hungarian-born writer

It is hard to tell where the MCC ends and the Church of England begins.

J. B. Priestley 1894-1984 English novelist, dramatist, and critic

An Englishman thinks he is moral when he is only uncomfortable.

George Bernard Shaw 1856–1950 Irish dramatist

Wensleydale lies between Tuesleydale and Thursleydale.

Arthur Smith 1954– English comedian

You should study the Peerage, Gerald ... It is the best thing in fiction the English have ever done.

Oscar Wilde 1854–1900 Irish dramatist and poet

I did a picture in England one winter and it was so cold I almost got married.

Shelley Winters 1922–2006 American actress

Epitaphs
see also DEATH

invited to write his own epitaph:

He finally met his deadline.

Douglas Adams 1952–2001 English science fiction writer

on the death of US President Warren G. Harding:

The only man, woman or child who wrote a simple declarative sentence with seven grammatical errors is dead.

e. e. cummings 1894–1962 American poet

Here lies W. C. Fields. I would rather be living in Philadelphia.

W. C. Fields 1880–1946 American humorist

epitaph for a waiter:

By and by
God caught his eye.

David McCord 1897-1997 American poet

Here lies Spike Milligan. I told you I was ill.

Spike Milligan 1918-2002 Irish comedian, *his chosen epitaph*

Excuse My Dust.

Dorothy Parker 1893-1967 American critic and humorist

when asked what he would like to see on his tombstone:

Keep off the grass.

Peter Ustinov 1921-2004 British actor, director, and writer

I always thought I'd like my tombstone to be blank. No epitaph, and no name. Well, actually I'd like it to say 'figment'.

Andy Warhol 1927-87 American artist

Examinations

Truth is no more at issue in an examination than thirst at a wine-tasting or fashion at a striptease.

Alan Bennett 1934- English dramatist and actor

He had ambitions, at one time, to become a sex maniac, but he failed his practical.

Les Dawson 1934-93 English comedian

I evidently knew more about economics than my examiners.

John Maynard Keynes 1883-1946 English economist, *explaining why he performed badly in the Civil Service examinations*

In examinations those who do not wish to know ask questions of those who cannot tell.

Walter Raleigh 1861-1922 English lecturer and critic

Do not on any account attempt to write on both sides of the paper at once.

W. C. Sellar 1898-1951 and **R. J. Yeatman** 1898-1968 British writers

Whistler had been found 'deficient in chemistry' in a West Point examination:

Had silicon been a gas, I would have been a major-general by now.

James McNeill Whistler 1834-1903 American-born painter

Excuses
see **APOLOGY**

Exercise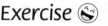

I'd love to go to the gym, but I just can't get my head around the footwear.

Victoria Beckham 1974- British pop singer

The only reason I would take up jogging is so that I could hear heavy breathing again.

Erma Bombeck 1927-96 American humorist

on exercise:

I'm at an age when my back goes out more than I do.
   Phyllis Diller 1917-2012 American actress

Exercise is the yuppie version of bulimia.
   Barbara Ehrenreich 1941- American sociologist and writer

For exercise, I wind my watch.
   Robert Maxwell 1923-91 Czech-born British publisher

The only exercise I take is walking behind the coffins of friends who took exercise.
   Peter O'Toole 1932-2013 British actor

If God had wanted us to bend over, He would have put diamonds on the floor.
   Joan Rivers 1933-2014 American comedienne

I used to jog but the ice cubes kept falling out of my glass.
   Dave Lee Roth 1955- American rock singer

I try to keep fit. I've got these parallel bars at home. I run at them and try to buy a drink from both of them.
   Arthur Smith 1954- English comedian

 # Faces

see also APPEARANCE

Frazier is so ugly that he should donate his face to the US Bureau of Wild Life.
   Muhammad Ali 1942-2016 American boxer

My face looks like a wedding cake left out in the rain.
> **W. H. Auden** 1907-73 English poet

In appearance Dior is like a bland country curate made out of pink marzipan.
> **Cecil Beaton** 1904-80 English photographer

of W. H. Auden's heavily wrinkled face:

Were a fly to attempt to cross it, it would break its leg.
> **Lord David Cecil** 1902-86 British biographer and critic

thanking Botox:

You have no idea how much money you've made me. I can't look surprised but...
> **Simon Cowell** 1959- English music executive and broadcaster

DOLLY PARTON: Time marches on and eventually you realize it is marching across your face.
> **Robert Harling** 1951- American writer, *in the film* Steel Magnolias

I tried to shave off my eyebrows once and my trousers fell down.
> **Denis Healey** 1917-2015 British Labour politician

A face made of broken commandments.
> **John Masefield** 1878-1967 English poet, *in* Sard Harker

Failure 🦢

Ever tried. Ever failed. No matter. Try again. Fail again. Fail better.
> **Samuel Beckett** 1906-89 Irish dramatist, novelist, and poet

Failure is the condiment that gives success its flavour.
  Truman Capote 1924-84 American writer

I have not failed. I've just found 10,000 ways that won't work.
  Thomas Alva Edison 1847-1931 American inventor

If at first you don't succeed, try, try again. Then quit. No use being a damn fool about it.
  W. C. Fields 1880-1946 American humorist

HOMER SIMPSON: Kids, you tried your best, and you failed miserably. The lesson is, never try.
  Matt Groening 1954- American humorist and satirist

Come forth, Lazarus! And he came fifth and lost the job.
  James Joyce 1882-1941 Irish novelist

Whoever said 'It's not whether you win or lose that counts' probably lost.
  Martina Navratilova 1956- Czech-born American tennis player

Anybody seen in a bus over the age of 30 has been a failure in life.
  Loelia, Duchess of Westminster 1902-93

Fame

Someone once asked me if my dream was to live on in the hearts of people, and I said I would prefer to live on in my apartment.
  Woody Allen 1935- American film director, writer, and actor

Oh, the self-importance of fading stars. Never mind, they will be black holes one day.

Jeffrey Bernard 1932–97 English journalist

I'm an instant star, just add water and stir.

David Bowie 1947–2016 English rock musician

They were so far down the bill I thought they were the printers.

Eddie Braben 1930–2013 English comedy writer, *on Morecambe and Wise in early posters and playbills*

Becoming famous has taken the place of going to heaven.

Jarvis Cocker 1963– English musician

One dreams of the goddess Fame and winds up with the bitch Publicity.

Peter De Vries 1910–93 American novelist

Fancy being remembered around the world for the invention of a mouse!

Walt Disney 1901–66 American animator and film producer

The main advantage of being famous is that when you bore people at dinner parties they think it is their fault.

Henry Kissinger 1923– American politician

Recognition has its upside, its downside and, you might say, its backside.

Pippa Middleton 1983– , *on the worldwide coverage of her rear view as bridesmaid at her sister's wedding to the Duke of Cambridge*

Kim Kardashian tweeted a nude selfie today. If Kim wants us to see a part of her we've never seen, she's gonna have to swallow the camera.

Bette Midler 1945- American actress

You can't shame or humiliate modern celebrities. What used to be called shame and humiliation is now called publicity.

P. J. O'Rourke 1947- American humorous writer

on being approached by a fan a few years after her retirement:
Get away dear, I don't need you anymore.

Norma Talmadge 1893-1957 American film actress

on rumours she would be posing for Playboy:
Oh sure—and next month I'm dressing up as a sea bass for the front cover of *Field and Stream*!

Elizabeth Taylor 1932-2011 English-born American actress

One day you are a signature, next day you're an autograph.

Billy Wilder 1906-2002 American screenwriter and director

 # The Family
see also **CHILDREN, PARENTS**

And my parents finally realize that I'm kidnapped and they snap into action immediately: They rent out my room.

Woody Allen 1935- American film director, writer, and actor

My mother-in-law broke up my marriage. My wife came home from work one day and found us in bed together.

Lenny Bruce 1925-66 American comedian

The first half of our lives is ruined by our parents, the second half by our children.

Clarence Darrow 1857-1938 American lawyer

My grandmother started walking five miles a day when she was sixty. She's ninety-seven now, and we don't know where the hell she is.

Ellen DeGeneres 1958- American comedian and actress

When your children are teenagers, it's important to have a dog so that someone in the house is happy to see you.

Nora Ephron 1941-2012 American screenwriter and director

As a child my family's menu consisted of two choices: take it or leave it.

Buddy Hackett 1924-2003 American comedian

MIRANDA: Good morning Mum how are you?
PENNY: Don't get emotional, we're not Spanish.

Miranda Hart 1972- English comedian

A dysfunctional family is any family with more than one person in it.

Mary Karr 1955- American poet

We kept Mommy on a pedestal—it was the only way we could keep Daddy off her.

Dolly Parton 1946- American singer and songwriter, *of family life as one of twelve children*

If a man's character is to be abused, say what you will, there's nobody like a relation to do the business.

William Makepeace Thackeray 1811-63 English novelist

I suppose that the high-water mark of my youth in Columbus, Ohio, was the night the bed fell on my father.

James Thurber 1894-1961 American humorist

Familiarity breeds contempt—and children.

Mark Twain 1835-1910 American writer

Wherever my dad is now, he's looking down on me...not because he's dead but because he is very condescending.

Jack Whitehall 1988- British comedian

To lose one parent, Mr Worthing, may be regarded as a misfortune; to lose both looks like carelessness.

Oscar Wilde 1854-1900 Irish dramatist and poet

It is no use telling me that there are bad aunts and good aunts. At the core, they are all alike. Sooner or later, out pops the cloven hoof.

P. G. Wodehouse 1881-1975 English-born writer

😄 Family Life

The truth is that parents are not really interested in justice. They just want quiet.

Bill Cosby 1937- American comedian and actor

The awe and dread with which the untutored savage contemplates his mother-in-law are amongst the most familiar facts of anthropology.

James George Frazer 1854-1941 Scottish anthropologist

A man...is *so* in the way in the house!
Elizabeth Gaskell 1810-65 English novelist

I was decorating, so I got out my step-ladder. I don't get on with my real ladder.
Harry Hill 1964- English comedian

Living with a teenage daughter is like living under the Taliban. Mothers are not allowed to dance, sing, flirt, laugh loudly or wear short skirts.
Kathy Lette 1958- Australian writer

The reason grandparents and grandchildren get along so well is that they have a common enemy.
Sam Levenson 1911-80 American humorist

I knew I was an unwanted baby when I saw that my bath toys were a toaster and a radio.
Joan Rivers 1933-2014 American comedienne

There's no such thing as fun for the whole family.
Jerry Seinfeld 1954- American comedian

What ought to be done to the man who invented the celebrating of anniversaries? Mere killing would be too light.
Mark Twain 1835-1910 American writer

Children and zip fasteners do not respond to force...Except occasionally.
Katharine Whitehorn 1928- English journalist

After a good dinner one can forgive anybody, even one's own relations.
Oscar Wilde 1854-1900 Irish dramatist and poet

 Fashion

see also DRESS

It is totally impossible to be well dressed in cheap shoes.

Hardy Amies 1909-2003 English fashion designer

I never cared for fashion much. Amusing little seams and witty little pleats. It was the girls I liked.

David Bailey 1938- English photographer

of Dior's New Look:

Clothes by a man who doesn't know women, never had one, and dreams of being one!

Coco Chanel 1883-1971 French fashion designer

Saint Laurent has excellent taste. The more he copies me, the better taste he displays.

Coco Chanel 1883-1971 French fashion designer

Wearing underwear is as formal as I ever hope to get.

Ernest Hemingway 1899-1961 American novelist

My only complaint about having a father in fashion is that every time I'm about to go to bed with a guy I have to look at my dad's name all over his underwear.

Marci Klein 1967- American television producer

I base my fashion sense on what doesn't itch.

Gilda Radner 1946-89 American comedian and actress

Don't wear perfume in the garden—unless you want to be pollinated by bees.

Anne Raver American journalist

his only regret:

I wish I had invented blue jeans.
   Yves Saint Laurent 1936-2008 French fashion designer

His socks compelled one's attention without losing one's
respect.
   Saki 1870-1916 Scottish writer

Women dress alike all over the world: they dress to be
annoying to other women.
   Elsa Schiaparelli 1896-1973 Italian-born French fashion designer

I blame the women's movement for 10 years in a boiler suit.
   Jill Tweedie 1936-93 British journalist

I like to dress egos. If you haven't got an ego today, you can
forget it.
   Gianni Versace 1949-97 Italian fashion designer

It is charming to totter into vogue.
   Horace Walpole 1717-97 English writer and connoisseur

Feminism
see also WOMEN

The suffragettes were triumphant. Woman's place was in
the gaol.
   Caryl Brahms 1901-82 and **S. J. Simon** 1904-48

A good part—and definitely the most fun part—of being a
feminist is about frightening men.
   Julie Burchill 1960- English journalist and writer

The feminist movement seems to have beaten the manners out of men, but I didn't see them put up a lot of resistance.

Clarissa Dickson Wright 1947-2014 English chef and broadcaster

Make policy, not coffee.

Betty Friedan 1921-2006 American feminist, *slogan for the National Organisation for Women's Political Caucus*

Militant feminists, I take my hat off to them. They don't like that.

Milton Jones 1964- English comedian

BETTY FRIEDAN: Don't you hate women being treated as a sexual plaything?
JESSICA MITFORD: But Betty, you're not a plaything, you're a war toy!

Jessica Mitford 1917-96 British writer

God made man and then said I can do better than *that* and made woman.

Adela Rogers St Johns 1894-1988 American journalist

We can't reduce women to equality. Equality is a step down for most women.

Phyllis Schlafly 1924-2016 American lawyer

Like every good little feminist-in-training in the sixties, I burned my bra—and now it's the nineties and I realize Playtex had supported me better than any man I have ever known.

Susan Sweetzer

Film Producers and Directors

see also CINEMA, HOLLYWOOD

resigning from the Motion Picture Producers and Distributors of America in 1933:

Gentlemen, include me out.

Sam Goldwyn 1882–1974 American film producer

PRODUCTION ASSISTANT: But Mr Goldwyn, you said you wanted a spectacle.
GOLDWYN: Yes, but goddam it, I wanted an intimate spectacle!

Sam Goldwyn 1882–1974 American film producer

That's the way with these directors, they're always biting the hand that lays the golden egg.

Sam Goldwyn 1882–1974 American film producer

Hitchcock was more careful about how the birds were treated than he was about me. I was just there to be pecked.

Tippi Hedren 1930– American actress, *on the filming of* The Birds

If I made Cinderella, the audience would immediately be looking for a body in the coach.

Alfred Hitchcock 1899–1980 British-born film director

Tsar of all the rushes.

B. P. Schulberg 1892–1957 American film producer, *of Louis B. Mayer*

Once a month the sky falls on my head, I come to, and I see another movie I want to make.

   Steven Spielberg 1947- American film director and producer

on Roman Polanski:

The four foot Pole you wouldn't want to touch with a ten foot pole.

   Kenneth Tynan 1927-80 English theatre critic

To Raoul Walsh a tender love scene is burning down a whorehouse.

   Jack Warner 1892-1978 Canadian-born American film producer

I like the old masters, by which I mean John Ford, John Ford, and John Ford.

   Orson Welles 1915-85 American actor and film director

Johnny, it's the usual slashed-wrist shot...Keep it out of focus. I want to win the foreign picture award.

   Billy Wilder 1906-2002 American screenwriter and director

An actor entering through the door, you've got nothing. But if he enters through the window, you've got a situation.

   Billy Wilder 1906-2002 American screenwriter and director

 Film Stars

see also CINEMA, HOLLYWOOD

Can't act. Slightly bald. Also dances.

   Anonymous, *studio official's comment on Fred Astaire*

They used to shoot her through gauze. You should shoot me through linoleum.

Tallulah Bankhead 1903-68 American actress, *on Shirley Temple*

JOE GILLIS: You used to be in pictures. You used to be big.
NORMA DESMOND: I am big. It's the pictures that got small.

Charles Brackett 1892-1969 and **Billy Wilder** 1906-2002 screenwriters, *in the film* Sunset Boulevard

Nowadays Mitchum doesn't so much act as point his suit at people.

Russell Davies 1946- British journalist

That man's ears make him look like a taxi-cab with both doors open.

Howard Hughes Jr. 1905-76 American businessman and film producer, *of Clark Gable*

approaching an unwelcoming Greta Garbo and peering up under the brim of her floppy hat:

Pardon me, Ma'am...I thought you were a guy I knew in Pittsburgh.

Groucho Marx 1890-1977 American film comedian

asked if she really had nothing on in a calendar photograph:

I had the radio on.

Marilyn Monroe 1926-62 American actress

Elizabeth [Taylor] is a wonderful movie actress: she has a deal with the film lab—she gets better in the bath overnight.

Mike Nichols 1931- American film director

on hearing that Ronald Reagan was seeking nomination as Governor of California:

No, *no. Jimmy Stewart* for governor—Reagan for his best friend.

Jack Warner 1892-1978 Canadian-born American film producer

It's not what I do, but the way I do it. It's not what I say, but the way I say it.

Mae West 1892-1980 American film actress

on Marilyn Monroe's unpunctuality:

My Aunt Minnie would always be punctual and never hold up production, but who would pay to see my Aunt Minnie?

Billy Wilder 1906-2002 American screenwriter and director

Fishing

If fishing is a religion, fly fishing is high church.

Tom Brokaw 1940- American journalist

I love fishing. It's like transcendental meditation with a punch-line.

Billy Connolly 1942- Scottish comedian

Fishing is unquestionably a form of madness but, happily, for the once-bitten there is no cure.

Lord Home 1903-95 British Conservative statesman

Fly fishing may be a very pleasant amusement; but angling or float fishing I can only compare to a stick and a string, with a worm at one end and a fool at the other.

Samuel Johnson 1709-84 English poet, critic, and lexicographer

It has always been my private conviction that any man who pits his intelligence against a fish and loses has it coming.

John Steinbeck 1902–68 American novelist

Flattery

see PRAISE *and Flattery*

Flying

Airline travel is hours of boredom interrupted by moments of stark terror.

Al Boliska Canadian broadcaster

My inclination to go by the Air Express is confirmed by the crash they had yesterday, which will make them more careful in the immediate future.

A. E. Housman 1859–1936 English poet

I feel about airplanes the way I feel about diets. It seems to me that they are wonderful things for other people to go on.

Jean Kerr 1923–2003 American writer

You know the oxygen masks on airplanes? I don't think there's really any oxygen. They're just to muffle the screams.

Rita Rudner 1953– American comedienne and writer

Food

see also COOKERY, DIETS

I will not eat oysters. I want my food dead—not sick, not wounded—dead.

Woody Allen 1935– American film director, writer, and actor

DAVID MITCHELL: Frosties are just cornflakes for people who can't deal with reality.

Jesse Armstrong and **Sam Bain** 1971- British screenwriters, *in the TV show Peep Show*

There's no such thing as a little garlic.

Arthur Baer 1886-1969 American journalist

Snails. I find this a somewhat disturbing dish, but the sauce is divine. What I do is order escargots, and tell them to 'hold' the snails.

Henry Beard 1945- American humorist, *Miss Piggy's view*

A gourmet who thinks of calories is like a tart who looks at her watch.

James Beard 1903-85 American chef

I've always thought Alfred showed a marked lack of ingenuity over cakes—why didn't he cut off the burnt bits, and ice the rest?

Madeline Bingham English writer

asked if he liked vegetables:

I don't know. I have never eaten them . . . No, that is not quite true. I once ate a pea.

Beau Brummell 1778-1840 English dandy

I'm President of the United States, and I'm not going to eat any more broccoli!

George Bush 1924- American Republican statesman

If you are afraid of butter, use cream.

Julia Child 1912-2004 American cook

[Cheese is] milk's leap toward immortality.
   Clifton Fadiman 1904-99 American critic

Roast Beef, Medium, is not only a food. It is a philosophy.
   Edna Ferber 1887-1968 American writer

It takes some skill to spoil a breakfast—even the English can't do it.
   J. K. Galbraith 1908-2006 Canadian-born American economist

HOMER SIMPSON: Donuts. Is there anything they *can't* do?
   Matt Groening 1954- American humorist and satirist

ANTHONY HOPKINS: I ate his liver with some fava beans and a nice chianti.
   Thomas Harris 1940- and **Ted Tally** 1952- screenwriters, *in the film* The Silence of the Lambs

explaining toad-in-the-hole to an American audience:

It has nothing to do with frogs' legs. No amphibian is harmed in the making of this dish.
   Nigella Lawson 1960- British journalist and cookery writer

Large, naked, raw carrots are acceptable as food only to those who live in hutches eagerly awaiting Easter.
   Fran Lebowitz 1950- American writer

her anti-aging secrets:

A love of life, spaghetti and the odd bath in virgin olive oil. Everything I have I owe to spaghetti.
   Sophia Loren 1934- Italian actress

The piece of cod passeth all understanding.
   Edwin Lutyens 1869-1944 English architect

You are offered a piece of bread and butter that feels like a damp handkerchief and sometimes, when cucumber is added to it, like a wet one.

Compton Mackenzie 1883–1972 English novelist

For those who want to eat efficiently, God made the banana, complete with its own colour-co-ordinated carrying case.

Judith Martin 1938– American journalist

to a friend who had said that he hated English food:
All you have to do is eat breakfast three times a day.

W. Somerset Maugham 1874–1965 English novelist

on having matzo balls for the third time at Arthur Miller's parents:
Isn't there any other part of the matzo you can eat?

Marilyn Monroe 1926–62 American actress

No man is lonely eating spaghetti; it requires so much attention.

Christopher Morley 1890–1957 American writer

Parsley
Is gharsley.

Ogden Nash 1902–71 American humorist

Botticelli isn't a wine, you Juggins! Botticelli's a *cheese*!

Punch 1841–1992 English humorous weekly periodical

BISHOP: I'm afraid you've got a bad egg, Mr Jones.
CURATE: Oh no, my Lord, I assure you! Parts of it are excellent!

Punch 1841–1992 English humorous weekly periodical

Does your chewing-gum lose its flavour on the bedpost overnight?

Billy Rose 1899-1966 and **Marty Bloom** American songwriters

Madam, I have been looking for a person who disliked gravy all my life; let us swear eternal friendship.

Sydney Smith 1771-1845 English clergyman and essayist

My idea of heaven is, eating *pâté de foie gras* to the sound of trumpets.

Sydney Smith 1771-1845 English clergyman and essayist, *reporting the view of his friend Henry Luttrell*

Cauliflower is nothing but cabbage with a college education.

Mark Twain 1835-1910 American writer

Beulah, peel me a grape.

Mae West 1892-1980 American film actress

MOTHER: It's broccoli, dear.
CHILD: I say it's spinach, and I say the hell with it.

E. B. White 1899-1985 American humorist

When I ask for a watercress sandwich, I do not mean a loaf with a field in the middle of it.

Oscar Wilde 1854-1900 Irish dramatist and poet

One doughnut doesn't do a thing. You've got to eat 20 a day for five weeks before you get results.

Renee Zellweger 1969- American actress, *on plumping up to play Bridget Jones*

 Foolishness

see also IGNORANCE

I sometimes wonder if the manufacturers of foolproof items keep a fool or two on their payroll to test things.

Alan Coren 1938-2007 English humorist

Two things are infinite, the universe and human stupidity, and I am not yet completely sure about the universe.

Albert Einstein 1879-1955 German-born theoretical physicist

Every man is a damn fool for at least five minutes every day. Wisdom consists in not exceeding that limit.

Elbert Hubbard 1859-1915 American writer

GROUCHO MARX: Chicolini here may talk like an idiot, and look like an idiot, but don't let that fool you: he really is an idiot.

Bert Kalmar 1884-1947 and **others** screenwriters, *in the film Duck Soup*

I could name eight people—half of those eight are barmy. How many apples short of a picnic?

John Major 1943- British Conservative statesman, *on his Tory critics*

A man may be a fool and not know it, but not if he is married.

H. L. Mencken 1880-1956 American journalist and literary critic

Hain't we got all the fools in town on our side? and ain't that a big enough majority in any town?

Mark Twain 1835-1910 American writer

Football

see also SPORTS

on meetings with players:

We talk about it for 20 minutes and then we decide I was right.

Brian Clough 1935-2004 English football manager

Football's football; if that weren't the case, it wouldn't be the game it is.

Garth Crooks 1958- English football player

when asked by Sir Stanley Rous whether she thought anyone had played well in a particularly dull football Cup Final:

Yes, the band.

Elizabeth II 1926- British queen

The only thing that Norwich didn't get was the goal that they finally got.

Jimmy Greaves 1940- English footballer

The natural state of the football fan is bitter disappointment, no matter what the score.

Nick Hornby 1957- British novelist and journalist

I don't think some of the people who come to Old Trafford can spell football, never mind understand it.

Roy Keane 1971- Irish football player and manager

Football is a simple game; 22 men chase a ball for 90 minutes and at the end, the Germans win.

Gary Lineker 1960- English footballer

What's a geriatric? A German footballer scoring three goals.

Bob Monkhouse 1928-2003 English entertainer

I think football would become an even better game if someone could invent a ball that kicks back.

Eric Morecambe 1926-84 English comedian

We didn't underestimate them. They were a lot better than we thought.

Bobby Robson 1933-2009 English footballer and manager, *on Cameroon's football team*

The first ninety minutes are the most important.

Bobby Robson 1933-2009 English footballer and manager

Some people think football is a matter of life and death... I can assure them it is much more serious than that.

Bill Shankly 1913-81 Scottish footballer and football manager

REPORTER: So, Gordon, in what areas do you think Middlesbrough were better than you today?
GORDON STRACHAN: What areas? Mainly that big green one out there...

Gordon Strachan 1957- Scottish football manager

 # France

France is the only place where you can make love in the afternoon without people hammering on your door.

Barbara Cartland 1901-2000 English writer

How can you govern a country which has 246 varieties of cheese?

Charles de Gaulle 1890-1970 French soldier and statesman

GROUNDSKEEPER WILLIE AS FRENCH TEACHER: Bonjourr, you cheese-eating surrender monkeys.

Matt Groening 1954- American humorist and satirist

The French are always too wordy and need cutting by half before they start.

Miles Kington 1941-2008 English humorist

No matter how politely or distinctly you ask a Parisian a question he will persist in answering you in French.

Fran Lebowitz 1950- American writer

Boy, those French, they have a different word for everything!

Steve Martin 1945- American comedian

The Riviera isn't only a sunny place for shady people.

W. Somerset Maugham 1874-1965 English novelist

Yet, who can help loving the land that has taught us
Six hundred and eighty-five ways to dress eggs?

Thomas Moore 1779-1852 Irish musician and songwriter

Cannes is where you lie on the beach and stare at the stars—or vice versa.

Rex Reed 1938- American critic

France is a country where the money falls apart in your hands and you can't tear the toilet paper.

Billy Wilder 1906-2002 American screenwriter and director

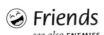 Friends

see also ENEMIES

I may be wrong, but I have never found deserting friends conciliates enemies.

Margot Asquith 1864-1945 British political hostess

Champagne for my real friends, and real pain for my sham friends.

Francis Bacon 1909-92 Irish painter, *his favourite toast*

Rough diamonds are a girl's best friend.

Jilly Cooper 1937- English writer

To find a friend one must close one eye. To keep him—two.

Norman Douglas 1868-1952 Scottish-born novelist and essayist

Most of my friends seem either to be dead, extremely deaf, or living in the wrong part of Kent.

John Gielgud 1904-2000 English actor

[Friends are] God's apology for relations.

Hugh Kingsmill 1889-1949 English man of letters

Money couldn't buy friends but you got a better class of enemy.

Spike Milligan 1918-2002 Irish comedian

Scratch a lover, and find a foe.

Dorothy Parker 1893-1967 American critic and humorist

on Harold Macmillan's sacking seven of his Cabinet:

Greater love hath no man than this, that he lay down his friends for his life.

Jeremy Thorpe 1929-2014 British Liberal politician

It takes your enemy and your friend, working together, to hurt you to the heart: the one to slander you and the other to get the news to you.

Mark Twain 1835-1910 American writer

He [Bernard Shaw] hasn't an enemy in the world, and none of his friends like him.

Oscar Wilde 1854-1900 Irish dramatist and poet

Funerals 😊

said at the funeral of the escapologist Harry Houdini, while carrying his coffin:

I bet you a hundred bucks he ain't in here.

Charles Bancroft Dillingham 1868-1934 American theatrical manager

You can't get buried quickly at Bexhill on Sea—it's like getting a table at the Caprice.

David Hare 1947- English dramatist

At his funeral in Omaha he filled the church to capacity. He was a draw right to the finish.

Jack Hurley, *after the death of the boxer Vince Foster*

fax sent to Harry Secombe:

I hope you go before me because I don't want you singing at my funeral.

Spike Milligan 1918-2002 Irish comedian

I have nothing against undertakers personally. It's just that I wouldn't want one to bury my sister.

Jessica Mitford 1917-96 British writer

on the crowds attending the funeral of the movie tycoon Harry Cohn:

Well, it only proves what they always say—give the public something they want to see, and they'll come out for it.

Red Skelton 1913-97 American comedian

 # The Future

see PAST, *Present, and Future*

 # Gambling

see BETTING *and Gambling*

 # Games

see SPORTS *and Games*

 # Gardens

A delectable sward, shaved as close as a bridegroom and looking just as green.

Basil Boothroyd 1910-88 English humorist

Eleven months' hard work and one month's acute disappointment.

John Heathcoat-Amory, *on gardening*

All really grim gardeners possess a keen sense of humus.

W. C. Sellar 1898-1951 and **R. J. Yeatman** 1898-1968 British writers

A flower is a weed with an advertising budget.

Rory Sutherland 1965- British advertising executive

What a man needs in gardening is a cast iron back, with a hinge in it.

Charles Dudley Warner 1829-1900 American writer

Perennials are the ones that grow like weeds, biennials are the ones that die this year instead of next and hardy annuals are the ones that never come up at all.

Katharine Whitehorn 1928- English journalist

The Generation Gap

on the similarities between teenagers and their grandparents:

They're both on drugs, they both detest you, and neither of them has a job.

Jasper Carrott 1945- English comedian

What's the point in growing old if you can't hound and persecute the young?

Kenneth Clarke 1940- British Conservative politician

It is the one war in which everyone changes sides.

Cyril Connolly 1903-74 English writer

When I was young, the old regarded me as an outrageous young fellow, and now that I'm old the young regard me as an outrageous old fellow.

Fred Hoyle 1915-2001 English astrophysicist

There is more felicity on the far side of baldness than young men can possibly imagine.

Logan Pearsall Smith 1865-1946 American-born man of letters

When I was a boy of 14, my father was so ignorant I could hardly stand to have the old man around. But when I got to be 21, I was astonished at how much the old man had learned in seven years.

Mark Twain 1835-1910 American writer

Gifts

To a woman, having flowers sent to her is thoughtful. To a man, sending flowers is a way of being thoughtful without putting any thought in to it.

Roy Blount Jr 1941- American writer

I kinda like it when you forget to give me presents. It makes me feel like we're married.

Abe Burrows 1910-85 American librettist

Mrs Thatcher tells us she has given the French president a piece of her mind...not a gift I would receive with alacrity.

Denis Healey 1917-2015 British Labour politician

Ever since Eve gave Adam the apple, there has been a misunderstanding between the sexes about gifts.

Nan Robertson 1926-2009 American journalist

From my experience of life I believe my personal motto should be 'Beware of men bearing flowers.'

Muriel Spark 1918-2006 British novelist

on ex-husband Rod Stewart:

What do you give to the man who's had everyone?

Alana Stewart 1945- American actress

God

see also RELIGION

If it turns out that there is a God, I don't think that he's evil. But the worst that you can say about him is that basically he's an underachiever.

Woody Allen 1935- American film director, writer, and actor

If only God would give me some clear sign! Like making a large deposit in my name at a Swiss bank.

Woody Allen 1935- American film director, writer, and actor

CLAIRE: How do you know you're...God?
EARL OF GURNEY: Simple. When I pray to Him I find I'm talking to myself.

Peter Barnes 1931-2004 English dramatist

If I were Her what would really piss me off the worst is that they cannot even get My gender right for Christsakes.

Roseanne Barr 1952- American comedienne and actress

God will not always be a Tory.

Lord Byron 1788-1824 English poet

I'm sorry, we don't do God.

Alastair Campbell 1957- British journalist, *Tony Blair's Director of Communications, when Blair was asked about his Christian faith in an interview*

Brian's mother to his would-be followers:

TERRY JONES: He's not the Messiah! He's a very naughty boy!

Graham Chapman 1941-89, **John Cleese** 1939- , and **others** British comedians, *in the film* Monty Python's Life of Brian

I am prepared to meet my Maker. Whether my Maker is prepared for the great ordeal of meeting me is another matter.
   Winston Churchill 1874-1965 British Conservative statesman

Thou shalt have one God only; who
Would be at the expense of two?
   Arthur Hugh Clough 1819-61 English poet

I've absolutely no idea if God exists. It seems unlikely to me, but then—does a trout know that I exist?
   Billy Connolly 1942- Scottish comedian

Our only hope rests on the off-chance that God does exist.
   Alice Thomas Ellis 1932-2005 English novelist

The world is disgracefully managed, one hardly knows to whom to complain.
   Ronald Firbank 1886-1926 English novelist

God will pardon me, it is His trade.
   Heinrich Heine 1797-1856 German poet, *see Catherine at* ROYALTY

God is love, but get it in writing.
   Gypsy Rose Lee 1914-70 American striptease artist

The chief contribution of Protestantism to human thought is its massive proof that God is a bore.
   H. L. Mencken 1880-1956 American journalist and literary critic

Satan probably wouldn't have talked so big if God had been his wife.
   P. J. O'Rourke 1947- American humorous writer

God can stand being told by Professor Ayer and Marghanita Laski that He doesn't exist.

J. B. Priestley 1894-1984 English novelist, dramatist, and critic

what he plans to say to God when they meet:

I've made a lot of mistakes, but, boy, you've made a lot more.

Burt Reynolds 1936- American actor

Those who set out to serve both God and Mammon soon discover that there is no God.

Logan Pearsall Smith 1865-1946 American-born man of letters

Only one thing, is impossible for God: to find any sense in any copyright law on the planet.

Mark Twain 1835-1910 American writer

God was left out of the Constitution but was furnished a front seat on the coins of the country.

Mark Twain 1835-1910 American writer

Golf

see also SPORTS

on the golf course, on being asked by Nancy Cunard, 'What is your handicap?'

Drink and debauchery.

Lord Castlerosse 1891-1943

QUESTION: What is your handicap?
ANSWER: I'm a colored, one-eyed Jew—do I need anything else?

Sammy Davis Jnr. 1925-90 American entertainer

definition of a Coarse Golfer:
One who has to shout 'Fore' when he putts.
   Michael Green 1927-2018 English writer

If you watch a game, it's fun. If you play it, it's recreation. If you work at it, it's golf.
   Bob Hope 1903-2003 American comedian

I consider it unsportsmanlike to hit a sitting ball.
   Ernest Hornung 1866-1921 English novelist, *on why he disliked golf*

I'm playing like Tarzan and scoring like Jane.
   Chi Chi Rodriguez 1935- Puerto Rican golfer

Golf is a good walk spoiled.
   Mark Twain 1835-1910 American writer

The least thing upset him on the links. He missed short putts because of the uproar of the butterflies in the adjoining meadows.
   P. G. Wodehouse 1881-1975 English writer

Gossip

They come together like the Coroner's Inquest, to sit upon the murdered reputations of the week.
   William Congreve 1670-1729 English dramatist

It's the gossip columnist's business to write about what is none of his business.
   Louis Kronenberger 1904-80 American critic

I hate to spread rumours, but what else can one do with them?

Amanda Lear 1939- French singer

If you haven't got anything good to say about anyone come and sit by me.

Alice Roosevelt Longworth 1884-1980 American socialite

I hope there's a tinge of disgrace about me. Hopefully, there's one good scandal left in me yet.

Diana Rigg 1938- British actress

No one gossips about other people's secret virtues.

Bertrand Russell 1872-1970 British philosopher and mathematician

Here is the whole set! a character dead at every word.

Richard Brinsley Sheridan 1751-1816 Irish dramatist and Whig politician

Gossip is just news running ahead of itself in a red satin dress.

Liz Smith 1923-2017 American journalist

It is perfectly monstrous the way people go about, nowadays, saying things against one behind one's back that are absolutely and entirely true.

Oscar Wilde 1854-1900 Irish dramatist and poet

There is only one thing in the world worse than being talked about, and that is not being talked about.

Oscar Wilde 1854-1900 Irish dramatist and poet

 Government

see also DEMOCRACY, POLITICS

The first requirement of a statesman is that he be dull.
Dean Acheson 1893-1971 American politician

Democracy means government by the uneducated, while aristocracy means government by the badly educated.
G. K. Chesterton 1874-1936 English essayist, novelist, and poet

'Do you pray for the senators, Dr Hale?' 'No, I look at the senators and I pray for the country.'
Edward Everett Hale 1822-1909 American Unitarian clergyman

People must not do things for fun. We are not here for fun. There is no reference to fun in any Act of Parliament.
A. P. Herbert 1890-1971 English writer and humorist

Office hours are from 12 to 1 with an hour off for lunch.
George S. Kaufman 1889-1961 American dramatist, *of the US Senate*

I work for a Government I despise for ends I think criminal.
John Maynard Keynes 1883-1946 English economist

How is the world ruled and how do wars start? Diplomats tell lies to journalists and then believe what they read.
Karl Kraus 1874-1936 Austrian satirist

on suggestions that the US should draft a Constitution for Iraq:
We might as well give them ours. We aren't using it.
Jay Leno 1950- American comedian

One of these days the people of Louisiana are going to get good government—and they aren't going to like it.

Huey Long 1893-1935 American Democratic politician

I don't want to abolish government. I simply want to reduce it to the size where I can drag it into the bathroom and drown it in the bathtub.

Grover Norquist 1956- American lobbyist

The nine most terrifying words in the English language are, 'I'm from the government and I'm here to help.'

Ronald Reagan 1911-2004 American Republican statesman

When you stop being a minister, you get in the back of the car and it doesn't go anywhere.

Malcolm Rifkind 1946- British Conservative politician

Are you labouring under the impression that I read these memoranda of yours? I can't even lift them.

Franklin D. Roosevelt 1882-1945 American Democratic statesman

We all know that Prime Ministers are wedded to the truth, but like other married couples they sometimes live apart.

Saki 1870-1916 Scottish writer

A government which robs Peter to pay Paul can always depend on the support of Paul.

George Bernard Shaw 1856-1950 Irish dramatist

It's a very sobering feeling to be up in space and realize that one's safety factor was determined by the lowest bidder on a government contract.

Alan Shepard 1923-98 American astronaut

I don't mind how much my Ministers talk, so long as they do what I say.

Margaret Thatcher 1925-2013 British Conservative stateswoman

of his first Cabinet meeting as Prime Minister:

An extraordinary affair. I gave them their orders and they wanted to stay and discuss them.

Duke of Wellington 1769-1852 British soldier and statesman

Hair

when asked by his barber how he would like his hair cut:

In silence.

Archelaus d. 399 BC Macedonian king

Libby...was what we used to call a 'suicide blonde' (dyed by her own hand).

Saul Bellow 1915-2005 American novelist

I have learned—and this may be the most important thing I say to you today—hair matters. Pay attention to your hair, because everyone else will.

Hillary Rodham Clinton 1947- American lawyer and politician

Not having to worry about your hair any more is the secret upside of death.

Nora Ephron 1941-2012 American screenwriter and director

Ronald Reagan doesn't dye his hair, he's just prematurely orange.

Gerald Ford 1909-2006 American Republican statesman

A hair in the head is worth two in the brush.

Oliver Herford 1863-1935 English-born American humorist

Handwriting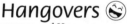

That exquisite handwriting like a fly which has been trained at the Russian ballet.

James Agate 1877-1947 British drama critic and novelist, *of George Bernard Shaw's handwriting*

The dawn of legibility in his handwriting has revealed his utter inability to spell.

Ian Hay 1876-1952 Scottish novelist and dramatist

No individual word was decipherable, but, with a bold reader, groups could be made to conform to a scheme based on probabilities.

Edith Œ. Somerville 1858-1949 and **Martin Ross** 1862-1915 Irish writers

I know that handwriting...I remember it perfectly. The ten commandments in every stroke of the pen, and the moral law all over the page.

Oscar Wilde 1854-1900 Irish dramatist and poet

Hangovers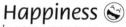
see DRUNKENNESS *and* Hangovers

Happiness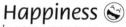
see also HOPE, SATISFACTION

The great pleasure in life is doing what people say you cannot do.

Walter Bagehot 1826-77 English economist and essayist

Happiness is good health—and a bad memory.

Ingrid Bergman 1915-82 Swedish actress

Happiness is having a large, loving, caring, close-knit family in another city.

George Burns 1896-1996 American comedian

Happiness is... finding two olives in your martini when you're hungry.

Johnny Carson 1925-2005 American broadcaster and comedian

There's no pleasure on earth that's worth sacrificing for the sake of an extra five years in the geriatric ward of the Sunset Old People's Home, Weston-Super-Mare.

John Mortimer 1923-2009 English writer and barrister

Men who are unhappy, like men who sleep badly, are always proud of the fact.

Bertrand Russell 1872-1970 British philosopher and mathematician

There are two tragedies in life. One is not to get your heart's desire. The other is to get it.

George Bernard Shaw 1856-1950 Irish dramatist

Life would be very pleasant if it were not for its enjoyments.

R. S. Surtees 1805-64 English sporting journalist and novelist

A cigarette is the perfect type of a perfect pleasure. It is exquisite, and it leaves one unsatisfied. What more can one want?

Oscar Wilde 1854-1900 Irish dramatist and poet

All the things I really like to do are either illegal, immoral, or fattening.

Alexander Woollcott 1887-1943 American writer

Headlines

Headless Body in Topless Bar.

Anonymous

Sticks nix hick pix.

Anonymous, *on the lack of enthusiasm for farm dramas among rural populations*

If I rescued a child from drowning, the Press would no doubt headline the story 'Benn grabs child.'

Tony Benn 1925-2014 British Labour politician

with which Cockburn claimed to have won a competition at The Times *for the dullest headline:*

Small earthquake in Chile. Not many dead.

Claud Cockburn 1904-81 British writer and journalist

SIXTY HORSES WEDGED IN CHIMNEY
The story to fit this sensational headline has not turned up yet.

J. B. Morton 1893-1975 British journalist

Health
see SICKNESS *and Health*

Heroes

The important thing when you are going to do something brave is to have someone on hand to witness it.

Michael Howard 1922- English historian

I'm a hero wid coward's legs, I'm a hero from the waist up.

Spike Milligan 1918-2002 Irish comedian

Genghis Khan was not exactly lovable but I suppose he is my favourite historical character because he was damned efficient.

Kerry Packer 1937-2005 Australian media tycoon

We can't all be heroes because someone has to sit on the curb and clap as they go by.

Will Rogers 1879-1935 American actor and humorist

 History

I often think it odd that it should be so dull, for a great deal of it must be invention.

Jane Austen 1775-1817 English novelist, *on history*

History is a commentary on the various and continuing incapabilities of men. What is history? History is women following behind with the bucket.

Alan Bennett 1934- English dramatist and actor

I was still a medieval historian, not a profession, I imagine, with a high sexual strike rate.

Alan Bennett 1934- English dramatist and actor

History repeats itself; historians repeat one other.

Rupert Brooke 1887-1915 English poet

People who make history know nothing about history. You can see that in the sort of history they make.

G. K. Chesterton 1874-1936 English essayist, novelist, and poet

One of the lessons of history is Nothing is often a good thing to do and always a clever thing to say.

Will Durant 1855-1981 American historian

History is more or less bunk.

Henry Ford 1863-1947 American car manufacturer and businessman

TONY HANCOCK: Does Magna Carta mean nothing to you? Did she die in vain?

Ray Galton 1930- and **Alan Simpson** 1929-2017 English scriptwriters

The Cavaliers (Wrong but Wromantic) and the Roundheads (Right but Repulsive).

W. C. Sellar 1898-1951 and **R. J. Yeatman** 1898-1968 British writers

AMERICA was thus clearly top nation, and History came to a .

W. C. Sellar 1898-1951 and **R. J. Yeatman** 1898-1968 British writers

SWINDON: What will history say?
BURGOYNE: History, sir, will tell lies as usual.

George Bernard Shaw 1856-1950 Irish dramatist

History is about arrogance, vanity and vapidity—who better than me to present it?

David Starkey 1945- English historian

Like most of those who study history, he [Napoleon III] learned from the mistakes of the past how to make new ones.

A. J. P. Taylor 1906-90 British historian

on being asked what would have happened in 1963, had Khrushchev and not Kennedy been assassinated:

With history one can never be certain, but I think I can safely say that Aristotle Onassis would not have married Mrs Khrushchev.

Gore Vidal 1925-2012 American novelist and critic

The one duty we owe to history is to rewrite it.

Oscar Wilde 1854-1900 Irish dramatist and poet

History started badly and hav been geting steadily worse.

Geoffrey Willans 1911-58 and **Ronald Searle** 1920-2011 English humorous writers

 # Holidays
see also WORK

There's sand in the porridge and sand in the bed,
And if this is pleasure we'd rather be dead.

Noël Coward 1899-1973 English dramatist, actor, and composer

After all, the best part of a holiday is perhaps not so much to be resting yourself, as to see all the other fellows busy working.

Kenneth Grahame 1859-1932 Scottish-born writer

supposedly quoting a letter from a Tyrolean landlord:

Standing among savage scenery, the hotel offers stupendous revelations. There is a French widow in every bedroom, affording delightful prospects.

Gerard Hoffnung 1925-59 German-born artist and musician

Twenty-four hour room service generally refers to the length of time that it takes for the club sandwich to arrive.

Fran Lebowitz 1950- American writer

I suppose we all have our recollections of our earlier holidays, all bristling with horror.

Flann O'Brien 1911-66 Irish novelist and journalist

The great advantage of a hotel is that it's a refuge from home life.

George Bernard Shaw 1856-1950 Irish dramatist

I like to have exciting evenings on holiday, because after you've spent 8 hours reading on the beach you don't feel like turning in early with a good book.

Arthur Smith 1954- English comedian

Hollywood
see also CINEMA

Hollywood is the only place in the world where an amicable divorce means each one gets 50 per cent of the publicity.

Lauren Bacall 1924-2014 American actress

Hollywood is the only place on earth where you can get stabbed in the back while you're climbing a ladder.

William Faulkner 1897-1962 American novelist

Every country gets the circus it deserves. Spain gets bullfights. Italy gets the Catholic Church. America Hollywood.

Erica Jong 1942- American novelist

Lunch Hollywood-style—a hot dog and vintage wine.

Harry Kurnitz 1907-68 American dramatist

Behind the phoney tinsel of Hollywood lies the real tinsel.

Oscar Levant 1906-72 American pianist

Working for Warner Bros is like fucking a porcupine: it's a hundred pricks against one.

Wilson Mizner 1876-1933 American dramatist

Hollywood is a place where they'll pay you a thousand dollars for a kiss and fifty cents for your soul.

Marilyn Monroe 1926-62 American actress

Gandhi was everything the voting members of the Academy would like to be: moral, tanned and thin.

Joe Morgenstern 1932- American film critic

Hollywood money isn't money. It's congealed snow, melts in your hand, and there you are.

Dorothy Parker 1893-1967 American critic and humorist

This is the biggest electric train any boy ever had!

Orson Welles 1915-85 American actor and film director

 # Honours

see AWARDS *and* Honours

Hope and Despair

see also OPTIMISM

Hope is the feeling you have that the feeling you have isn't permanent.

Jean Kerr 1923-2003 American writer

'Blessed is the man who expects nothing, for he shall never be disappointed' was the ninth beatitude.

Alexander Pope 1688-1744 English poet

Despair is a black leather jacket that everyone looks good in. Hope is a frilly, pink dress that exposes the knees.

Rebecca Solnit 1961- American writer

If you think nobody cares if you're alive, try missing a couple of car payments.

Earl Wilson 1907-87 American journalist

Hospitality

see PARTIES *and* Hospitality

Housework

WIFE: Cooking! Cleaning! Why should women do it?
HUSBAND: You're quite right—let's get an au pair girl.

Mel Calman 1931-94 English cartoonist

Conran's Law of Housework—it expands to fill the time available plus half an hour.

Shirley Conran 1932- English writer

There was no need to do any housework at all. After the first four years the dirt doesn't get any worse.

Quentin Crisp 1908-99 English writer

The graveyards are full of women whose houses were so spotless you could eat off the floor. Remember the second wife always has a maid.

Heloise Cruse 1919-77 American writer

Housework can't kill you, but why take a chance?

Phyllis Diller 1917-2012 American actress

Cleaning your house while your kids are still growing is like shovelling the walk before it stops snowing.

Phyllis Diller 1917-2012 American actress

The worst thing about work in the house or home is that whatever you do it is destroyed, laid waste or eaten within twenty-four hours.

Alexandra Hasluck 1908-93 Australian writer

All I need is room enough to lay a hat and a few friends.

Dorothy Parker 1893-1967 American critic and humorist

I hate housework! You make the beds, you do the dishes—and six months later you have to start all over again.

Joan Rivers 1933-2014 American comedienne

The only advantage of not being too good a housekeeper is that your guests are so pleased to feel how very much better they are.

Eleanor Roosevelt 1884-1962 American humanitarian and diplomat

It looks different when you're sober. I thought I had twice as much furniture.

Neil Simon 1927- American dramatist

Hatred of domestic work is a natural and admirable result of civilization.

Rebecca West 1892-1983 English novelist and journalist

When it comes to housework the one thing no book of household management can ever tell you is how to begin. Or maybe I mean *why*.

Katharine Whitehorn 1928- English journalist

Everything's getting on top of me. I can't switch off. I've got a self-cleaning oven—I have to get up in the night to see if it's doing it.

Victoria Wood 1953-2016 British writer and comedienne

The Human Race

We are all here on Earth to help others; what on earth the others are here for I don't know.

W. H. Auden 1907-73 English poet

Well, of course, people are only human...But it really does not seem much for them to be.

Ivy Compton-Burnett 1884-1969 English novelist

Human beings can get used to virtually anything, given plenty of time and no choice in the matter whatsoever.

Tom Holt 1961- English novelist

All God's children are not beautiful. Most of God's children are, in fact, barely presentable.

Fran Lebowitz 1950- American writer

Man is one of the toughest of animated creatures. Only the anthrax bacillus can stand so unfavourable an environment for so long a time.

H. L. Mencken 1880-1956 American journalist and literary critic

People differ. Some object to the fan dancer, and others to the fan.

Elizabeth W. Spalding

I'm dealing in rock'n'roll. I'm, like, I'm not a bona fide human being.

Phil Spector 1940- American record producer and songwriter

The only man who wasn't spoilt by being lionized was Daniel.

Herbert Beerbohm Tree 1852-1917 English actor-manager

Man is the Only Animal that Blushes. Or needs to.

Mark Twain 1835-1910 American writer

This world is a comedy to those that think, a tragedy to those that feel.

Horace Walpole 1717-97 English writer and connoisseur

The real problem of humanity is the following: we have Paleolithic emotions, medieval institutions, and god-like technology.

Edward O. Wilson 1929- American sociobiologist

Humour

see also **WIT**

The marvellous thing about a joke with a double meaning is that it can only mean one thing.

Ronnie Barker 1929-2005 English comedian

Mark my words, when a society has to resort to the lavatory for its humour, the writing is on the wall.

Alan Bennett 1934- English dramatist and actor

I worked for a while as a stripper—that's when I realised I had a flair for comedy.

Jeanine Burnier American comedienne

Good jests ought to bite like lambs, not dogs: they should cut, not wound.

Charles II 1630-85 British king

A difference of taste in jokes is a great strain on the affections.

George Eliot 1819-80 English novelist

What do you mean, funny? Funny-peculiar or funny ha-ha?

Ian Hay 1876-1952 Scottish novelist and dramatist

The only way to amuse some people is to slip and fall on an icy pavement.

E. W. Howe 1853-1937 American novelist and editor

It's an odd job, making decent people laugh.

Molière 1622-73 French comic dramatist

They laughed when I said I was going to be a comedian…
They're not laughing now.
   Bob Monkhouse 1928-2003 English entertainer

Good taste and humour…are a contradiction in terms,
like a chaste whore.
   Malcolm Muggeridge 1903-90 British journalist

Satire is a lesson, parody is a game.
   Vladimir Nabokov 1899-1977 Russian novelist

That's the Irish people all over—they treat a joke as a
serious thing and a serious thing as a joke.
   Sean O'Casey 1880-1964 Irish dramatist

Laughter is pleasant, but the exertion is too much for me.
   Thomas Love Peacock 1785-1866 English novelist and poet

Everything is funny as long as it is happening to
Somebody Else.
   Will Rogers 1879-1935 American actor and humorist

There are three basic rules for great comedy. Unfortunately
no-one can remember what they are.
   Arthur Smith 1954- English comedian

Humour is emotional chaos remembered in tranquillity.
   James Thurber 1894-1961 American humorist

Laughter would be bereaved if snobbery died.
   Peter Ustinov 1921-2004 British actor, director, and writer

It's hard to be funny when you have to be clean.
   Mae West 1892-1980 American film actress

Husbands

see also MARRIAGE

The most popular labour-saving device today is still a husband with money.

Joey Adams 1911-99 American comedian

showing Lord Esher the corpse of her notoriously unfaithful husband, King Edward VII:

Now at least I know where he is!

Queen Alexandra 1844-1925

My husband will never chase another woman. He's too fine, too decent, too old.

Gracie Allen 1895-1964 American comedienne

My husband said he needed more space, so I locked him outside.

Roseanne Barr 1952- American comedienne and actress

Being a husband is a whole-time job. That is why so many husbands fail. They cannot give their entire attention to it.

Arnold Bennett 1867-1931 English novelist

Never marry a man who hates his mother, because he'll end up hating you.

Jill Bennett 1931-90 English actress

A girl can wait for the right man, but in the meantime that doesn't mean she can't have a wonderful time with the wrong ones.

Cher 1946- American singer and actress

Husbands

Every woman should marry an archaeologist because she grows increasingly attractive to him as she grows increasingly to resemble a ruin.

Agatha Christie 1890-1976 English writer of detective fiction

I've never yet met a man who could look after me. I don't need a husband. What I need is a wife.

Joan Collins 1933- British actress

To catch a husband is an art, to keep him a job.

Simone de Beauvoir 1908-86 French novelist and feminist

The desire to get married is a basic and primal instinct in women. It's followed by another basic and primal instinct: the desire to be single again.

Nora Ephron 1941-2012 American screenwriter and director

Husbands are like fires. They go out when unattended.

Zsa Zsa Gabor 1917-2016 Hungarian-born actress

when asked how many husbands she had had:
You mean apart from my own?

Zsa Zsa Gabor 1917-2016 Hungarian-born actress

The husband who wants a happy marriage should learn to keep his mouth shut and his cheque book open.

Groucho Marx 1890-1977 American film comedian

Trust your husband, adore your husband, and get as much as you can in your own name.

Joan Rivers 1933-2014 American comedienne

A husband is what is left of a lover, after the nerve has been extracted.

Helen Rowland 1875-1950 American writer

When you see what some girls marry, you realise how they must hate to work for a living.

Helen Rowland 1875-1950 American writer

He would grab me in his arms, hold me close—and tell me how wonderful he was.

Shelley Winters 1922-2006 American actress, *of her ex-husband Vittorio Gassman*

Hypocrisy

We are so very 'umble.

Charles Dickens 1812-70 English novelist, *Uriah Heep*

If I were two-faced would I be wearing this one?

Abraham Lincoln 1809-65 American statesman

An orgy looks particularly alluring seen through the mists of righteous indignation.

Malcolm Muggeridge 1903-90 British journalist

Most people sell their souls, and live with a good conscience on the proceeds.

Logan Pearsall Smith 1865-1946 American-born man of letters

I hope you have not been leading a double life, pretending to be wicked and being really good all the time. That would be hypocrisy.

Oscar Wilde 1854-1900 Irish dramatist and poet

Ideas

I ran into Isosceles. He has a great idea for a new triangle!

Woody Allen 1935- American film director, writer, and actor

An original idea. That can't be too hard. The library must be full of them.

Stephen Fry 1957- English comedian, actor, and writer

The chief end of man is to frame general ideas—and . . . no general idea is worth a damn.

Oliver Wendell Holmes Jr. 1841-1935 American lawyer

It is better to entertain an idea than to take it home to live with you for the rest of your life.

Randall Jarrell 1914-65 American poet

There are some ideas so wrong that only a very intelligent person could believe in them.

George Orwell 1903-50 English novelist

The English approach to ideas is not to kill them, but to let them die of neglect.

Jeremy Paxman 1950- British journalist and broadcaster

My sole inspiration is a telephone call from a producer.

Cole Porter 1891-1964 American songwriter

 Idleness

If I am doing nothing, I like to be doing nothing to some purpose. That is what leisure means.

Alan Bennett 1934- English dramatist and actor

I do nothing, granted. But I see the hours pass—which is better than trying to fill them.

E. M. Cioran 1911-95 Romanian-born French philosopher

It is impossible to enjoy idling thoroughly unless one has plenty of work to do.

Jerome K. Jerome 1859-1927 English writer

My son's taken up meditation—at least it's better than sitting doing nothing.

Max Kauffman American artist

on being accused of idleness:

I'm burning the midday oil!

Ronald Reagan 1911-2004 American Republican statesman

Ignorance

on being asked why he had defined pastern *in his dictionary as the 'knee' of a horse:*

Ignorance, madam, pure ignorance.

Samuel Johnson 1709-84 English poet, critic, and lexicographer

You know everybody is ignorant, only on different subjects.

Will Rogers 1879-1935 American actor and humorist

There are known knowns; there are things we know we know. We also know there are known unknowns; that is to say we know there are some things we do not know. But there are also unknown unknowns—the ones we don't know we don't know.

Donald Rumsfeld 1932- American Republican politician and businessman

Ignorance is like a delicate exotic fruit; touch it and the bloom is gone.

Oscar Wilde 1854–1900 Irish dramatist and poet

Insults

see also COMEBACKS

The reason Michael Jackson entitled his album *Bad* was because he couldn't spell *Indescribable*.

Anonymous

Lord Birkenhead is very clever but sometimes his brains go to his head.

Margot Asquith 1864–1945 British political hostess

The *t* is silent, as in *Harlow*.

Margot Asquith 1864–1945 British political hostess, *to Jean Harlow, who had been mispronouncing her first name*

I didn't know he'd been knighted. I knew he'd been doctored.

Thomas Beecham 1879–1961 English conductor, *on rival conductor Malcolm Sargent's knighthood*

If there is anybody here that I have forgotten to insult, I apologize.

Johannes Brahms 1833–97 German composer, *leaving a gathering*

shouting at his whist partner:

Ye stupid auld bitch—I beg yer pardon, mem. I mistook ye for my wife.

Lord Braxfield 1722–99

The 'g' is silent—the only thing about her that is.

Julie Burchill 1960- English journalist and writer, *of Camille Paglia*

When he said we were trying to make a fool of him I could only murmur that the Creator had beat us to it.

Ilka Chase 1905-78 American actress and writer

She's been kissed oftener than a police-court Bible and by much the same class of people.

Robertson Davies 1913-95 Canadian novelist

Why am I so good at playing bitches? I think it's because I'm not a bitch. Maybe that why Miss Crawford always plays ladies.

Bette Davis 1908-89 American actress

He is just about the nastiest little man I've ever known. He struts sitting down.

Lillian Dykstra American journalist, *on American politician Thomas E. Dewey*

on hearing that Nancy Mitford was borrowing a friend's villa 'to finish her book':

Oh really? What exactly is she reading?

Edith Evans 1888-1976 English actress

[Ernest Hemingway's *The Sun Also Rises* is about] bullfighting, bullslinging, and bull—.

Zelda Fitzgerald 1900-47

There never was a Churchill from John of Marlborough down that had either morals or principles.

W. E. Gladstone 1809-98 British Liberal statesman

A very weak-minded fellow I am afraid, and, like the feather pillow, bears the marks of the last person who has sat on him!

Earl Haig 1861–1928 British general, *of Lord Derby*

on being criticized by Geoffrey Howe:
Like being savaged by a dead sheep.

Denis Healey 1917–2015 British Labour politician

Some men are born mediocre, some men achieve mediocrity, and some men have mediocrity thrust upon them. With Major Major it had been all three.

Joseph Heller 1923–99 American novelist

When you cannot answer your opponent's logic, do not be discouraged—You can still call him vile names.

Elbert Hubbard 1859–1915 American writer

to a subordinate:
You couldn't pour piss out of a boot if the instructions were printed on the heel.

Lyndon Baines Johnson 1908–73 American Democratic statesman

This little flower, this delicate little beauty, this cream puff, is supposed to be beyond personal criticism... He is simply a shiver looking for a spine to run up.

Paul Keating 1944– Australian Labor statesman, *of John Hewson, the Australian Liberal leader*

The truckman, the trashman and the policeman on the block may call me Alice but you may not.

Alice Roosevelt Longworth 1884–1980 American socialite, *to Senator Joseph McCarthy*

I never forget a face, but in your case I'll be glad to make an exception.

Groucho Marx 1890-1977 American film comedian

I've had a perfectly wonderful evening, but this wasn't it.

Groucho Marx 1890-1977 American film comedian

The only thing Madonna will ever do like a virgin is give birth in a stable.

Bette Midler 1945- American actress

The affair between Margot Asquith and Margot Asquith will live as one of the prettiest love stories in all literature.

Dorothy Parker 1893-1967 American critic and humorist

on hearing that a well-known English actress, famous for her love affairs with members of the legal profession, had broken her leg:

She must have done it sliding down a barrister.

Dorothy Parker 1893-1967 American critic and humorist

I'm not offended at all, because I know I'm not a dumb blonde. I also know I'm not blonde.

Dolly Parton 1946- American singer and songwriter

Elizabeth Taylor is wearing Orson Welles designer jeans.

Joan Rivers 1933-2014 American comedienne

Diana Rigg is built like a brick mausoleum with insufficient flying buttresses.

John Simon 1925- American critic

JUDGE: You are extremely offensive, young man.

SMITH: As a matter of fact, we both are, and the only difference between us is that I am trying to be, and you can't help it.

   F. E. Smith 1872-1930 British Conservative politician and lawyer

on a proposal to surround St Paul's with a wooden pavement:

Let the Dean and Canons lay their heads together and the thing will be done.

   Sydney Smith 1771-1845 English clergyman and essayist

[Richard Nixon is] the kind of politician who would cut down a redwood tree, and then mount the stump and make a speech on conservation.

   Adlai Stevenson 1900-65 American Democratic politician

I regard you with an indifference closely bordering on aversion.

   Robert Louis Stevenson 1850-94 Scottish novelist

when pressed by a gramophone company for a written testimonial:

Sirs, I have tested your machine. It adds a new terror to life and makes death a long-felt want.

   Herbert Beerbohm Tree 1852-1917 English actor-manager

There, standing at the piano, was the original good time who had been had by all.

   Kenneth Tynan 1927-80 English theatre critic

Looking and sounding not unlike Hitler, but without the charm.

   Gore Vidal 1925-2012 American novelist and critic, *on William F. Buckley Jr.*

Every other inch a gentleman.
Rebecca West 1892–1983 English novelist and journalist

CECILY: When I see a spade I call it a spade.
GWENDOLEN: I am glad to say that I have never seen a spade.
Oscar Wilde 1854–1900 Irish dramatist and poet

She's been on more laps than a napkin.
Walter Winchell 1897–1972 American journalist

Intelligence and Intellectuals

see also MIND

No one, however smart, however well-educated, however experienced, is the suppository of all wisdom.
Tony Abbott 1957– Australian Liberal statesman

definition of an intellectual:
Someone who can listen to the William Tell Overture without thinking of the Lone Ranger.
Anonymous

I'm not young enough to know everything.
J. M. Barrie 1860–1937 Scottish writer and dramatist

to H. G. Wells:
It is all very well to be able to write books, but can you wag your ears?
J. M. Barrie 1860–1937 Scottish writer and dramatist

Genius is one per cent inspiration, ninety-nine per cent perspiration.

Thomas Alva Edison 1847-1931 American inventor

Probably the greatest concentration of talent and genius in this house except for perhaps those times when Thomas Jefferson ate alone.

John F. Kennedy 1917-63 American Democratic statesman, *of a dinner for Nobel Prizewinners at the White House*

I think, therefore I am is the statement of an intellectual who underrates toothaches.

Milan Kundera 1929- Czech novelist

She does not understand the concept of Roman numerals. She thinks we just fought World War Eleven.

Joan Rivers 1933-2014 American comedienne

What is a highbrow? He is a man who has found something more interesting than women.

Edgar Wallace 1875-1932 English thriller writer

I have nothing to declare except my genius.

Oscar Wilde 1854-1900 Irish dramatist and poet

I know I've got a degree. Why does that mean I have to spend my life with intellectuals? I've got a life-saving certificate but I don't spend my evenings diving for a rubber brick with my pyjamas on.

Victoria Wood 1953-2016 British writer and comedienne

 # The Internet
see COMPUTERS *and the Internet*

Ireland and the Irish

see also **COUNTRIES**

We've never been cool, we're hot. Irish people are Italians who can't dress, Jamaicans who can't dance.
Bono 1960- Irish rock star

Where would the Irish be without someone to be Irish at?
Elizabeth Bowen 1899-1973 British novelist and short-story writer, born in Ireland

In some parts of Ireland the sleep which knows no waking is always followed by a wake which knows no sleeping.
Mary Wilson Little

I'm Irish. We think sideways.
Spike Milligan 1918-2002 Irish comedian

An Irishman's heart is nothing but his imagination.
George Bernard Shaw 1856-1950 Irish dramatist

denying that he was Irish:
Because a man is born in a stable, that does not make him a horse.
Duke of Wellington 1769-1852 British soldier and statesman

Jewellery

Every engagement ring should have at least one diamond or there is something very wrong—with the ring and the relationship.
Francis Boulle 1988- British businessman

Don't ever wear artistic jewellery; it *wrecks* a woman's reputation.
Colette 1873-1954 French novelist

You've got so much ice on your hands I could skate on them.
John Curry 1949-94 British skater, *to Liberace*

I never hated a man enough to give him diamonds back.
Zsa Zsa Gabor 1917-2016 Hungarian-born actress

A diamond is the only kind of ice that keeps a girl warm.
Elizabeth Taylor 1932-2011 English-born American actress

Big girls need big diamonds.
Elizabeth Taylor 1932-2011 English-born American actress, *originally said by the 6 foot tall American model Margaux Hemingway in the 1970s, and later much associated with Taylor*

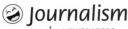 # Journalism
see also NEWSPAPERS

When a dog bites a man, that is not news, because it happens so often. But if a man bites a dog, that is news.
John B. Bogart 1848-1921 American journalist

I've been watching the TV News for forty years. It hasn't got any better.
Michele Brown 1947- British writer and publisher

Let's face it, sports writers, we're not hanging around with brain surgeons.
Jimmy Cannon 1910-73 American journalist

When seagulls follow a trawler, it is because they think
sardines will be thrown into the sea.

Eric Cantona 1966- French footballer, *at a press conference*

Journalism largely consists in saying 'Lord Jones Dead' to
people who never knew that Lord Jones was alive.

G. K. Chesterton 1874-1936 English essayist, novelist,
and poet

Everything is copy.

Phoebe Ephron 1914-71 American writer

News is something which somebody wants suppressed—
all the rest is advertising.

William Randolph Hearst 1863-1951 American newspaper
publisher and tycoon

Power without responsibility: the prerogative of the harlot
throughout the ages.

Rudyard Kipling 1865-1936 English writer and poet, *summing
up the view of Lord Beaverbrook*

If as Graham Greene said every novelist needs an icicle in
his heart, a successful editor needs a small iceberg.

Ferdinand Mount 1939- British writer and politician

Comment is free but facts are on expenses.

Tom Stoppard 1937- British dramatist

Freedom of the press in Britain means freedom to print
such of the proprietor's prejudices as the advertisers don't
object to.

Hannen Swaffer 1879-1962 British journalist

There are laws to protect the freedom of the press's speech, but none that are worth anything to protect the people from the press.

   Mark Twain 1835-1910 American writer

the difference between journalism and literature:

Journalism is unreadable, and literature is not read.

   Oscar Wilde 1854-1900 Irish dramatist and poet

Rock journalism is people who can't write interviewing people who can't talk for people who can't read.

   Frank Zappa 1940-93 American rock musician

 Judges

see also CRIME, LAW

Reform! Reform! Aren't things bad enough already?

   Mr Justice Astbury 1860-1939 British judge

CONVICTED CRIMINAL: As God is my judge—I am innocent.

LORD BIRKETT: He isn't; I am, and you're not!

   Lord Birkett 1883-1962 English barrister and judge

I don't want to know what the law is, I want to know who the judge is.

   Roy M. Cohn 1927-86 American lawyer

the judge Sir James Mansfield had suggested that the Court might sit on Good Friday:

If your Lordship pleases. But your Lordship will be the first judge who has done so since Pontius Pilate.

   William Davy d. 1780, *the Court did not sit*

I always feel that there should be some comfort derived from any question from the bench. It is clear proof that the inquiring Justice is not asleep.

Robert H. Jackson 1892-1954 American lawyer and judge

JUDGE: I have read your case, Mr Smith, and I am no wiser now than I was when I started.
SMITH: Possibly not, My Lord, but far better informed.

F. E. Smith 1872-1930 British Conservative politician and lawyer

JUDGE: What do you suppose I am on the Bench for, Mr Smith?
SMITH: It is not for me, Your Honour, to attempt to fathom the inscrutable workings of Providence.

F. E. Smith 1872-1930 British Conservative politician and lawyer

Kissing

asked what it was like to kiss Marilyn Monroe:
It's like kissing Hitler.

Tony Curtis 1925-2010 American actor

To let a fool kiss you is stupid,
To let a kiss fool you is worse.

E. Y. Harburg 1898-1981 American songwriter

on being discovered by his wife with a chorus girl:
I wasn't kissing her, I was just whispering in her mouth.

Chico Marx 1891-1961 American film comedian

When women kiss it always reminds one of prize-fighters shaking hands.

H. L. Mencken 1880-1956 American journalist and literary critic

Kissing don't last: cookery do!

George Meredith 1828-1909 English novelist and poet

A kiss can be a comma, a question mark or an exclamation point. That's basic spelling that every woman ought to know.

Mistinguett 1875-1956 French actress

I smoked my first cigarette and kissed my first woman on the same day. I have never had time for tobacco since.

Arturo Toscanini 1867-1957 Italian conductor

Language

see also LANGUAGES, WORDS

Sentence structure is innate but whining is acquired.

Woody Allen 1935- American film director, writer, and actor

Don't swear, boy. It shows a lack of vocabulary.

Alan Bennett 1934- English dramatist and actor

This is the sort of English up with which I will not put.

Winston Churchill 1874-1965 British Conservative statesman

There was so little English in that answer that President Chirac would have been happy with it.

William Hague 1961- British Conservative politician

The only person entitled to use the imperial 'we' in speaking of himself is a king, an editor, and a man with a tapeworm.

Robert G. Ingersoll 1833-99 American agnostic

The Achilles heel which has bitten us in the backside all year has stood out like a sore thumb.

Andy King 1956- English footballer

The subjunctive mood is in its death throes, and the best thing to do is to put it out of its misery as soon as possible.

W. Somerset Maugham 1874-1965 English novelist

My spelling is Wobbly. It's good spelling but it Wobbles, and the letters get in the wrong places.

A. A. Milne 1882-1956 English writer

All those exclamation marks, you notice? Five? A sure sign of someone who wears his underpants on his head.

Terry Pratchett 1948-2015 English fantasy writer

Save the gerund and screw the whale.

Tom Stoppard 1937- British dramatist

The four most beautiful words in our common language: I told you so.

Gore Vidal 1925-2012 American novelist and critic

title for a language-monitoring organization:

Association for the Annihilation of the Aberrant Apostrophe.

Keith Waterhouse 1929-2009 English writer

Good intentions are invariably ungrammatical.
> **Oscar Wilde** 1854-1900 Irish dramatist and poet

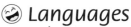 Languages

see also LANGUAGE, WORDS

If you understand English, press 1. If you do not understand English, press 2.
> **Anonymous**, *recorded message on Australian tax helpline*

Is there no Latin word for Tea? Upon my soul, if I had known that I would have let the vulgar stuff alone.
> **Hilaire Belloc** 1870-1953 British writer and Liberal politician

You know the trouble with the French, they don't even have a word for entrepreneur.
> **George W. Bush** 1946- American Republican statesman

Speak in French when you can't think of the English for a thing.
> **Lewis Carroll** 1832-98 English writer and logician

If the King's English was good enough for Jesus Christ, it's good enough for Texas.
> **Miriam A. 'Ma' Ferguson** 1875-1961 American Democratic politician

All pro athletes are bilingual. They speak English and profanity.
> **Gordie Howe** 1928-2016 Canadian ice-hockey player

when Khrushchev began banging his shoe on the desk:

Perhaps we could have a translation, I could not quite follow.

Harold Macmillan 1894-1986 British Conservative statesman

Listen, someone's screaming in agony—fortunately I speak it fluently.

Spike Milligan 1918-2002 Irish comedian

Waiting for the German verb is surely the ultimate thrill.

Flann O'Brien 1911-66 Irish novelist and journalist

KENNETH: If you're so hot, you'd better tell me how to say she has ideas above her station.
BRIAN: Oh, yes, I forgot. It's fairly easy, old boy. *Elle a des idées au-dessus de sa gare.*

Terence Rattigan 1911-77 English dramatist

They spell it Vinci and pronounce it Vinchy; foreigners always spell better than they pronounce.

Mark Twain 1835-1910 American writer

I once heard a Californian student in Heidelberg say, in one of his calmest moods, that he would rather decline two drinks than one German adjective.

Mark Twain 1835-1910 American writer

An unalterable and unquestioned law of the musical world required that the German text of French operas sung by Swedish artists should be translated into Italian for the clearer understanding of English-speaking audiences.

Edith Wharton 1862-1937 American novelist

There had crept a look of furtive shame, the shifty, hangdog look which announces that an Englishman is about to talk French.

P. G. Wodehouse 1881–1975 English writer

 Last Words

see also DEATH

Do you know the famous last words of the Fatted Calf? 'I hear the young master has returned.'

Monja Danischewsky 1911–94 Russian-born British screenwriter and producer

I will not go down to posterity talking bad grammar.

Benjamin Disraeli 1804–81 British Tory statesman and novelist, *while correcting proofs of his last Parliamentary speech*

No it is better not. She would only ask me to take a message to Albert.

Benjamin Disraeli 1804–81 British Tory statesman and novelist, *near death, declining a proposed visit from Queen Victoria*

on his deathbed, when someone remarked 'Cheer up, your Majesty, you will soon be at Bognor again':

Bugger Bognor.

George V 1865–1936 British king, *the remark may have been made earlier*

Leave the shower curtain on the inside of the tub.

Conrad Hilton 1887–1979 American hotelier

Dying is easy. Comedy is hard.

Edmund Kean c.1787–1833 English actor

Die, my dear Doctor, that's the last thing I shall do!
Lord Palmerston 1784–1865 British statesman

last words, as the priest was leaving her room:
One moment, Monsieur Le Curé, and we will depart together.
Madame de Pompadour 1721–64 French favourite of Louis XV

Bring down the curtain, the farce is played out.
François Rabelais c.1494–c.1553 French humanist

Put that bloody cigarette out!
Saki 1870–1916 Scottish writer, *before being shot by a sniper in World War One*

They couldn't hit an elephant at this distance…
John Sedgwick 1813–64 American Union general, *immediately prior to being killed by enemy fire at the battle of Spotsylvania*

If this is dying, then I don't think much of it.
Lytton Strachey 1880–1932 English biographer

on being asked to renounce the Devil, on his deathbed:
This is no time for making new enemies.
Voltaire 1694–1778 French writer and philosopher

The Law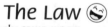
see also CRIME, JUDGES

Laws are like sausages. It's better not to see them being made.
Otto von Bismarck 1815–98 German statesman

The one great principle of the English law is, to make business for itself.

Charles Dickens 1812-70 English novelist

This contract is so one-sided that I am surprised to find it written on both sides of the paper.

Lord Evershed 1899-1966 British judge

A jury consists of twelve persons chosen to decide who has the better lawyer.

Robert Frost 1874-1963 American poet

I was sued by a woman who claimed that she became pregnant because she watched me on the television and I bent her contraceptive coil.

Uri Geller 1946- Israeli magician and illusionist

on the award of £600,000 libel damages to Sonia Sutcliffe against Private Eye:

If this is justice, I am a banana.

Ian Hislop 1960- English satirical journalist

No-one obeys the speed limit except a motorised rickshaw.

Boris Johnson 1964- British Conservative politician

If you want to get ahead in this world get a lawyer—not a book.

Fran Lebowitz 1950- American writer, *on self-help books*

In England, justice is open to all—like the Ritz Hotel.

James Mathew 1830-1908 Irish judge

However harmless a thing is, if the law forbids it most people will think it wrong.

W. Somerset Maugham 1874-1965 English novelist

Injustice is relatively easy to bear; what stings is justice.

H. L. Mencken 1880-1956 American journalist and literary critic

Here [in Paris] they hang a man first, and try him afterwards.

Molière 1622-73 French comic dramatist

MASTER OF THE ROLLS: Really, Mr Smith, do give this court credit for some little intelligence.
SMITH: That is the mistake I made in the court below, my lord

F. E. Smith 1872-1930 British Conservative politician and lawyer

Some circumstantial evidence is very strong, as when you find a trout in the milk.

Henry David Thoreau 1817-62 American writer

JUDGE: Are you trying to show contempt for this court?
WEST: No, I'm doing my best to hide it.

Mae West 1892-1980 American film actress

on juries:

Asking the ignorant to use the incomprehensible to decide the unknowable.

Hiller B. Zobel 1932- American judge, *see Wilde at* SPORTS

😄 Lawyers

I have knowingly defended a number of guilty men. But the guilty never escape unscathed. My fees are sufficient punishment for anyone.

F. Lee Bailey 1933- American lawyer

I don't know as I want a lawyer to tell me what I cannot do. I hire him to tell me how to do what I want to do.

J. P. Morgan 1837-1913 American financier and philanthropist

No brilliance is needed in the law. Nothing but common sense, and relatively clean finger nails.

John Mortimer 1923-2009 English writer and barrister

Professional men, they have no cares;
Whatever happens, they get theirs.

Ogden Nash 1902-71 American humorist

If law school is so hard to get through, how come there are so many lawyers?

Calvin Trillin 1935- American journalist and writer

What chance has the ignorant, uncultivated liar against the educated expert? What chance have I ... against a lawyer?

Mark Twain 1835-1910 American writer

😄 Letters

I would have answered your letter sooner, but you didn't send one.

Goodman Ace 1899-1982 American humorist

formula with which to return unsolicited manuscripts:

Mr James Agate regrets that he has no time to bother about the enclosed in which he has been greatly interested.

James Agate 1877–1947 British drama critic and novelist

using Lawrence's military number:

Dear 338171 (May I call you 338?).

Noël Coward 1899–1973 English dramatist, actor, and composer

in reply to a letter from executives of CBS headed 'From the desk of':

Dear Desk, . . .

Noël Coward 1899–1973 English dramatist, actor, and composer

Sir, My pa requests me to write to you, the doctors considering it doubtful whether he will ever recuvver the use of his legs which prevents his holding a pen.

Charles Dickens 1812–70 English novelist

It is wonderful how much news there is when people write every other day; if they wait for a month, there is nothing that seems worth telling.

O. Douglas 1877–1948 Scottish writer

I have made this [letter] longer than usual, only because I have not had the time to make it shorter.

Blaise Pascal 1623–62 French mathematician, physicist, and moralist

circular sent out to forestall unwanted visitors:

Mr J. Ruskin is about to begin a work of great importance and therefore begs that in reference to calls and correspondence you will consider him dead for the next two months.

John Ruskin 1819–1900 English art and social critic

Wilde had written to the Daily Telegraph, *but explained in a covering letter:*

I don't wish to sign my name, though I am afraid everybody will know who the writer is: one's style is one's signature always.

Oscar Wilde 1854-1900 Irish dramatist and poet

Libraries

see also BOOKS

RUTH: They'll sack you.
NORMAN: They daren't. I reorganized the Main Index. When I die, the secret dies with me.

Alan Ayckbourn 1939- English dramatist

There is nowhere in the world where sleep is so deep as in the libraries of the House of Commons.

Chips Channon 1897-1958 American-born British Conservative politician

Th' first thing to have in a libry is a shelf. Fr'm time to time this can be decorated with lithrachure. But th' shelf is th' main thing.

Finley Peter Dunne 1867-1936 American humorous writer

I've been drunk for about a week now, and I thought it might sober me up to sit in a library.

F. Scott Fitzgerald 1896-1940 American novelist

Mr Cobb took me into his library and showed me his books, of which he had a complete set.

Ring Lardner 1885-1933 American writer

Lies

see also TRUTH

She [Lady Desborough] tells enough white lies to ice a wedding cake.

Margot Asquith 1864-1945 British political hostess

of propaganda:

That branch of the art of lying which consists in very nearly deceiving your friends without quite deceiving your enemies.

Francis M. Cornford 1874-1943 English academic

Telling lies is a bit like tiling bathrooms—if you don't know how to do it properly, it's best not to try.

Tom Holt 1961- English novelist

on being told that Lord Astor claimed that her allegations concerning himself were untrue:

He would, wouldn't he?

Mandy Rice-Davies 1944-2014 English model and showgirl

A little inaccuracy sometimes saves tons of explanation.

Saki 1870-1916 Scottish writer

In exceptional circumstances it is necessary to say something that is untrue in the House of Commons.

William Waldegrave 1946- British Conservative politician

Untruthful! My nephew Algernon? Impossible! He is an Oxonian.

Oscar Wilde 1854-1900 Irish dramatist and poet

Life and its Challenges

see also LIFESTYLE

If you can't be a good example, then you'll just have to be a horrible warning.

Catherine Aird 1930- English writer

WOODY ALLEN: I feel that life is—is divided up into the horrible and the miserable.

Woody Allen 1935- American film director, writer, and actor, *in the film* Annie Hall, *written with* **Marshall Brickman** (1941-)

WOODY ALLEN: Life doesn't imitate art. It imitates bad television.

Woody Allen 1935- American film director, writer, and actor, *in the film* Husbands and Wives

I have yet to see any problem, however complicated, which, when you looked at it in the right way, did not become still more complicated.

Poul Anderson 1926-2001 American science fiction writer

Nothing matters very much and very few things matter at all.

Arthur James Balfour 1848-1930 British Conservative statesman

Life, you know, is rather like opening a tin of sardines. We are all of us looking for the key.

Alan Bennett 1934- English dramatist and actor

W. C. FIELDS: It's a funny old world—a man's lucky if he gets out of it alive.

Walter de Leon and **Paul M. Jones** screenwriters, *in the film* You're Telling Me

I find I always have to write something on a steamed mirror.

Elaine Dundy 1921-2008 American writer

Life is like riding a bicycle. To keep your balance you must keep moving.

Albert Einstein 1879-1955 German-born theoretical physicist

All men are equal—all men, that is to say, who possess umbrellas.

E. M. Forster 1879-1970 English novelist

Drama is life with the dull bits cut out.

Alfred Hitchcock 1899-1980 British-born film director

Life is just one damned thing after another.

Elbert Hubbard 1859-1915 American writer

Most of one's life . . . is one prolonged effort to prevent oneself thinking.

Aldous Huxley 1894-1963 English novelist

Do you know how helpless you feel if you have a full cup of coffee in your hand and you start to sneeze?

Jean Kerr 1923-2003 American writer

Life doesn't wait to be asked: it comes grinning in, sits down uninvited and helps itself to bread and cheese, and comments uninhibitedly on the decorations.

Philip Larkin 1922-85 English poet

Life is something to do when you can't get to sleep.

Fran Lebowitz 1950- American writer

For the happiest life, days should be rigorously planned, nights left open to chance.

Mignon McLaughlin 1913-83 American writer

There's one thing to be said for inviting trouble: it generally accepts.

Mae Maloo

Whenever I investigate a smell, I find that the answer is always bad. It's never: 'What is that? [sniff] muffins'!

Demetri Martin 1973- American comedian

It's not true that life is one damn thing after another—it's one damn thing over and over.

Edna St Vincent Millay 1892-1950 American poet

There are three ingredients in the good life: learning, earning, and yearning.

Christopher Morley 1890-1957 American writer

There are few things in this world more reassuring than an unhappy lottery winner.

Tony Parsons 1953- English writer

You're born naked and the rest is drag.

RuPaul 1960- American drag queen

I *love* living. I have some problems with my *life*, but living is the best thing they've come up with so far.

Neil Simon 1927- American dramatist

Life is a gamble at terrible odds—if it was a bet, you wouldn't take it.

Tom Stoppard 1937- British dramatist

We're all in this together—by ourselves.
   Lily Tomlin 1939- American comedienne and actress

What a queer thing Life is! So unlike anything else, don't you know, if you see what I mean.
   P. G. Wodehouse 1881-1975 English-born writer

Lifestyle 😄

What is the secret of my long life? I really don't know—cigarettes, whisky and wild, wild women!
   Henry Allingham 1896-2009 English airman, *the oldest British survivor of the First World War*

The only thing I regret about my life is the length of it. If I had to live my life again I'd make all the same mistakes—only sooner.
   Tallulah Bankhead 1903-68 American actress

Never try to keep up with the Joneses. Drag them down to your level.
   Quentin Crisp 1908-99 English writer

If A is a success in life, then A equals x plus y plus z. Work is x; y is play; and z is keeping your mouth shut.
   Albert Einstein 1879-1955 German-born theoretical physicist

Most people die without ever having lived. Luckily for them, they don't realize it.
   Henrik Ibsen 1828-1906 Norwegian dramatist

You only live once, and the way I live, once is enough.
   Frank Sinatra 1915-98 American singer and actor

 Literature

see also POETRY, WRITING

Literature's always a good card to play for Honours. It makes people think that Cabinet ministers are educated.
   Arnold Bennett 1867-1931 English novelist

'What is the use of a book', thought Alice, 'without pictures or conversations?'
   Lewis Carroll 1832-98 English writer and logician

If my books had been any worse, I should not have been invited to Hollywood, and if they had been any better, I should not have come.
   Raymond Chandler 1888-1959 American writer

on encountering a footnote:

Like going downstairs to answer the doorbell while making love.
   Noël Coward 1899-1973 English dramatist, actor, and composer

When I want to read a novel, I write one.
   Benjamin Disraeli 1804-81 British Tory statesman and novelist

listening to readings from Tolkien's Lord of the Rings:

Oh fuck, not another elf!
   Hugo Dyson 1896-1975 English academic

How rare, how precious is frivolity! How few writers can prostitute all their powers! They are always implying, 'I am capable of higher things.'
   E. M. Forster 1879-1970 English novelist

What greater service could I have performed for German literature than that I didn't bother with it?
Frederick the Great 1712-86 Prussian king

It takes a great deal of history to produce a little literature.
Henry James 1843-1916 American novelist

A beginning, a muddle, and an end.
Philip Larkin 1922-85 English poet, *on the 'classic formula' for a novel*

Literature is mostly about having sex and not much about having children. Life is the other way round.
David Lodge 1935- English novelist

From the moment I picked up your book until I laid it down, I was convulsed with laughter. Some day I intend reading it.
Groucho Marx 1890-1977 American film comedian

In literature as in love, we are astonished at what is chosen by others.
André Maurois 1885-1967 French writer

Is Moby Dick the whale or the man?
Harold Ross 1892-1951 American journalist and editor

You're familiar with the tragedies of antiquity, are you? The great homicidal classics?
Tom Stoppard 1937- British dramatist

Like playing Beethoven on the kazoo.
John Sutherland 1938- English writer, *on his translation of Shakespeare into text messages*

Love

see also DATING, SEX

Even logical positivists are capable of love.
A. J. Ayer 1910–89 English philosopher

The test for true love is whether you can endure the thought of cutting your sweetheart's toe-nails.
W. N. P. Barbellion 1889–1919 English diarist

Make love to every woman you meet. If you get five percent on your outlays it's a good investment.
Arnold Bennett 1867–1931 English novelist

It is a curious thought, but it is only when you see people looking ridiculous, that you realize just how much you love them.
Agatha Christie 1890–1976 English writer

Love and a cottage! Eh, Fanny! Ah, give me indifference and a coach and six!
George Colman, the Elder 1732–94 and **David Garrick** 1717–79 English dramatists

The magic of first love is our ignorance that it can ever end.
Benjamin Disraeli 1804–81 British Tory statesman and novelist

What is commonly called love, namely the desire of satisfying a voracious appetite with a certain quantity of delicate white human flesh.
Henry Fielding 1707–54 English novelist and dramatist

Love is a perky elf dancing a merry little jig and then suddenly he turns on you with a miniature machine gun.

Matt Groening 1954- American humorist and satirist

When I'm not near the girl I love,
I love the girl I'm near.

E. Y. Harburg 1898-1981 American songwriter

Love's like the measles—all the worse when it comes late in life.

Douglas Jerrold 1803-57 English dramatist and journalist

Tell me, George, if you had to do it all over would you fall in love with yourself again.

Oscar Levant 1906-72 American pianist, *to George Gershwin*

Love's a disease. But curable.

Rose Macaulay 1881-1958 English novelist

Love is the delusion that one woman differs from another.

H. L. Mencken 1880-1956 American journalist and literary critic

If love is the answer, could you rephrase the question?

Lily Tomlin 1939- American comedienne and actress

Love conquers all things—except poverty and toothache.

Mae West 1892-1980 American film actress

To love oneself is the beginning of a lifelong romance.

Oscar Wilde 1854-1900 Irish dramatist and poet

 Management

see also BUREAUCRACY

The most important thing in communication is to hear what isn't being said.

Peter F. Drucker 1909-2005 Austrian-born American management consultant

Meetings are a great trap...However, they are indispensable when you don't want to do anything.

J. K. Galbraith 1908-2006 Canadian-born American economist

Only the paranoid survive.

Andrew Grove 1936-2016 Hungarian-born American businessman, *dictum on which he long ran his company, the Intel Corporation*

I was to learn later in life that...we tend...to meet any new situation by reorganizing; and a wonderful method it can be for creating the illusion of progress while producing confusion, inefficiency, and demoralization.

Charlton Ogburn Jr 1911-98 American writer, *frequently wrongly attributed to Petronius Arbiter (d.* AD 65)

The man who is denied the opportunity of taking decisions of importance begins to regard as important the decisions he is allowed to take.

C. Northcote Parkinson 1909-93 English writer

It is difficult to get a man to understand something when his salary depends on his not understanding it.

Upton Sinclair 1878-1968 American novelist and social reformer

MICHAEL DOUGLAS: Lunch is for wimps.
> **Stanley Weiser** and **Oliver Stone** 1946- screenwriters, *in the film* Wall Street

Don't say yes until I finish talking!
> **Darryl F. Zanuck** 1902-79 American film producer, *characteristic instruction*

Manners

My grandmother took a bath every year, whether she was dirty or not.
> **Brendan Behan** 1923-64 Irish dramatist

INTERVIEWER: You've been accused of vulgarity.
MEL BROOKS: Bullshit!
> **Mel Brooks** 1926- American film director and comic actor

Curtsey while you're thinking what to say. It saves time.
> **Lewis Carroll** 1832-98 English writer and logician

Vulgarity is the garlic in the salad of charm.
> **Cyril Connolly** 1903-74 English writer

NOTE FROM FELLOW DINNER GUEST: Talk to the woman on your left.
HEATH (PASSING THE NOTE BACK): I have.
> **Edward Heath** 1916-2005 British Conservative statesman

To Americans, English manners are far more frightening than none at all.
> **Randall Jarrell** 1914-65 American poet

'What are you doing for dinner tonight?'
'Digesting it.'

> **George S. Kaufman** 1889-1961 American dramatist, *replying to a dinner invitation arriving at 8.30 pm*

I've always had good manners. I always take the cigarette out of my mouth before kissing someone.

> **Ian Kilminster** (known as 'Lemmy') 1945-2015 English pop singer

as the pantomime dame Mother Goose:

The bus was so crowded—even the men were standing.

> **Dan Leno** 1860-1904 English entertainer

I have noticed that the people who are late are often so much jollier than the people who have to wait for them.

> **E. V. Lucas** 1868-1938 English journalist, essayist, and critic

aged four, having had hot coffee spilt over his legs:

Thank you, madam, the agony is abated.

> **Lord Macaulay** 1800-59 English politician and historian

GROUCHO MARX: Do you suppose I could buy back my introduction to you?

> **S. J. Perelman** 1904-79 and **others** screenwriters, *in the film* Monkey Business

Everyone knows that the real business of a ball is either to look out for a wife, to look after a wife, or to look after somebody else's wife.

> **R. S. Surtees** 1805-64 English sporting journalist and novelist

Somerset Maugham excused his leaving early when dining with Lady Tree by saying, 'I must look after my youth':

Next time do bring him. We adore those sort of people.

> **Lady Tree** 1863-1937 English actress

Orthodoxy is my doxy; heterodoxy is another man's doxy.

William Warburton 1698-1779 English theologian and bishop

Manners are especially the need of the plain. The pretty can get away with anything.

Evelyn Waugh 1903-66 English novelist

Duty is what one expects from others, it is not what one does oneself.

Oscar Wilde 1854-1900 Irish dramatist and poet

Marriage

see also DIVORCE, HUSBANDS, WEDDINGS

WOODY ALLEN: I think people should mate for life. Like pigeons, or Catholics.

Woody Allen 1935- American film director, writer, and actor, *in the film* Manhattan

A man cannot marry before he has studied anatomy and has dissected at the least one woman.

Honoré de Balzac 1799-1850 French novelist

I'm not going to make the same mistake once.

Warren Beatty 1937- American actor, film director, and screenwriter, *on marriage*

Love matches are formed by people who pay for a month of honey with a life of vinegar.

Countess of Blessington 1789-1849 Irish novelist

It was very good of God to let Carlyle and Mrs Carlyle marry one another and so make only two people miserable instead of four.

Samuel Butler 1835–1902 English novelist

The deep, deep peace of the double-bed after the hurly-burly of the chaise-longue.

Mrs Patrick Campbell 1865–1940 English actress

He has a future and I have a past so we should be all right.

Jennie Churchill 1851–1921 American-born society hostess, *on her marriage to Montagu Porch in 1918 (he was forty-one, three years younger than her son Winston)*

If you're married for more than ten minutes, you're going to have to forgive somebody for something.

Hillary Rodham Clinton 1947– American lawyer and politician

The most happy marriage I can picture or imagine to myself would be the union of a deaf man to a blind woman.

Samuel Taylor Coleridge 1772–1834 English poet, critic, and philosopher

asked, on returning from their honeymoon, about the age difference with her husband, 32 years her junior:

If he dies, he dies.

Joan Collins 1933– British actress

Marriage is a feast where the grace is sometimes better than the dinner.

Charles Caleb Colton 1780–1832 English clergyman and writer

Marriage is a wonderful invention; but, then again, so is a bicycle repair kit.

Billy Connolly 1942- Scottish comedian

One of those looks which only a quarter-century of wedlock can adequately marinate.

Alan Coren 1938-2007 English humorist

I have always thought that every woman should marry, and no man.

Benjamin Disraeli 1804-81 British Tory statesman and novelist

Keep your eyes wide open before marriage, half shut afterwards.

Benjamin Franklin 1706-90 American politician, inventor, and scientist

I support gay marriage because I believe they have a right to be just as miserable as the rest of us.

Kinky Friedman 1944- American singer and politician

A man in love is incomplete until he has married. Then he's finished.

Zsa Zsa Gabor 1917-2016 Hungarian-born film actress

My mother said it was simple to keep a man, you must be a maid in the living room, a cook in the kitchen and a whore in the bedroom. I said I'd hire the other two and take care of the bedroom bit.

Jerry Hall 1956- American model

Marriage is a good deal like a circus: there is not as much in it as is represented in the advertising.

E. W. Howe 1853–1937 American novelist and editor

Do you think I'd marry anyone who would marry *me*?

Henry James 1843–1916 American novelist

of a man who remarried immediately after the death of a wife with whom he had been unhappy:

The triumph of hope over experience.

Samuel Johnson 1709–84 English poet, critic, and lexicographer

The most difficult year of marriage is the one you're in.

Franklin P. Jones 1887–1929 American businessman

The honeymoon is over when he phones that he'll be late for supper—and she has already left a note that it's in the refrigerator.

Bill Lawrence 1968– American screenwriter

Many a man in love with a dimple makes the mistake of marrying the whole girl.

Stephen Leacock 1869–1944 Canadian humorist

Some people claim that marriage interferes with romance. There is no doubt about it. Anytime you have a romance, your wife is bound to interfere.

Groucho Marx 1890–1977 American film comedian

to her husband, who had asked the age of a flirtatious starlet with noticeably thick legs:

For God's sake, Walter, why don't you chop off her legs and read the rings?

Carol Matthau 1925–2003 American actress

No matter how happily a woman may be married, it always pleases her to discover that there is a nice man who wishes she were not.

H. L. Mencken 1880-1956 American journalist and literary critic

One doesn't have to get anywhere in a marriage. It's not a public conveyance.

Iris Murdoch 1919-99 English novelist

Marriage is the alliance of two people one of whom never remembers birthdays and the other never forgetsam.

Ogden Nash 1902-71 American humorist

BISHOP: Who is it that sees and hears all we do, and before whom even I am but as a crushed worm?
PAGE: The Missus, my Lord.

Punch 1841-1992 English humorous weekly periodical

the Lord Chief Justice was once asked by a lady what was the maximum punishment for bigamy:

Two mothers-in-law.

Lord Russell of Killowen 1832-1900 Irish lawyer and politician

Marriage is popular because it combines the maximum of temptation with the maximum of opportunity.

George Bernard Shaw 1856-1950 Irish dramatist

Take care of him. And make him feel important. And if you can do that, you'll have a happy and wonderful marriage. Like two out of every ten couples.

Neil Simon 1927- American dramatist

My definition of marriage ... it resembles a pair of shears, so joined that they cannot be separated; often moving in opposite directions, yet always punishing anyone who comes between them.

Sydney Smith 1771–1845 English clergyman and essayist

My brother Toby, quoth she, is going to be married to Mrs Wadman. Then he will never, quoth my father, lie *diagonally* in his bed again as long as he lives.

Laurence Sterne 1713–68 English novelist

asked who wore the trousers at home:

I do. I wear the trousers. And I wash and iron them, too.

Denis Thatcher 1915–2003 English businessman

It should be a very happy marriage—they are both so much in love with *him*.

Irene Thomas 1919–2001 British broadcaster

Marriage isn't a word…it's a *sentence*!

King Vidor 1895–1982 American film director

Marriage is a great institution, but I'm not ready for an institution yet.

Mae West 1892–1980 American film actress

A good marriage is like Dr Who's Tardis, only small and banal from the outside, but spacious and interesting from within.

Katharine Whitehorn 1928– English journalist

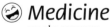

Medicine

see also SICKNESS

I am dying with the help of too many physicians.

Alexander the Great 356–323 BC Greek king

I was in for ten hours and had 40 pints, beating my previous record by 20 minutes.

George Best 1946-2005 Northern Irish footballer, *comparing transfusions after his liver transplant with drinking*

I used to believe that chiropractors were charlatans, but then I went to one and now I stand corrected.

Shmuel Breban American comedian

A fashionable surgeon, like a pelican, can be recognized by the size of his bill.

John Chalmers DaCosta 1863-1933 American surgeon

A Harvard medical school study has determined that rectal thermometers are still the best way to tell a baby's temperature. Plus it really teaches the baby who's boss.

Tina Fey 1970- American comedian and actress

A cousin of mine who was a casualty surgeon in Manhattan tells me that he and his colleagues had a one-word nickname for bikers: Donors.

Stephen Fry 1957- English comedian, actor, and writer

TONY HANCOCK: I came in here in all good faith to help my country. I don't mind giving a reasonable amount [of blood], but a pint...why that's very nearly an armful.

Ray Galton 1930- and **Alan Simpson** 1929-2017 English writers

A hospital is no place to be sick.

Sam Goldwyn 1882-1974 American film producer

If you have a stomach ache, in France you get a suppository, in Germany a health spa, in the United States they cut your stomach open and in Britain they put you on a waiting list.

Phil Hammond 1955- and **Michael Mosley** 1957- writers and presenters

No families take so little medicine as those of doctors, except those of apothecaries.

Oliver Wendell Holmes 1809-94 American physician and writer

The kind of doctor I want is one who, when he's not examining me, is home studying medicine.

George S. Kaufman 1889-1961 American dramatist

In disease Medical Men guess: if they cannot ascertain a disease, they call it nervous.

John Keats 1795-1821 English poet

One of the most difficult things to contend with in a hospital is the assumption on the part of the staff that because you have lost your gall bladder you have also lost your mind.

Jean Kerr 1923-2003 American writer

A specialist is a man who knows more and more about less and less.

William Mayo 1861-1939 American physician

The desire to take medicine is perhaps the greatest feature which distinguishes man from animals.

William Osler 1849-1919 Canadian-born physician

Cured yesterday of my disease,
I died last night of my physician.

Matthew Prior 1664-1721 English poet

A friend of mine confused her Valium with her birth control pills—she had 14 kids but didn't give a shit.

Joan Rivers 1933-2014 American comedienne

There is at bottom only one genuinely scientific treatment for all diseases, and that is to stimulate the phagocytes.

George Bernard Shaw 1856-1950 Irish dramatist

I can't stand whispering. Every time a doctor whispers in the hospital, next day there's a funeral.

Neil Simon 1927- American dramatist

Memory 😄

Our memories are card-indexes consulted, and then put back in disorder by authorities whom we do not control.

Cyril Connolly 1903-74 English writer

The older I get, the better I used to be.

John McEnroe 1959- American tennis player, *quoting basketball star Connie Hawkins*

The fondest memory I have is not really of the Goons. It is a girl called Julia with enormous breasts.

Spike Milligan 1918-2002 Irish comedian

The selective memory isn't selective enough.

Blake Morrison 1950- English poet

Men

see also MEN AND WOMEN

My mother's two categories: nice men did things for you, bad men did things to you.

Margaret Atwood 1939- Canadian novelist

It is a truth universally acknowledged, that a single man in possession of a good fortune, must be in want of a wife.

Jane Austen 1775-1817 English novelist

A man is two people, himself and his cock. A man always takes his friend to the party. Of the two, the friend is the nicer, being more able to show his feelings.

Beryl Bainbridge 1934-2010 English novelist

A man who correctly guesses a woman's age may be smart, but he's not very bright.

Lucille Ball 1911-89 American actress

Women were brought up to believe that men were the answer. They weren't. They weren't even one of the questions.

Julian Barnes 1946- English novelist

All men are children anyway and if you understand that, a woman understands everything.

Coco Chanel 1883-1971 French fashion designer

My mother wanted me to be a nice boy. I didn't let her down. I don't smoke, drink or mess around with women.

Julian Clary 1959- English comedian

Beware of men who cry. It's true that men who cry are sensitive to and in touch with feelings, but the only feelings they tend to be sensitive to and in touch with are their own.

Nora Ephron 1941-2012 American screenwriter and director

I want a man who's kind and understanding. Is that too much to ask of a millionaire?

Zsa Zsa Gabor 1917-2016 Hungarian-born actress

Behind every successful man stands a surprised mother-in-law.

Hubert Humphrey 1911-78 American Democratic politician

To men, porno movies are beautiful love stories with all the boring stuff taken out.

Richard Jeni 1957-2007 American comedian

When a man brings his wife flowers for no reason—there's a reason!

Marian Jordan 1898-1961 American actress

Years ago, manhood was an opportunity for achievement, and now it is a problem to be overcome.

Garrison Keillor 1942- American humorous writer and broadcaster

Most men think monogamy is something you make dining-room tables out of.

Kathy Lette 1958- Australian writer

A man's home may seem to be his castle on the outside; inside it is more often his nursery.

Clare Booth Luce 1903-87 American diplomat, politician, and writer

Men are those creatures with two legs and eight hands.
Jayne Mansfield 1933-67 American actress

If you want to scare your boyfriend next Halloween, come dressed as what he fears most. Commitment.
Peter Nelson

The follies which a man regrets most, in his life, are those which he didn't commit when he had the opportunity.
Helen Rowland 1875-1950 American writer

The typical public schoolboy is acceptable at a dance and invaluable in a shipwreck.
J. F. Roxburgh 1885-1951 English headmaster

Men's bums never grow up. Like school satchels, they evoke in an instant memories of childhood.
Arundhati Roy 1961- Indian novelist

I like men to behave like men—strong and childish.
Françoise Sagan 1935-2004 French novelist

God made him, and therefore let him pass for a man.
William Shakespeare 1564-1616 English dramatist

A hard man is good to find.
Mae West 1892-1980 American film actress

A man in the house is worth two in the street.
Mae West 1892-1980 American film actress

A fox is a wolf who sends flowers.
Ruth Weston 1906-55 American actress

Men and Women

see also DATING, MEN, WIVES, WOMEN

In passing, also, I would like to say that the first time
Adam had a chance he laid the blame on woman...

Nancy Astor 1879-1964 American-born British Conservative
politician

You never see a man walking down the street with a
woman who has a little pot belly and a bald spot.

Elayne Boosler 1952- American comedian

Guys are like dogs. They keep coming back. Ladies are like
cats. Yell at a cat one time, they're gone.

Lenny Bruce 1925-66 American comedian

A woman can become a man's friend only in the following
stages—first an acquaintance, next a mistress, and only
then a friend.

Anton Chekhov 1860-1904 Russian dramatist and short-story
writer

Certain women should be struck regularly, like gongs.

Noël Coward 1899-1973 English dramatist, actor, and composer

I wouldn't be seen dead with a woman old enough to be
my wife.

Tony Curtis 1925-2010 American actor

Last year my wife ran off with the fellow next door and
I must admit, I still miss him.

Les Dawson 1934-93 English comedian

If they ever invent a vibrator that can open pickle jars, we've had it.

Jeff Green 1964- English comedian, *on the bleak future facing men*

Women and cats do as they please, and men and dogs might as well relax to it.

Robert Heinlein 1907-88 American science fiction writer

A woman's mind is cleaner than a man's; she changes it more often.

Oliver Herford 1863-1935 English-born American humorist

Can you imagine a world without men? No crime and lots of happy fat women.

Nicole Hollander 1939- American cartoonist

Women speak because they wish to speak, whereas a man speaks only when driven to speech by something outside himself—like, for instance, he can't find any clean socks.

Jean Kerr 1923-2003 American writer

No one will ever win the battle of the sexes; there's too much fraternizing with the enemy.

Henry Kissinger 1923- American politician

JIM CARREY: Behind every great man is a woman rolling her eyes.

Steve Koren, **Mark O'Keefe**, and **Steve Oedekerk** screenwriters, *in the film* Bruce Almighty

Why do men like smart women? Because opposites attract.

Kathy Lette 1958- Australian writer

Women are brighter than men. That's true, but it should be kept very quiet or it ruins the whole racket.

Anita Loos 1893-1981 American writer

Men talk to women so they can sleep with them and women sleep with men so they can talk to them.

Jay McInerney 1955- American writer

A little incompatibility is the spice of life, particularly if he has income and she is pattable.

Ogden Nash 1902-71 American humorist

Men seldom make passes
At girls who wear glasses.

Dorothy Parker 1893-1967 American critic and humorist

When a man opens the car door for his wife, it's either a new car or a new wife.

Philip, Duke of Edinburgh 1921- husband of Elizabeth II

All my life I've loved a womanly woman and admired a manly man, but I never could stand a boily boy.

Lord Rosebery 1847-1929 British Liberal statesman

The material for this book was collected directly from nature at great personal risk by the author.

Helen Rowland 1875-1950 American writer, *in capitals, on the flyleaf of her book* A Guide to Men

Men hate to lose. I once beat my husband at tennis. I asked him 'Are we going to have sex again?' He said 'Yes, but not with each other'.

Rita Rudner 1953- American comedienne and writer

It was always women who did the choosing, and men's place was to be grateful if they were lucky enough to be the chosen ones.

Salman Rushdie 1947- Indian-born British novelist

LYDIA: Every great man has had a woman behind him.
JANET: And every great woman has had some man or other in front of her, tripping her up.

Dorothy L. Sayers 1893-1957 English writer

Men want the same thing from their underwear that they want from women: a little bit of support and a little bit of freedom.

Jerry Seinfeld 1954- American comedian

If you want anything said, ask a man. If you want anything done, ask a woman.

Margaret Thatcher 1925-2013 British Conservative stateswoman

Sure he was great, but don't forget that Ginger Rogers did everything he did backwards...and in high heels!

Bob Thaves 1924-2006 American cartoonist, *caption to cartoon showing a Fred Astaire film festival*

A man has one hundred dollars and you leave him with two dollars, that's subtraction.

Mae West 1892-1980 American film actress

Is that a gun in your pocket, or are you just glad to see me?

Mae West 1892-1980 American film actress, *usually quoted as 'Is that a pistol in your pocket...'*

When women go wrong, men go right after them.

Mae West 1892-1980 American film actress

asked by the gossip columnist Hedda Hopper how she knew so much about men:

Baby, I went to night school.

Mae West 1892-1980 American film actress

Whatever women do they must do twice as well as men to be thought half as good. Luckily, this is not difficult.

Charlotte Whitton 1896-1975 Canadian writer and politician

The only time a woman really succeeds in changing a man is when he's a baby.

Natalie Wood 1938-81 American actress

A man is designed to walk three miles in the rain to phone for help when the car breaks down—and a woman is designed to say, 'You took your time' when he comes back dripping wet.

Victoria Wood 1953-2016 British writer and comedienne

Mental Health

see also MIND

The statistics on sanity are that one out of every four Americans is suffering from some form of mental illness. Think of your three best friends. If they're okay, then it's you.

Rita Mae Brown 1944- American novelist and poet

I told my wife the truth. I told her I was seeing a psychiatrist. Then she told *me* the truth; that she was seeing a psychiatrist, two plumbers and a bartender.

Rodney Dangerfield 1921-2004 American comedian

Any man who goes to a psychiatrist should have his head examined.

Sam Goldwyn 1882-1974 American film producer

Psychiatry is a waste of good couches. Why should I make a psychiatrist laugh, and then pay him?

Kathy Lette 1958- Australian writer

O Lord, Sir—when a heroine goes mad she always goes into white satin.

Richard Brinsley Sheridan 1751-1816 Irish dramatist and Whig politician

A psychiatrist is a man who goes to the Folies-Bergère and looks at the audience.

Mervyn Stockwood 1913-95 English clergyman

You're only given a little spark of madness. You mustn't lose it.

Robin Williams 1951-2014 American actor

 # Middle Age
see also OLD AGE, YOUTH

I recently turned 60. Practically a third of my life is over.

Woody Allen 1935- American film director, writer, and actor

You are thirty-two. You are rapidly approaching the age when your body, whether it embarrasses you or not, begins to embarrass other people.

Alan Bennett 1934- English dramatist and actor

Whenever the talk turns to age, I say I am 49 plus VAT.

Lionel Blair 1936- British actor and dancer

Middle age is when your broad mind and narrow waist begin to change places.

E. Joseph Cossman

of Zsa Zsa Gabor:

She's discovered the secret of perpetual middle age.

Oscar Levant 1906-72 American pianist

The lovely thing about being forty is that you can appreciate twenty-five-year-old men more.

Colleen McCullough 1937-2015 Australian writer

Maturity is a high price to pay for growing up.

Tom Stoppard 1937- British dramatist

From birth to 18 a girl needs good parents. From 18 to 35, she needs good looks. From 35 to 55, good personality. From 55 on, she needs good cash.

Sophie Tucker 1884-1966 Russian-born American vaudeville artist

Youth is when you are allowed to stay up late on New Year's Eve. Middle age is when you are forced to.

Bill Vaughan 1915-77 American columnist

Thirty-five is a very attractive age. London society is full of women of the very highest birth who have, of their own free choice, remained thirty-five for years.

Oscar Wilde 1854-1900 Irish dramatist and poet

# The Mind

see also INTELLIGENCE, MENTAL HEALTH

WOODY ALLEN: My brain? It's my second favourite organ.

Woody Allen 1935- American film director, writer, and actor and **Marshall Brickman** 1941-*in the film* Sleeper

definition of the brain:

An apparatus with which we think that we think.

Ambrose Bierce 1842-c.1914 American writer

Minds are like parachutes. They only function when they are open.

Lord Dewar 1864-1930 British industrialist

Insanity is hereditary. You can get it from your children.

Sam Levenson 1911-80 American humorist

If I knew what I was so anxious about I wouldn't be anxious.

Mignon McLaughlin 1913-83 American writer

The trouble with having an open mind, of course, is that people will insist on coming along and trying to put things in it.

Terry Pratchett 1948-2015 English fantasy writer

Not body enough to cover his mind decently with; his intellect is improperly exposed.

Sydney Smith 1771–1845 English clergyman and essayist

I must have a prodigious quantity of mind; it takes me as much as a week, sometimes, to make it up.

Mark Twain 1835–1910 American writer

A neurosis is a secret you don't know you're keeping.

Kenneth Tynan 1927–80 English theatre critic

Right now I'm having amnesia and déja vu at the same time. I think I've forgotten this before.

Steven Wright 1955– American comedian

Mistakes and Misfortunes

STRIKER: Surely you can't be serious.
DR RUMACK: I am serious. And don't call me Shirley.

Jim Abrahams and **others** screenwriters, *in the film* Airplane!

waiter delivering champagne to George Best's hotel room:
Tell me, Mr Best, where did it all go wrong?

Anonymous, *£20,000 in cash was scattered on the bed, which also contained Miss World*

My only solution for the problem of habitual accidents… is to stay in bed all day. Even then, there is always the chance that you will fall out.

Robert Benchley 1889–1945 American humorist

on being told by her son that lesbians are women who sleep together:

MRS HOPKINS: Well, that's nothing. I slept with your Auntie Phyllis all during the air raids.

Alan Bennett 1934- English dramatist and actor

Calamities are of two kinds: misfortune to ourselves, and good fortune to others.

Ambrose Bierce 1842-c.1914 American writer

I've learned from my mistakes, and I'm sure I can repeat them.

Peter Cook 1937-95 English comedian and actor, *as Sir Arthur Streeb-Greebling*

If Gladstone fell into the Thames, that would be misfortune; and if anybody pulled him out, that, I suppose, would be a calamity.

Benjamin Disraeli 1804-81 British Tory statesman and novelist

I left the room with silent dignity, but caught my foot in the mat.

George Grossmith 1847-1912 and **Weedon Grossmith** 1854-1919 English writers

If, of all words of tongue and pen,
The saddest are, 'It might have been,'
More sad are these we daily see:
'It is, but hadn't ought to be!'

Bret Harte 1836-1902 American poet

My father told me all about the birds and the bees, the liar—I went steady with a woodpecker until I was 21.

Bob Hope 1903-2003 American comedian

MICHAEL CAINE: You were only supposed to blow the
bloody doors off!

Troy Kennedy-Martin 1932-2009 British screenwriter, *in the film*
The Italian Job

No snowflake in an avalanche ever feels responsible.

Stanislaw Lec 1909-66 Polish writer

I had never had a piece of toast
Particularly long and wide,
But fell upon the sanded floor,
And always on the buttered side.

James Payn 1830-98 English writer

I actually slipped on a hamburger in Hamburg once, and
almost fell off stage.

Keith Richards 1943- English rock musician

a postcard of the Venus de Milo sent to his niece:

See what'll happen to you if you don't stop biting your
finger-nails.

Will Rogers 1879-1935 American actor and humorist

For Pheasant *read* Peasant, throughout.

W. C. Sellar 1898-1951 and **R. J. Yeatman** 1898-1968 British
writers

Well, if I called the wrong number, why did you answer
the phone?

James Thurber 1894-1961 American humorist

If we had had more time for discussion we should
probably have made a great many more mistakes.

Leon Trotsky 1879-1940 Russian revolutionary

Unseen, in the background, Fate was quietly slipping the lead into the boxing gloves.

P. G. Wodehouse 1881–1975 English writer

He felt like a man who, chasing rainbows, has had one of them suddenly turn and bite him in the leg.

P. G. Wodehouse 1881–1975 English writer

😄 Modern Life

Facebook is for people who can't face books.

Madeleine Beard English writer

I don't like little chip and pin machines. I don't like that they tell you what to do. 'Hand me back to the merchant!' like a bossy toddler.

Russell Brand 1975– British comedian

The other line moves faster...And don't try to change lines. The other line—the one you were in originally—will then move faster.

Barbara Ettore, *usually quoted as 'The other line always moves faster'*

Change is inevitable—except from a vending machine.

Robert C. Gallagher

I was standing behind a man in Starbucks the other day, he was ordering 'a tall skinny black Americano'. I said, 'What are you ordering, coffee or a President?'

Michael McIntyre 1976– English comedian

Men who blow themselves up are promised 72 virgins in paradise. That's a high price to pay for a shag.

Shazia Mirza 1976- English comedian

Starbucks says they are going to start putting religious quotes on cups. The very first one will say, 'Jesus! This cup is expensive!'

Conan O'Brien 1963- American comedian and broadcaster

Why would I tweet when I've not yet read *The Brothers Karamazov*?

Michael Palin 1953- British comedian and broadcaster

The trouble with the rat race is that even if you win you're still a rat.

Lily Tomlin 1939- American comedienne and actress

I'm the modern, intelligent, independent-type woman—in other words, a girl who can't get a man.

Shelley Winters 1922-2006 American actress

Money

see also DEBT, POVERTY, WEALTH

Money is better than poverty, if only for financial reasons.

Woody Allen 1935- American film director, writer, and actor

Money, it turned out, was exactly like sex, you thought of nothing else if you didn't have it and thought of other things if you did.

James Baldwin 1924-87 American novelist and essayist

We live by the Golden Rule. Those who have the gold make the rules.

Buzzie Bavasi 1914-2008 American baseball manager

HOLDUP MAN: Quit stalling—I said your money or your life.
JACK BENNY: I'm thinking it over!

Jack Benny 1894-1974 American comedian and actor

I live in a two-income household, but who knows how long my mom can keep that up.

Shmuel Breban American comedian

My rule is, if it flies, floats, or fornicates, rent it. It's cheaper in the long run.

Felix Dennis 1947-2014 English publisher

When you don't have any money, the problem is food. When you have money, it's sex. When you have both it's health.

J. P. Donleavy 1926-2017 Irish-American novelist

We don't wake up for less than $10,000 a day.

Linda Evangelista 1965- Canadian supermodel, *of herself and supermodel Christy Turlington; often quoted as, 'I don't get out of bed for less than $10,000 a day'*

A fool and his money are soon parted. What I want to know is how they got together in the first place.

Cyril Fletcher 1913-2005 English comedian

My main problem is reconciling my gross habits with my net income.

Errol Flynn 1909-59 Australian-born American actor

A bank is a place where they lend you an umbrella in fair weather and ask for it back when it begins to rain.

Robert Frost 1874-1963 American poet

on being told that money doesn't buy happiness:

But it upgrades despair so beautifully.

Richard Greenberg 1958- American dramatist

A bank is a place that will lend you money if you can prove that you don't need it.

Bob Hope 1903-2003 American comedian

When a feller says, 'It hain't the money, but th' principle o' th' thing', it's the money.

Frank McKinney Hubbard 1868-1930 American humorist

Nobody works as hard for his money as the man who marries it.

Frank McKinney Hubbard 1868-1930 American humorist

Never say you know a man until you have divided an inheritance with him.

Johann Kaspar Lavater 1741-1801 Swiss theologian

All I ask is the chance to prove that money can't make me happy.

Spike Milligan 1918-2002 Irish comedian

Money is like manure. If you spread it around it does a lot of good, but if you pile it up in one place it stinks like hell.

Clint Murchison 1923-87 American businessman

'My boy,' he says, 'always try to rub up against money, for if you rub up against money long enough, some of it may rub off on you.'
Damon Runyon 1884–1946 American writer

I'm living so far beyond my income that we may also be said to be living apart.
Saki 1870–1916 Scottish writer

I do want to get rich but I never want to do what there is to do to get rich.
Gertrude Stein 1874–1946 American writer

If someone's dumb enough to offer me a million dollars to make a picture, I'm certainly not dumb enough to turn it down.
Elizabeth Taylor 1932–2011 English-born American actress, *on her role of Cleopatra in Joseph L. Mankiewicz's block-buster film* Antony and Cleopatra; *'If someone was stupid enough…' as originally recounted by David Niven*

Money talks, but credit has an echo.
Bob Thaves 1924–2006 American cartoonist

Pennies don't fall from heaven. They have to be earned on earth.
Margaret Thatcher 1925–2013 British Conservative stateswoman

Money won't buy happiness, but it will pay the salaries of a large research staff to study the problem.
Bill Vaughan

Morality
see also VIRTUE

Guilt: the gift that keeps on giving.
   Erma Bombeck 1927-96 American humorist

Throwing acid is wrong—in some people's eyes.
   Jimmy Carr 1972- Irish comedian

To be absolutely honest, what I feel really bad about is that
I don't feel worse. That's the ineffectual liberal's problem in
a nutshell.
   Michael Frayn 1933- English writer

When it comes to the morality of our ancestors, none of us
can boast much; the records do not show that Adam and
Eve were married.
   E. W. Howe 1853-1937 American novelist and editor

If people want a sense of purpose, they should get it from
their archbishops. They should not hope to receive it from
their politicians.
   Harold Macmillan 1894-1986 British Conservative
statesman

Those are my principles, and if you don't like them...well,
I have others.
   Groucho Marx 1890-1977 American film comedian

Being moral isn't what you *do*...it's what you *mean* to do.
   Bette Midler 1945- American actress

That woman speaks eighteen languages, and can't say No in any of them.

Dorothy Parker 1893-1967 American critic and humorist

And there was that wholesale libel on a Yale prom. If all the girls attending it were laid end to end, Mrs Parker said, she wouldn't be at all surprised.

Dorothy Parker 1893-1967 American critic and humorist

Dost thou think, because thou art virtuous, there shall be no more cakes and ale?

William Shakespeare 1564-1616 English dramatist

When a stupid man is doing something he is ashamed of, he always declares that it is his duty.

George Bernard Shaw 1856-1950 Irish dramatist

PICKERING: Have you no morals, man?
DOOLITTLE: Can't afford them, Governor.

George Bernard Shaw 1856-1950 Irish dramatist

Do not do unto others as you would that they should do unto you. Their tastes may not be the same.

George Bernard Shaw 1856-1950 Irish dramatist

If your morals make you dreary, depend upon it they are wrong.

Robert Louis Stevenson 1850-94 Scottish novelist

BELINDA: Ay, but you know we must return good for evil.
LADY BRUTE: That may be a mistake in the translation.

John Vanbrugh 1664-1726 English architect and dramatist

Moral indignation is jealousy with a halo.
H. G. Wells 1866–1946 English novelist

On an occasion of this kind it becomes more than a moral duty to speak one's mind. It becomes a pleasure.
Oscar Wilde 1854–1900 Irish dramatist and poet

A Tory minister can sleep in ten different women's beds in a week. A Labour minister gets it in the neck if he looks at his neighbour's wife over the garden fence.
Harold Wilson 1916–95 British Labour statesman

Mothers

When your mother asks, 'Do you want a piece of advice?' it's a mere formality. It doesn't matter if you answer yes or no. You're going to get it anyway.
Erma Bombeck 1927–96 American humorist

I have reached the age when a woman begins to perceive that she is growing into the person she least plans to resemble: her mother.
Anita Brookner 1928–2016 British novelist and art historian

People often ask me 'How are you sleeping?' and I say: 'I sleep like a baby—I wake up every hour calling for my mother'.
David Cameron 1966– British Conservative statesman, *on his unexpected resignation as Prime Minister*

Any suburban mother can state her role sardonically enough in a sentence: it is to deliver children obstetrically once and by car forever after.
Peter De Vries 1910–93 American novelist and humorist

Few misfortunes can befall a boy which bring worse consequences than to have a really affectionate mother.
   W. Somerset Maugham 1874-1965 English novelist

My mother had a good deal of trouble with me, but I think she enjoyed it.
   Mark Twain 1835-1910 American writer

Movies
see CINEMA

Murder

Every murderer is probably somebody's old friend.
   Agatha Christie 1890-1976 English writer

Television has brought back murder into the home—where it belongs.
   Alfred Hitchcock 1899-1980 British-born film director

English law does not permit good persons, as such, to strangle bad persons, as such.
   T. H. Huxley 1825-95 English biologist

The National Rifle Association says guns don't kill people, people do. But I think the gun helps. Just standing there, going 'Bang!'—that's not going to kill too many people.
   Eddie Izzard 1962- British comedian

You can always count on a murderer for a fancy prose style.
   Vladimir Nabokov 1899-1977 Russian novelist

Julius Caesar of his assassins:

KENNETH WILLIAMS: Infamy, infamy, they've all got it in for me!

Talbot Rothwell 1916–74 English screenwriter, *in the film* Carry On, Cleo

justification for poisoning his sister-in-law:

She had very thick ankles.

Thomas Griffiths Wainewright 1794–1847 English artist

Music

see also MUSICIANS, OPERA, SONGS

Whenever I don't know what to write about, I just close my eyes and think of Essex.

Damon Albarn 1968– English musician

I can't listen to too much Wagner, ya know? I start to get the urge to conquer Poland.

Woody Allen 1935– American film director, writer, and actor

All music is folk music, I ain't never heard no horse sing a song.

Louis Armstrong 1901–71 American singer and jazz musician

when asked what jazz is:

If you still have to ask…shame on you.

Louis Armstrong 1901–71 American singer and jazz musician

There is nothing to it. You only have to hit the right notes at the right time and the instrument plays itself.

Johann Sebastian Bach 1685–1750 German composer, *when complimented on his organ playing*

I love Wagner, but the music I prefer is that of a cat hung up by its tail outside a window and trying to stick to the panes of glass with its claws.

Charles Baudelaire 1821-67 French poet and critic

What can you do with it? It's like a lot of yaks jumping about.

Thomas Beecham 1879-1961 English conductor, *on the third movement of Beethoven's Seventh Symphony*

The musical equivalent of the Towers of St Pancras Station.

Thomas Beecham 1879-1961 English conductor, *describing Elgar's 1st Symphony*

There are two golden rules for an orchestra: start together and finish together. The public doesn't give a damn what goes on in between.

Thomas Beecham 1879-1961 English conductor

ANDRÉ PREVIN: You're playing all the wrong notes.
ERIC MORECAMBE: I'm playing all the *right* notes. But not *necessarily* in the right order.

Eddie Braben 1930-2013 English comedy writer

Extraordinary how potent cheap music is.

Noël Coward 1899-1973 English dramatist, actor, and composer

The tuba is certainly the most intestinal of instruments— the very lower bowel of music.

Peter De Vries 1910-93 American novelist

I hate music, especially when it's played.

Jimmy Durante 1893-1980 American comedian and singer

Playing 'Bop' is like scrabble with all the vowels missing.

Duke Ellington 1899-1974 American jazz pianist, composer, and band-leader

message sent after the Grenadier Guards had played an arrangement of Richard Strauss' Elektra:

His Majesty does not know what the Band has just played, but it is *never* to be played again.

George V 1865-1936 British king

I only know two tunes. One of them is 'Yankee Doodle' and the other isn't.

Ulysses S. Grant 1822-85 American Unionist general and statesman

Classic music is th'kind that we keep thinkin'll turn into a tune.

Frank McKinney Hubbard 1868-1930 American humorist

on the performance of a celebrated violinist:

Difficult do you call it, Sir? I wish it were impossible.

Samuel Johnson 1709-84 English poet, critic, and lexicographer

to another musician:

Very well, my dear. You continue to play Bach your way and I'll continue to play him *his* way.

Wanda Landowska 1877-1959 Polish-born American pianist and harpsichordist

I don't like my music, but what is my opinion against that of millions of others.

Frederick Loewe 1904-88 American composer

on seeing Niagara Falls:
Fortissimo at last!
    Gustav Mahler 1860–1911 Austrian composer

If you're in jazz and more than ten people like you, you're labelled commercial.
    Herbie Mann 1930– American jazz musician

Writing about music is like dancing about architecture.
    Martin Mull 1943– American actor and comedian

I don't like country music, but I don't mean to denigrate those who do. And for the people who like country music, denigrate means 'put down'.
    Bob Newhart 1929– American comedian

I have been told that Wagner's music is better than it sounds.
    Bill Nye 1850–96 American humorist

If anyone has conducted a Beethoven performance, and then doesn't have to go to an osteopath, then there's something wrong.
    Simon Rattle 1955– English conductor

Wagner has lovely moments but awful quarters of an hour.
    Gioacchino Rossini 1792–1868 Italian composer

Applause is a receipt, not a note of demand.
    Artur Schnabel 1882–1951 Austrian-born pianist

You are there and I am here; but where is Beethoven?
    Artur Schnabel 1882–1951 Austrian-born pianist, *to his conductor during a Beethoven rehearsal*

I am delighted to add another unplayable work to the repertoire. I want the Concerto to be difficult and I want the little finger to become longer. I can wait.

Arnold Schoenberg 1874–1951 Austrian-born American composer, *of his Violin Concerto*

of the piano:

A large, rectangular monster that screams when you touch its teeth.

Andrés Segovia 1893–1987 Spanish guitarist

Hell is full of musical amateurs: music is the brandy of the damned.

George Bernard Shaw 1856–1950 Irish dramatist

I play all my country and western music backwards. Your lover returns, your dog comes back to life and you cease to be an alcoholic.

Linda Smith 1958–2006 British comedian

Musical people are so absurdly unreasonable. They always want one to be perfectly dumb at the very moment when one is longing to be absolutely deaf.

Oscar Wilde 1854–1900 Irish dramatist and poet

You have Van Gogh's ear for music.

Billy Wilder 1906–2002 American screenwriter and director

Musicians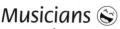

see also MUSIC

The music teacher came twice each week to bridge the awful gap between Dorothy and Chopin.

George Ade 1866–1944 American humorist and dramatist

printed notice in an American dancing saloon:
Please do not shoot the pianist. He is doing his best.
Anonymous

A musicologist is a man who can read music but can't hear it.
Thomas Beecham 1879-1961 English conductor

Why do we have to have all these third-rate foreign conductors around—when we have so many second-rate ones of our own?
Thomas Beecham 1879-1961 English conductor

No wonder Bob Geldof is such an expert on famine. He's been feeding off 'I Don't Like Mondays' for 30 years.
Russell Brand 1975- British comedian

JOURNALIST: Why do you continue to practise the cello for several hours each day?
CASALS (AGED OVER 90): Because I think I'm improving.
Pablo Casals 1876-1973 Spanish cellist

QUESTION: Do you play the guitar with your teeth?
HENDRIX: No, with my ears.
Jimi Hendrix 1942-70 American rock musician

ANONYMOUS: Is Ringo the best drummer in the world?
JOHN LENNON: He's not even the best drummer in the band.
John Lennon 1940-80 English pop singer and songwriter

on Stravinsky's Symphony of Wind Instruments in memory of Debussy:
I had no idea Stravinsky disliked Debussy so much as this.
Ernest Newman 1868-1959 English music critic

asked how he could play so well when he was loaded:

I practise when I'm loaded.

Zoot Sims 1925–85 American jazz musician

'What do you think of Beethoven?'
'I love him, especially his poems.'

Ringo Starr 1940– English rock musician

On matters of intonation and technicalities I am more than a martinet—I am a martinetissimo!

Leopold Stokowski 1882–1977 English-born American conductor

After I die, I shall return to earth as the doorkeeper of a bordello and I won't let one of you in.

Arturo Toscanini 1867–1957 Italian conductor, *to his orchestra during a difficult rehearsal*

Names

I never really needed a nickname at school. Although it was bad for me it was much worse for my sister Ophelia.

Ed Balls 1967– British Labour politician

Remember, they only name things after you when you're dead or really old.

Barbara Bush 1925– American First Lady, *at the naming ceremony for the George Bush Centre for Intelligence*

of Alfred Bossom:

Who is this man whose name is neither one thing nor the other?

Winston Churchill 1874–1965 British Conservative statesman

If you don't give your child a middle name, how are they ever to know when you are cross with them?

Vivienne Clore British showbusiness agent

Colin is the sort of name you give your goldfish for a joke.

Colin Firth 1960- British actor

to Arthur Hornblow, who was planning to name his son Arthur:

Every Tom, Dick and Harry is called Arthur.

Sam Goldwyn 1882-1974 American film producer

comment at a Test Match as Michael Holding faced Peter Willey:

The batsman's Holding, the bowler's Willey.

Brian Johnston 1912-94 British cricket commentator

In the last Parliament, the House of Commons had more MPs called John than all the women MPs put together.

Tessa Jowell 1947- British Labour politician

when asked if Groucho were his real name:

No, I'm breaking it in for a friend.

Groucho Marx 1890-1977 American film comedian

But I must not go on singling out names. One must not be a name-dropper, as Her Majesty remarked to me yesterday.

Lord St John of Fawsley 1929-2012 British Conservative politician

I remember your name perfectly; but I just can't think of your face.

William Archibald Spooner 1844-1930 English clergyman and academic

A good name will wear out; a bad one may be turned; a nickname lasts forever.

Johann Georg Zimmerman 1728-95 Swiss physician and writer

Nature and the Country

I am at two with nature.

Woody Allen 1935- American film director, writer, and actor

Hedgehogs—why can't they just share the hedge?

Dan Antopolski 1972- English comedian

I'm proud of George. He's learned a lot about ranching since that first year when he tried to milk the horse. What's worse, it was a male horse.

Laura Bush 1946- American First Lady

Worms have played a more important part in the history of the world than most persons would at first suppose.

Charles Darwin 1809-82 English natural historian

There is nothing good to be had in the country, or if there is, they will not let you have it.

William Hazlitt 1778-1830 English essayist

a London clubman's view of the country:

A damp sort of place where all sorts of birds fly about uncooked.

Joseph Wood Krutch 1893-1970 American critic and naturalist

So *that's* what hay looks like.

Queen Mary 1867-1953 British Queen Consort, *said at Badminton House, where she was evacuated during the Second World War*

It is no good putting up notices saying 'Beware of the bull' because very rude things are sometimes written on them. I have found that one of the most effective notices is 'Beware of the Agapanthus'.
Lord Massereene and Ferrard 1914–93

I have no relish for the country; it is a kind of healthy grave.
Sydney Smith 1771–1845 English clergyman and essayist

Anybody can be good in the country.
Oscar Wilde 1854–1900 Irish dramatist and poet

What do we see at once but a little robin! There is no need to burst into tears fotherington-tomas swete tho he be. Nor to buzz a brick at it, molesworth 2.
Geoffrey Willans 1911–58 and **Ronald Searle** 1920–2011 English humorous writers, *a nature walk at St Custards*

Newspapers
see also JOURNALISM

I read the newspapers avidly. It is my one form of continuous fiction.
Aneurin Bevan 1897–1960 British Labour politician

We have a saying in Fleet Street: the editor who writes for his own newspaper has a fool for a contributor.
Bill Deedes 1913–2007 British journalist and Conservative politician

If you can't get a job as a pianist in a brothel you become a royal reporter.
Max Hastings 1945– British journalist and historian

Editor: a person employed by a newspaper, whose business it is to separate the wheat from the chaff, and to see that the chaff is printed.

Elbert Hubbard 1859–1915 American writer

People don't actually read newspapers. They get into them every morning, like a hot bath.

Marshall McLuhan 1911–80 Canadian communications scholar

Exclusives aren't what they used to be. We tend to put 'exclusive' on everything just to annoy other papers. I once put 'exclusive' on the weather by mistake.

Piers Morgan 1965– English journalist

asked why he had allowed the unclothed models feature on Page 3 to develop:

I don't know. The editor did it when I was away.

Rupert Murdoch 1931– Australian-born American media entrepreneur

Four hostile newspapers are more to be feared than a thousand bayonets.

Napoleon I 1769–1821 French emperor

No self-respecting fish would be wrapped in a Murdoch newspaper.

Mike Royko 1932–97 American journalist

Ever noticed that no matter what happens in one day, it exactly fits in the newspaper?

Jerry Seinfeld 1954– American comedian

People who read tabloids deserve to be lied to.

Jerry Seinfeld 1954– American comedian

Accuracy to a newspaper is what virtue is to a lady; but a newspaper can always print a retraction.

Adlai Stevenson 1900-65 American Democratic politician

 Office Life

of the cramped office he shared with Dorothy Parker:

One square foot less and it would be adulterous.

Robert Benchley 1889-1945 American humorist

Meetings...are rather like cocktail parties. You don't want to go, but you're cross not to be asked.

Jilly Cooper 1937- English writer

What I don't like about office Christmas parties is looking for a job the next day.

Phyllis Diller 1917-2012 American actress

An office party is not, as is sometimes supposed, the Managing Director's chance to kiss the tea-girl. It is the tea-girl's chance to kiss the Managing Director.

Katharine Whitehorn 1928- English journalist

I yield to no one in my admiration for the office as a social centre, but it's no place actually to get any work done.

Katharine Whitehorn 1928- English journalist

A team effort is a lot of people doing what I say.

Michael Winner 1935-2013 British film director and producer

Sexual harassment at work—is it a problem for the self-employed?

Victoria Wood 1953-2016 British writer and comedienne

Old Age

see also AGEING, MIDDLE AGE, YOUTH

Mr Salteena was an elderly man of 42.

    Daisy Ashford 1881–1972 English child author

The only thing for old age is a brave face, a good tailor and comfortable shoes.

    Alan Ayckbourn 1939– English dramatist

To me old age is always fifteen years older than I am.

    Bernard Baruch 1870–1965 American financier and presidential adviser

If you live to be ninety in England and can still eat a boiled egg they think you deserve the Nobel Prize.

    Alan Bennett 1934– English dramatist and actor

on reaching the age of 100:

If I'd known I was gonna live this long, I'd have taken better care of myself.

    Eubie Blake 1883–1983 American ragtime pianist

in his old age Churchill overheard one of two new MPs whisper to the other, 'They say the old man's getting a bit past it':

And they say the old man's getting deaf as well.

    Winston Churchill 1874–1965 British Conservative statesman

it was pointed out to the aged Winston Churchill that his fly-button was undone:

No matter. The dead bird does not leave the nest.

    Winston Churchill 1874–1965 British Conservative statesman

To what do I attribute my longevity? Bad luck.
   Quentin Crisp 1908-99 English writer

approaching his 80th birthday:
While there's snow on the roof, it doesn't mean the fire has gone out in the furnace.
   John G. Diefenbaker 1895-1979 Canadian Progressive Conservative statesman

As Groucho Marx once said, 'Anyone can get old—all you have to do is to live long enough.'
   Elizabeth II 1926- British queen

Being an old maid is like death by drowning, a really delightful sensation after you cease to struggle.
   Edna Ferber 1887-1968 American writer

After the age of 80, you seem to be having breakfast every five minutes.
   Christopher Fry 1907-2005 English dramatist

It's amazing how much 'mature wisdom' resembles being too tired.
   Robert Heinlein 1907-88 American science fiction writer

I still go up my 44 stairs two at a time, but that is in hopes of dropping dead at the top.
   A. E. Housman 1859-1936 English poet

In one old people's home they changed the words of the song to 'When I'm 84' as they considered 64 to be young. I might do that.
   Paul McCartney 1942- English pop singer and songwriter

Growing old is like being increasingly penalized for a crime you haven't committed.
   Anthony Powell 1905-2000 English novelist

on the latest generation of stairlifts:
They go so fast you can still remember why you went upstairs.
   June Whitfield 1925- English actor

One should never make one's début with a scandal. One should reserve that to give an interest to one's old age.
   Oscar Wilde 1854-1900 Irish dramatist and poet

Opera 🦢

I do not mind what language an opera is sung in so long as it is a language I don't understand.
   Edward Appleton 1892-1965 English physicist

The opera ain't over 'til the fat lady sings.
   Dan Cook 1926-2008 American journalist

People are wrong when they say that the opera isn't what it used to be. It is what it used to be—that's what's wrong with it.
   Noël Coward 1899-1973 English dramatist, actor, and composer

Opera is when a guy gets stabbed in the back and, instead of bleeding, he sings.
   Ed Gardner 1901-63 American radio comedian

Parsifal is the kind of opera that starts at six o'clock. After it has been going three hours, you look at your watch and it says 6.20.

David Randolph 1914-2010 American conductor

It is a music one must hear several times. I am not going again.

Gioacchino Rossini 1792-1868 Italian composer, *of* Tannhäuser

The first act of the three occupied two hours. I enjoyed that in spite of the singing.

Mark Twain 1835-1910 American writer

Optimism and Pessimism

see also HOPE

A pessimist is a man who thinks all women are bad. An optimist is a man who hopes that they are.

Chauncey Depew 1834-1928 American businessman and politician

I guess I just prefer to see the dark side of things. The glass is always half empty. And cracked. And I just cut my lip on it. And chipped a tooth.

Janeane Garofalo 1964- American comedian

The people who live in a Golden Age usually go around complaining how yellow everything looks.

Randall Jarrell 1914-65 American poet

My friends, as I have discovered myself, there are no disasters, only opportunities. And, indeed, opportunities for fresh disasters.

Boris Johnson 1964- British Conservative politician

An optimist is a girl who mistakes a bulge for a curve.
   Ring Lardner 1885-1933 American writer

Isn't it nice to think that tomorrow is a new day with no mistakes in it yet?
   L. M. Montgomery 1874-1942 Canadian novelist

The nice part about being a pessimist is that you are constantly being either proven right or pleasantly surprised.
   George F. Will 1941- American columnist

The Paranormal

on spiritualism:
I always knew the living talked rot, but it's nothing to the rot the dead talk.
   Margot Asquith 1864-1945 British political hostess

I don't believe in astrology; I'm a Sagittarius and we're sceptical.
   Arthur C. Clarke 1917-2008 English science fiction writer

supposed opening words of a letter of dismissal to the Sun's astrologer:
As you will no doubt have foreseen...
   Kelvin Mackenzie 1946- British journalist

The only contact I ever made with the dead was when I spoke to a journalist from the *Sun*.
   Morrissey 1959- English singer and songwriter

Apart from the known and the unknown, what else is there?
   Harold Pinter 1930-2008 English dramatist

Mr Geller may have psychic powers by means of which he can bend spoons; if so, he appears to be doing it the hard way.
James Randi 1928- Canadian-born American conjuror

Parents

see also CHILDREN, FAMILY, MOTHERS

Maternity is a matter of fact. Paternity is a matter of opinion.
Walter Bagehot 1826-77 English economist

I'm still working. I need the money. Money, I've discovered, is the one thing keeping me in touch with my children.
Gyles Brandreth 1948- English writer and broadcaster

If you have never been hated by your child, you have never been a parent.
Bette Davis 1908-89 American actress

Most children threaten at times to run away from home. This is the only thing that keeps some parents going.
Phyllis Diller 1917-2012 American actress

[A successful parent is one] who raises a child who grows up and is able to pay for his or her own psychoanalysis.
Nora Ephron 1941-2012 American screenwriter and director

To be a successful father ... there's one absolute rule: when you have a kid, don't look at it for the first two years.
Ernest Hemingway 1899-1961 American novelist

Mom and Pop were just a couple of kids when they got married. He was eighteen, she was sixteen, and I was three.

Billie Holiday 1915-59 American singer

Having children makes you no more a parent than having a piano makes you a pianist.

Michael Levine

A Jewish man with parents alive is a fifteen-year-old boy, and will remain a fifteen-year-old boy until *they die*!

Philip Roth 1933- American novelist

If you must hold yourself up to your children as an object lesson (which is not at all necessary), hold yourself up as a warning and not as an example.

George Bernard Shaw 1856-1950 Irish dramatist

I have four sons and three stepsons. I have learnt what it is like to step on Lego with bare feet.

Fay Weldon 1931- British novelist and scriptwriter

All women become like their mothers. That is their tragedy. No man does. That's his.

Oscar Wilde 1854-1900 Irish dramatist and poet

Parliament

see also POLITICS

Being an MP is the sort of job all working-class parents want for their children—clean, indoors and no heavy lifting.

Diane Abbott 1953- British Labour politician

The difference between the House of Commons and the House of Lords is the difference between a newly poured glass of champagne and one that has stood for five days.

Clement Attlee 1883-1967 British Labour statesman

The British House of Lords is the British Outer Mongolia for retired politicians.

Tony Benn 1925-2014 British Labour politician

As an MP, you only meet two types of people: people with problems and people who are right.

Gyles Brandreth 1948- English writer and broadcaster

CHURCHILL: I am the humble servant of the Lord Jesus Christ and of the House of Commons.
CRIPPS: I hope you treat Jesus better than you treat the H of C.

Stafford Cripps 1889-1952 British Labour politician

The only safe pleasure for a parliamentarian is a bag of boiled sweets.

Julian Critchley 1930-2000 British Conservative politician and journalist

The occupational hazards are the three As: arrogance, alcoholism and adultery. If you suffer from only one, it's thought you're doing quite well.

Edwina Currie 1946- British Conservative politician, *advice for women MPs*

Under the present circumstances, I would rather be a lap dancer than a woman MP—the hours are better and unruly male members are shown the door.

Allison Pearson 1960- Welsh journalist

on the quality of debate in the House of Lords:

It is, I think, good evidence of life after death.

Donald Soper 1903-98 British Methodist minister

The House of Lords is a perfect eventide home.

Baroness Stocks 1891-1975 British writer

The House of Lords, an illusion to which I have never been able to subscribe—responsibility without power, the prerogative of the eunuch throughout the ages.

Tom Stoppard 1937- British dramatist

Parties and Hospitality

see also SOCIETY

It is amazing how nice people are to you when they know you are going away.

Michael Arlen 1895-1963 British novelist

on the arrival of the champagne after a series of poor dishes at a dinner:

Thank God for something warm!

Benjamin Disraeli 1804-81 British Tory statesman and novelist

Here you are again, older faces and younger clothes.

Mamie Stuyvesant Fish 1853-1915 American socialite, *habitual greeting to guests*

My idea of hell is a very large party in a cold room, where everybody has to play hockey properly.

Stella Gibbons 1902-89 English novelist

The best number for a dinner party is two—myself and a dam' good head waiter.

Nubar Gulbenkian 1896-1972 British industrialist and philanthropist

Some people can stay longer in an hour than others can in a week.

William Dean Howells 1837-1920 American novelist and critic

At every party there are two kinds of people—those who want to go home and those who don't. The trouble is, they are usually married to each other.

Ann Landers 1918-2002 American advice columnist

How VIP do we gotta get?

Paul McCartney 1942- English pop singer and songwriter, *on being refused entry by a doorman at rapper Tyga's party after the Grammy awards*

I really felt for you in the scene in which you tried to make the party go.

Queen Mary 1867-1953 British Queen Consort, *to Judith Anderson on her* Lady Macbeth

At a dinner party one should eat wisely but not too well, and talk well but not too wisely.

W. Somerset Maugham 1874-1965 English novelist

I once went to one of those parties where everyone throws their car keys into the middle of the room. I don't know who got my moped but I drove that Peugeot for years.

Victoria Wood 1953-2016 British writer and comedienne

😄 Past, Present, and Future

Nothing is more responsible for the good old days than a bad memory.

Franklin P. Adams 1881-1960 American journalist and humorist

Predictions can be very difficult—especially about the future.

Niels Bohr 1885-1962 Danish physicist

The rule is, jam to-morrow and jam yesterday—but never jam today.

Lewis Carroll 1832-98 English writer and logician

For my part, I consider that it will be found much better by all Parties to leave the past to history, especially as I propose to write that history myself.

Winston Churchill 1874-1965 British Conservative statesman

I never think of the future. It comes soon enough.

Albert Einstein 1879-1955 German-born theoretical physicist

In times like these, it helps to recall that there have always been times like these.

Paul Harvey 1918-2009 American radio broadcaster

Cheer up! the worst is yet to come!

Philander Chase Johnson 1866-1939 American journalist

Industrial archaeology...believes that a thing that doesn't work any more is far more interesting than a thing that still works.

Miles Kington 1941-2008 English humorist

Soon we'll be sliding down the razor-blade of life.

Tom Lehrer 1928- American humorist

They spend their time mostly looking forward to the past.

John Osborne 1929-94 English dramatist

Hindsight is always twenty-twenty.
Billy Wilder 1906-2002 American screenwriter and director

😄 People and Personalities

Jimmy [Connors] was such an out-and-out 'personality' that he managed to get into a legal dispute with the president of his own fan club.
Martin Amis 1949- English novelist

He was my knight on a shining bicycle.
Franny Armstrong 1972- British film director, *of Boris Johnson after he rescued her from a gang of girls*

Agatha Christie has given more pleasure in bed than any other woman.
Nancy Banks-Smith 1929- British journalist

I will take questions from the guys, but from the girls I want telephone numbers.
Silvio Berlusconi 1936- Italian statesman

of Viscount Montgomery:
In defeat unbeatable: in victory unbearable.
Winston Churchill 1874-1965 British Conservative statesman

after meeting Irving Berlin and supposing him to be Isaiah Berlin:
Berlin's just like most bureaucrats. Wonderful on paper but disappointing when you meet them face to face.
Winston Churchill 1874-1965 British Conservative statesman

He has all the virtues I dislike and none of the vices I admire.

> **Winston Churchill** 1874–1965 British Conservative statesman, *on Sir Stafford Cripps*

on a visit to Washington:

If there were anything I could take back to France with me, it would be Mrs Kennedy.

> **Charles de Gaulle** 1890–1970 French statesman

of David Steel, Leader of the Liberal Party:

He's passed from rising hope to elder statesman without any intervening period whatsoever.

> **Michael Foot** 1913–2010 British Labour politician

He's the angriest man you'll ever meet. He's like a man with a fork in a world of soup.

> **Noel Gallagher** 1967– English pop singer, *on his brother Liam*

Like a Goth swaggering around Rome wearing an onyx toilet seat for a collar, he exudes self-confidence.

> **Clive James** 1939– Australian critic and writer, *of Rupert Murdoch*

on her son Karl writing a book about capital:

If only Karl had made capital instead.

> **Henrietta Marx** German mother of Karl Marx

The thinking man's crumpet.

> **Frank Muir** 1920–98 English writer and broadcaster, *of Joan Bakewell*

of Errol Flynn:

You always knew precisely where you stood with him because he *always* let you down.

David Niven 1910-83 English actor

I was the toast of two continents: Greenland and Australia.

Dorothy Parker 1893-1967 American critic and humorist

on Mick Jagger:

The lips, the lips! He could French kiss a moose or blow a tuba from both ends at the same time.

Joan Rivers 1933-2014 American comedienne

on Marilyn Monroe:

Her body has gone to her head.

Barbara Stanwyck 1907-90 American actress

A genius with the IQ of a moron.

Gore Vidal 1925-2012 American novelist and critic, *of Andy Warhol*

I think his fate is rather like Humpty Dumpty's, quite as tragic and quite as impossible to put right.

Constance Wilde 1859-98, *on her husband, Oscar Wilde*

on Burt Reynolds:

He's the kind of guy who would stop on his way down the aisle to get married to say hello to a pretty girl.

Tammy Wynette 1942-98 American singer

Q: Who does George Michael sleep with?
A: Nobody. You can't get two on a sunbed.

Paula Yates 1959-2000 British television presenter

Peoples

see COUNTRIES *and Peoples*

Personalities

see PEOPLE *and Personalities*

Pessimism

see OPTIMISM *and Pessimism*

Philosophy

What if everything is an illusion and nothing exists? In that case I definitely overpaid for my carpet.

Woody Allen 1935- American film director, writer, and actor

Some people see things that are and ask, Why? Some people dream of things that never were and ask, Why not? Some people have to go to work and don't have time for all that.

George Carlin 1937-2008 American comedian

I have tried too in my time to be a philosopher; but, I don't know how, cheerfulness was always breaking in.

Oliver Edwards 1711-91 English lawyer

He thinks nothing empirical is Knowable—I asked him to admit that there was not a rhinoceros in the room, but he wouldn't.

Bertrand Russell 1872-1970 British philosopher and mathematician, *of Wittgenstein*

I have a new philosophy; I'm only going to dread one day at a time.

Charles Monroe Schulz 1922-2000 American cartoonist

The safest general characterization of the European philosophical tradition is that it consists of a series of footnotes to Plato.

Alfred North Whitehead 1861-1947 English philosopher and mathematician

What is your aim in philosophy?—To show the fly the way out of the fly-bottle.

Ludwig Wittgenstein 1889-1951 Austrian-born philosopher

You would not like Nietzsche, sir. He is fundamentally unsound.

P. G. Wodehouse 1881-1975 English-born writer, *Jeeves to Bertie Wooster*

 # Poetry

see also LITERATURE, POETS

Poets have been mysteriously silent on the subject of cheese.

G. K. Chesterton 1874-1936 English essayist, novelist, and poet

on the haiku:

To convey one's mood in seventeen syllables is very diffic.

John Cooper Clarke 1949- English poet

Immature poets imitate; mature poets steal.

T. S. Eliot 1888-1965 American-born British poet, critic, and dramatist

I'd as soon write free verse as play tennis with the net down.
Robert Frost 1874-1963 American poet

The notion of expressing sentiments in short lines having similar sounds at their ends seems as remote as mangoes on the moon.
Philip Larkin 1922-85 English poet

Writing a book of poetry is like dropping a rose petal down the Grand Canyon and waiting for the echo.
Don Marquis 1878-1937 American poet and journalist

My favourite poem is the one that starts 'Thirty days hath September' because it actually tells you something.
Groucho Marx 1890-1977 American film comedian

All that is not prose is verse; and all that is not verse is prose.
Molière 1622-73 French comic dramatist

to Rousseau, of his 'Ode to Posterity':
It will never reach its address.
Voltaire 1694-1778 French writer and philosopher

All bad poetry springs from genuine feeling.
Oscar Wilde 1854-1900 Irish dramatist and poet

Poets
see also POETRY

Even the greatest poets need something to cling to. Keats had Beauty; Milton had God. T. S. Eliot's standby was Worry.
John Carey 1934- British literary scholar

A poet who reads his work in public may have other nasty habits.

Robert Heinlein 1907-88 American science fiction writer

Dr Donne's verses are like the peace of God; they pass all understanding.

James I 1566-1625 British king

on the relative merits of two minor poets:

Sir, there is no settling the point of precedency between a louse and a flea.

Samuel Johnson 1709-84 English poet, critic, and lexicographer

We had the old crow over at Hull recently, looking like a Christmas present from Easter Island.

Philip Larkin 1922-85 English poet, *of Ted Hughes*

on being asked by Stephen Spender how a poet could serve the Communist cause in Spain:

Go and get killed, comrade, we need a Byron in the movement.

Harry Pollitt 1890-1960 British Communist politician

ACQUAINTANCE: How are you?
YEATS: Not very well. I can only write prose today.

W. B. Yeats 1865-1939 Irish poet

😄 Political Parties

Vote Labour and you build castles in the air. Vote Conservative and you can live in them.

David Frost 1939-2013 English broadcaster

I never dared be radical when young
For fear it would make me conservative when old.

Robert Frost 1874-1963 American poet

at a photocall when Lady Thatcher said to him 'You should be on my right':

That would be difficult.

Edward Heath 1916-2005 British Conservative statesman

Voting Tory will cause your wife to have bigger breasts and increase your chances of owning a BMW M3.

Boris Johnson 1964- British Conservative politician

The Tory Party only panics in a crisis.

Iain Macleod 1913-70 British Conservative politician

As usual the Liberals offer a mixture of sound and original ideas. Unfortunately none of the sound ideas is original and none of the original ideas is sound.

Harold Macmillan 1894-1986 British Conservative statesman

I have only one firm belief about the American political system, and that is this: God is a Republican and Santa Claus is a Democrat.

P. J. O'Rourke 1947- American humorous writer

I will make a bargain with the Republicans. If they will stop telling lies about Democrats, we will stop telling the truth about them.

Adlai Stevenson 1900-65 American Democratic politician

The Labour Party is going around stirring up apathy.

William Whitelaw 1918-99 British Conservative politician

 Politicians

see also PARLIAMENT, PRESIDENTS, PRIME MINISTERS

Dalton McGuinty: He's an evil reptilian kitten-eater from another planet.

Anonymous, *Canadian Conservative press release attacking the Liberal leader*

Beaverbrook is so pleased to be in the Government that he is like the town tart who has finally married the Mayor!

Beverley Baxter 1891-1964 Canadian-born British journalist and Conservative politician

The right kind of leader for the Labour Party... a desiccated calculating machine.

Aneurin Bevan 1897-1960 British Labour politician, *generally taken as referring to Hugh Gaitskell, although Bevan specifically denied it*

Attlee is said to have remarked that Herbert Morrison was his own worst enemy:

Not while I'm alive he ain't.

Ernest Bevin 1881-1951 British Labour politician and trade unionist

JONES: What's your favourite political joke?
CAMERON: Nick Clegg.

David Cameron 1966– British Conservative statesman

There but for the grace of God, goes God.

Winston Churchill 1874-1965 British Conservative statesman, *of Stafford Cripps*

He is loyal to his own career but only incidentally to anything or anyone else.

Hugh Dalton 1887-1962 British Labour politician, *of Richard Crossman*

It is not necessary that every time he rises he should give his famous imitation of a semi-house-trained polecat.

Michael Foot 1913-2010 British Labour politician, *of Norman Tebbit*

Peter Mandelson is someone who can skulk in broad daylight.

Simon Hoggart 1946-2014 English journalist

I once said cynically of a politician, 'He'll double-cross that bridge when he comes to it.'

Oscar Levant 1906-72 American pianist

You can put lipstick on a pig, but it's still a pig.

Barack Obama 1961- American Democratic statesman, *see Palin at* POLITICIANS *below*

The majority of the members of the Irish parliament are professional politicians, in the sense that otherwise they would not be given jobs minding mice at a crossroads.

Flann O'Brien 1911-66 Irish novelist and journalist

What's the difference between a hockey mom and a pitbull? Lipstick.

Sarah Palin 1964- American Republican politician, *see Obama at* POLITICIANS *above*

He may be a son of a bitch, but he's our son of a bitch.

Franklin D. Roosevelt 1882-1945 American Democratic statesman, *on President Somoza of Nicaragua*

on deciding to run for Governor of California:

The most difficult decision I've ever made in my entire life, except for the one in 1978 when I decided to get a bikini wax.

Arnold Schwarzenegger 1947- Austrian-born American actor and Republican politician

A politician is a man who understands government, and it takes a politician to run a government. A statesman is a politician who's been dead 10 or 15 years.

Harry S. Truman 1884-1972 American Democratic statesman

If you want a friend in Washington, get a dog.

Harry S. Truman 1884-1972 American Democratic statesman

I cannot bring myself to vote for a woman who has been voice-trained to speak to me as though my dog has just died.

Keith Waterhouse 1929-2009 British journalist and writer, *of Margaret Thatcher*

It's a pity, as my husband says, that more politicians are not bastards by birth instead of vocation.

Katharine Whitehorn 1928- English journalist

Politics

see also DEMOCRACY, DIPLOMACY, GOVERNMENT

Politics is the gentle art of getting votes from the poor and campaign funds from the rich by promising to protect each from the other.

Oscar Ameringer 1870-1943 American humorist

Vote for the man who promises least; he'll be the least disappointing.

Bernard Baruch 1870-1965 American financier and presidential adviser

Politics is the art of looking for trouble, finding it everywhere, diagnosing it wrongly and applying unsuitable remedies.

Ernest Benn 1875-1954 English publisher

There are two ways of getting into the Cabinet—you can crawl in or kick your way in.

Aneurin Bevan 1897-1960 British Labour politician

The liberals can understand everything but people who don't understand them.

Lenny Bruce 1925-66 American comedian

Have you ever seen a candidate talking to a rich person on television?

Art Buchwald 1925-2007 American humorist

Dear Chief Secretary, I'm afraid there is no money.

Liam Byrne 1970- British Labour politician

to Franklin Roosevelt on the likely duration of the Yalta conference:
I do not see any other way of realizing our hopes about World Organization in five or six days. Even the Almighty took seven.

Winston Churchill 1874-1965 British Conservative statesman

There are no true friends in politics. We are all sharks circling, and waiting, for traces of blood to appear in the water.

Alan Clark 1928-99 British Conservative politician

on being attacked by Egyptian protesters:

I felt bad that good tomatoes were wasted.

Hillary Rodham Clinton 1947- American lawyer and politician

on Mussolini's allowing himself to be photographed in a bathing suit:

A really great statesman doesn't do that.

Adolf Hitler 1889-1945 German dictator

My policy on cake is still pro having it and pro eating it!

Boris Johnson 1964- British Conservative politician

Politics is just show business for ugly people.

Jay Leno 1950- American comedian

If voting changed anything they'd abolish it.

Ken Livingstone 1945- British Labour politician

If you want to succeed in politics, you must keep your
conscience well under control.

David Lloyd George 1863-1945 British Liberal statesman

Being in politics is like being a football coach. You have to
be smart enough to understand the game, and dumb
enough to think it's important.

Eugene McCarthy 1916-2005 American Democratic politician

I have never found in a long experience of politics that
criticism is ever inhibited by ignorance.

Harold Macmillan 1894-1986 British Conservative statesman

on privatization:

First of all the Georgian silver goes, and then all that nice
furniture that used to be in the saloon. Then the Canalettos go.

Harold Macmillan 1894-1986 British Conservative statesman

WOMAN HECKLER: I wouldn't vote for you if you were the Archangel Gabriel.

MENZIES: If I were the Archangel Gabriel, madam, I'm afraid you would not be in my constituency.

Robert Gordon Menzies 1894–1978 Australian Liberal statesman

When I want a peerage, I shall buy it like an honest man.

Lord Northcliffe 1865–1922 British newspaper proprietor

Men enter local politics solely as a result of being unhappily married.

C. Northcote Parkinson 1909–93 English writer

Politics is supposed to be the second oldest profession. I have come to realize that it bears a very close resemblance to the first.

Ronald Reagan 1911–2004 American Republican statesman

Status quo, you know, that is Latin for 'the mess we're in'.

Ronald Reagan 1911–2004 American Republican statesman

Communism is like prohibition, it's a good idea but it won't work.

Will Rogers 1879–1935 American actor and humorist

He knows nothing; and he thinks he knows everything. That points clearly to a political career.

George Bernard Shaw 1856–1950 Irish dramatist

An independent is a guy who wants to take the politics out of politics.

Adlai Stevenson 1900–65 American Democratic politician

WOMAN AT A RALLY: Governor, every thinking person will be voting for you.

STEVENSON: Madam, that's not enough. I need a majority.

Adlai Stevenson 1900-65 American Democratic politician

I always cheer up immensely if an attack is particularly wounding because I think, well, if they attack me personally, it means they have not a single political argument left.

Margaret Thatcher 1925-2013 British Conservative stateswoman

The country is going down the drain, and they are squabbling about the size of the plughole.

Jeremy Thorpe 1929-2014 British Liberal politician

The people have spoke—the bastards.

Dick Tuck 1924- American Democratic politician, *after being defeated in the California Senate primary; usually quoted as 'The people have spoken—the bastards'*

on Marxism, from an expert on ants:

Wonderful theory, wrong species.

Edward O. Wilson 1929- American sociobiologist

 # Poverty

see also DEBT, MONEY

Anyone who has ever struggled with poverty knows how extremely expensive it is to be poor.

James Baldwin 1924-87 American novelist and essayist

It's no disgrace t'be poor, but it might as well be.

Frank McKinney Hubbard 1868–1930 American humorist

We were so poor that if we woke up on Christmas day without an erection, we had nothing to play with.

Frank McCourt 1930–2009 Irish writer

Poverty is no disgrace to a man, but it is confoundedly inconvenient.

Sydney Smith 1771–1845 English clergyman and essayist

As for the virtuous poor, one can pity them, of course, but one cannot possibly admire them.

Oscar Wilde 1854–1900 Irish dramatist and poet

Like dear St Francis of Assisi I am wedded to Poverty: but in my case the marriage is not a success.

Oscar Wilde 1854–1900 Irish dramatist and poet

Power

So long as men worship the Caesars and Napoleons, Caesars and Napoleons will duly arise and make them miserable.

Aldous Huxley 1894–1963 English novelist

I don't want loyalty. I want *loyalty*. I want him to kiss my ass in Macy's window at high noon and tell me it smells like roses. I want his pecker in my pocket.

Lyndon Baines Johnson 1908–73 American Democratic statesman

Powerful men often succeed through the help of their wives. Powerful women only succeed in spite of their husbands.

Lynda Lee-Potter 1935-2004 British journalist

Knowledge is power, if you know it about the right person.

Ethel Watts Mumford 1878-1940 American writer and humorist

Castro couldn't even go to the bathroom unless the Soviet Union put the nickel in the toilet.

Richard Milhous Nixon 1913-94 American Republican statesman

I'll make him an offer he can't refuse.

Mario Puzo 1920-99 American novelist

Seven months ago I could give a single command and 541,000 people would immediately obey it. Today I can't get a plumber to come to my house.

H. Norman Schwarzkopf III 1934-2012 American general

The Pope! How many divisions has *he* got?

Joseph Stalin 1879-1953 Soviet dictator, *on being asked to encourage Catholicism in Russia by way of conciliating the Pope*

🙂 Praise and Flattery

The advantage of doing one's praising for oneself is that one can lay it on so thick and exactly in the right places.

Samuel Butler 1835-1902 English novelist

If a man is vain, flatter. If timid, flatter. If boastful, flatter. In all history, too much flattery never lost a gentleman.
   Kathryn Cravens 1898–1991 American broadcaster

The others were only my wives. But you, my dear, will be my widow.
   Sacha Guitry 1885–1957 French actor and dramatist, *to his fifth wife*

To refuse to accept praise is to want to be praised twice over.
   Duc de La Rochefoucauld 1613–80 French moralist

Nine out of ten males will believe anything, especially if it confirms their virility.
   Andrea Martin 1947– American actress

What really flatters a man is that you think him worth flattering.
   George Bernard Shaw 1856–1950 Irish dramatist

I suppose flattery hurts no one, that is, if he doesn't inhale.
   Adlai Stevenson 1900–65 American Democratic politician

Pregnancy
see BIRTH *and Pregnancy*

Prejudice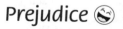

Being a star has made it possible for me to get insulted in places where the average Negro could never *hope* to go and get insulted.
   Sammy Davis Jnr. 1925–90 American entertainer

Prejudice

I am free of all prejudice. I hate everyone equally.

W. C. Fields 1880–1946 American humorist

CONGRESSMAN STARNES: You are quoting from this
Marlowe. Is he a Communist?
FLANAGAN: I am very sorry. I was quoting from
Christopher Marlowe.

Hallie Flanagan 1890–1969 American theatre director, *before
the House Un-American Activities Committee*

Wouldn't it be a hell of a thing if all this was burnt cork
and you people were being tolerant for nothing?

Dick Gregory 1932–2017 American comedian and civil rights
activist

When they call you articulate, that's another way of saying
'He talks good for a black guy'.

Ice-T 1958– American rap musician

refused admittance to a smart Californian beach club:

Since my daughter is only half-Jewish, could she go in the
water up to her knees?

Groucho Marx 1890–1977 American film comedian

The South African police would leave no stone unturned
to see that nothing disturbed the even terror of their
lives.

Tom Sharpe 1928–2013 British novelist

You must always look for the *Ulsterior motive*.

J. R. R. Tolkien 1892–1973 British philologist and writer, *of C. S.
Lewis as an Ulsterman*

Present
see PAST, *Present, and Future*

Presidents
see also POLITICIANS, POLITICS

Anybody that wants the presidency so much that he'll spend two years organizing and campaigning for it is not to be trusted with the office.

David Broder 1929-2011 American columnist

of President Nixon:

I worship the quicksand he walks on.

Art Buchwald 1925-2007 American humorist

The US presidency is a Tudor monarchy plus telephones.

Anthony Burgess 1917-93 English novelist and critic

God Almighty was satisfied with Ten Commandments. Mr Wilson requires Fourteen Points.

Georges Clemenceau 1841-1929 French statesman

Being president is like running a cemetery; you've got a lot of people under you and nobody's listening.

Bill Clinton 1946- American Democratic statesman

A hard dog to keep on the porch.

Hillary Rodham Clinton 1947- American lawyer and Democratic politician, *on her husband, Bill Clinton*

It is a great advantage to a President, and a major source of safety to the country, for him to know he is not a great man.

Calvin Coolidge 1872-1933 American Republican statesman

on his office:

The vice-presidency isn't worth a pitcher of warm piss.

John Nance Garner 1868-1967 American Democratic politician

So dumb he can't fart and chew gum at the same time.

Lyndon Baines Johnson 1908-73 American Democratic statesman, *of Gerald Ford*

Ronald Reagan, the President who never told bad news to the American people.

Garrison Keillor 1942- American humorous writer and broadcaster

The pay is good and I can walk to work.

John F. Kennedy 1917-63 American Democratic statesman, *on becoming President of the U.S.A.*

The battle for the mind of Ronald Reagan was like the trench warfare of World War I. Never have so many fought so hard for such barren terrain.

Peggy Noonan 1950- American writer

Poor George, he can't help it—he was born with a silver foot in his mouth.

Ann Richards 1933-2006 American Democratic politician, *of George Bush Snr*

McKinley has no more backbone than a chocolate éclair!

Theodore Roosevelt 1858-1919 American Republican statesman

He'll sit right here and he'll say do this, do that! And nothing will happen. Poor Ike—it won't be a bit like the Army.

Harry S. Truman 1884-1972 American Democratic statesman

A triumph of the embalmer's art.

Gore Vidal 1925-2012 American writer, *of Ronald Reagan*

Prime Ministers 🐌

see also POLITICIANS, POLITICS

He [Lloyd George] can't see a belt without hitting below it.

Margot Asquith 1864-1945 British political hostess

There are three classes which need sanctuary more than others—birds, wild flowers, and Prime Ministers.

Stanley Baldwin 1867-1947 British Conservative statesman

[Lloyd George] did not seem to care which way he travelled providing he was in the driver's seat.

Lord Beaverbrook 1879-1964 Canadian-born British newspaper proprietor and Conservative politician

Listening to a speech by Chamberlain is like paying a visit to Woolworth's: everything in its place and nothing above sixpence.

Aneurin Bevan 1897-1960 British Labour politician

If he ever went to school without any boots it was because he was too big for them.

Ivor Bulmer-Thomas 1905-93 British Conservative politician, *of Harold Wilson*

COMMENT: One never hears of Baldwin nowadays — he might as well be dead.
CHURCHILL: No, not dead. But the candle in that great turnip has gone out.

> **Winston Churchill** 1874-1965 British Conservative statesman

[Clement Attlee is] a modest man who has a good deal to be modest about.

> **Winston Churchill** 1874-1965 British Conservative statesman

A sheep in sheep's clothing.

> **Winston Churchill** 1874-1965 British Conservative statesman, *of Clement Attlee*

on stepping from his bath in the presence of a startled President Roosevelt:
The Prime Minister has nothing to hide from the President of the United States.

> **Winston Churchill** 1874-1965 British Conservative statesman

Margaret Thatcher has added the diplomacy of Alf Garnett to the economics of Arthur Daley.

> **Denis Healey** 1917-2015 British Labour politician

He is a mixture of Harry Houdini and a greased piglet… Nailing Blair is like trying to pin jelly to a wall.

> **Boris Johnson** 1964- British Conservative politician

on being asked what place Arthur Balfour would have in history:
He will be just like the scent on a pocket handkerchief.

> **David Lloyd George** 1863-1945 British Liberal statesman

[Churchill] would make a drum out of the skin of his mother in order to sound his own praises.

David Lloyd George 1863-1945 British Liberal statesman

Well, it was the best I could do, seated as I was between Jesus Christ and Napoleon Bonaparte.

David Lloyd George 1863-1945 British Liberal statesman, *on the Peace Conference negotiations in 1919 between himself, Woodrow Wilson, and Georges Clemenceau*

after forming the National Government, 1931:

Tomorrow every Duchess in London will be wanting to kiss me!

Ramsay MacDonald 1866-1937 British Labour statesman

A C-3PO made of ham. His resemblance to a slightly camp gammon robot is extraordinary.

Caitlin Moran 1975- English journalist, *on David Cameron*

A big cat detained briefly in a poodle parlour, sharpening her claws on the velvet.

Matthew Parris 1949- British journalist and former politician, *of Lady Thatcher in the House of Lords*

Every Prime Minister needs a Willie.

Margaret Thatcher 1925-2013 British Conservative stateswoman, *at the farewell dinner for William Whitelaw*

If my critics saw me walking over the Thames, they would say it was because I couldn't swim.

Margaret Thatcher 1925-2013 British Conservative stateswoman

 # Progress

see also SCIENCE, TECHNOLOGY

Now, *here*, you see, it takes all the running *you* can do, to keep in the same place. If you want to get somewhere else, you must run at least twice as fast as that!

Lewis Carroll 1832-98 English writer and logician

The civilized man has built a coach, but has lost the use of his feet.

Ralph Waldo Emerson 1803-82 American philosopher and poet

on being asked what he thought of modern civilization:

That would be a good idea.

Mahatma Gandhi 1869-1948 Indian statesman

Progress doesn't come from early risers—progress is made by lazy men looking for easier ways to do things.

Robert Heinlein 1907-88 American science fiction writer

Progress might have been all right once, but it has gone on too long.

Ogden Nash 1902-71 American humorist

You can't say civilization don't advance, however, for in every war they kill you in a new way.

Will Rogers 1879-1935 American actor and humorist

Publishing

The world needs your book, just not many copies of it.

Derek Brewer 1923-2008 British academic and publisher

The poem will please if it is lively—if it is stupid it will fail—but I will have none of your damned cutting and slashing.

Lord Byron 1788-1824 English poet

at a literary dinner during the Napoleonic Wars, proposing a toast to Napoleon:

Gentlemen, we must be just to our great enemy. We must not forget that he once shot a bookseller.

Thomas Campbell 1777-1844 Scottish poet

Aren't we due a royalty statement?

Charles, Prince of Wales 1948- heir apparent to the British throne, *to his literary agent*

Manuscript: something submitted in haste and returned at leisure.

Oliver Herford 1863-1935 English-born American humorist

The relationship of an agent to a publisher is that of a knife to a throat.

Marvin Josephson American agent

A publisher who writes is like a cow in a milk bar.

Arthur Koestler 1905-83 Hungarian-born writer

I suppose publishers are untrustworthy. They certainly always look it.

Oscar Wilde 1854-1900 Irish dramatist and poet

Being published by the Oxford University Press is rather like being married to a duchess: the honour is almost greater than the pleasure.

G. M. Young 1882-1959 English historian

 Punishment

see CRIME *and* Punishment

Puns

see also WIT

Hanging is too good for a man who makes puns; he should be drawn and quoted.

Fred Allen 1894–1956 American humorist

explaining her mother's insistence on taking her own bidet with her when she travelled:

My poor, dear mother suffers from a bidet-fixe.

Karen Lancaster d. 1964

DANNY KAYE: A jester unemployed is nobody's fool.

Norman Panama 1914–2003 and **Melvin Frank** 1913–88 American screenwriters, *in the film* The Court Jester

on her abortion:

It serves me right for putting all my eggs in one bastard.

Dorothy Parker 1893–1967 American critic and humorist

You can lead a horticulture, but you can't make her think.

Dorothy Parker 1893–1967 American critic and humorist

of Sir Charles Napier's conquest of Sindh:

Peccavi—I have Sindh.

Catherine Winkworth 1827–78 English hymnwriter, *reworking Latin* peccavi I have sinned

Quotations

I know heaps of quotations, so I can always make quite a fair show of knowledge.
O. Douglas 1877–1948 Scottish writer

Next to the originator of a good sentence is the first quoter of it.
Ralph Waldo Emerson 1803–82 American philosopher and poet

Pretentious quotations being the surest road to tedium.
H. W. Fowler 1858–1933 and **F. G. Fowler** 1870–1918 English lexicographers and grammarians

You can get a happy quotation anywhere if you have the eye.
Oliver Wendell Holmes Jr. 1841–1935 American lawyer

A widely-read man never quotes accurately, for the rather obvious reason that he has read too widely.
Hesketh Pearson 1887–1964 English actor and biographer

An anthology is like all the plums and orange peel picked out of a cake.
Walter Raleigh 1861–1922 English lecturer and critic

I always have a quotation for everything—it saves original thinking.
Dorothy L. Sayers 1893–1957 English writer

It's better to be quotable than honest.
Tom Stoppard 1937– British dramatist

What a good thing Adam had. When he said a good thing he knew nobody had said it before.

Mark Twain 1835–1910 American writer

Reading

see also BOOKS

The world may be full of fourth-rate writers but it's also full of fourth-rate readers.

Stan Barstow 1928–2011 English novelist

on the difficulties of reading the novels of Sir Walter Scott:
He shouldn't have written in such small print.

O. Douglas 1877–1948 Scottish writer

I read part of it all the way through.

Sam Goldwyn 1882–1974 American film producer

Reading isn't an occupation we encourage among police officers. We try to keep the paper work down to a minimum.

Joe Orton 1933–67 English dramatist

People say that life is the thing, but I prefer reading.

Logan Pearsall Smith 1865–1946 American-born man of letters

'*Classic*.' A book which people praise and don't read.

Mark Twain 1835–1910 American writer

Relationships

see also DATING

The feeling of friendship is like that of being comfortably filled with roast beef; love, like being enlivened with champagne.

James Boswell 1740-95 Scottish lawyer and biographer

Once a woman has forgiven her man, she must not reheat his sins for breakfast.

Marlene Dietrich 1901-92 German-born American actress and singer

Never go to bed mad. Stay up and fight.

Phyllis Diller 1917-2012 American actress

I know a lot of people didn't expect our relationship to last—but we've just celebrated our two months anniversary.

Britt Ekland 1942- Swedish actress

Men love women, women love children; children love hamsters—it's quite hopeless.

Alice Thomas Ellis 1932-2005 English novelist

The trouble with Ian [Fleming] is that he gets off with women because he can't get on with them.

Rosamund Lehmann 1901-90 English novelist

on Valentine's Day:

Just last week I wrote 'I still love you, see last year's card for full details.'

Michael McIntyre 1976- English comedian

Take me or leave me; or, as is the usual order of things, both.

Dorothy Parker 1893-1967 American critic and humorist

My love life is like a piece of Swiss cheese. Most of it's missing and what's there stinks.

Joan Rivers 1933-2014 American comedienne

We had a lot in common. I loved him and he loved him.

Shelley Winters 1922-2006 American actress, *on divorcing Vittorio Gassman*

 Religion

see also CLERGY, GOD

To be Catholic or Jewish isn't chic. Chic is Episcopalian.

Elizabeth Arden c.1880-1966 Canadian-born American businesswoman

I've a definite sense of spirituality. I want Brooklyn to be christened, but don't know into what religion yet.

David Beckham 1975- English footballer

FOSTER: I'm still a bit hazy about the Trinity, sir.
SCHOOLMASTER: Three in one, one in three, perfectly straightforward. Any doubts about that see your maths master.

Alan Bennett 1934- English dramatist and actor

The Vatican is against surrogate mothers. Good thing they didn't have that rule when Jesus was born.

Elayne Boosler 1952- American comedian

If Jesus had been killed 20 years ago, Catholic school children would be wearing little electric chairs around their necks instead of crosses.

Lenny Bruce 1925-66 American comedian

An atheist is a man who has no invisible means of support.
John Buchan 1875-1940 Scottish novelist

Thanks to God, I am still an atheist.
Luis Buñuel 1900-83 Spanish film director

The one excuse for being pagan is to enjoy it thoroughly.
Roy Campbell 1901-57 South African poet

Atheism is a non-prophet organization.
George Carlin 1937-2008 American comedian

Blessed are the cheesemakers.
Graham Chapman 1941-89, **John Cleese** 1939- , and **others**
British comedians, *a misheard beatitude, in the film* Monty
Python's Life of Brian

It is the test of a good religion whether you can joke
about it.
G. K. Chesterton 1874-1936 English essayist, novelist, and poet

Said Waldershare, 'Sensible men are all of the same
religion.' 'And pray what is that?' ... 'Sensible men never
tell.'
Benjamin Disraeli 1804-81 British Tory statesman and novelist

    What after all
Is a halo? It's only one more thing to keep clean.
Christopher Fry 1907-2005 English dramatist

I find it hard to understand why one should look for
sermons in stones when the inability to preach is so
attractive a feature of stones.
Northrop Frye 1912-91 Canadian literary critic

The three kinds of services you generally find in the
Episcopal churches. I call them either low-and-lazy,
broad-and-hazy, or high-and-crazy.

Willa Gibbs Canadian writer

*imagining how a Church of England Inquisition might have
worked*

'Cake or death?' 'Cake, please.'

Eddie Izzard 1962- British comedian

VISITOR: How many people work in the Vatican?
POPE JOHN: About half of them.

Pope John XXIII 1881-1963 Italian cleric

FATHER TED: It's nice to have a nun around. Gives the
place a bit of glamour.

Graham Linehan 1968- and **Arthur Mathews**
1959- screenwriters

You can't run the Church on Hail Marys.

Paul Marcinkus 1922-2006 American Roman Catholic
archbishop, *view of a Vatican banker*

on hearing an evangelical sermon:

Things have come to a pretty pass when religion is allowed
to invade the sphere of private life.

Lord Melbourne 1779-1848 British Whig statesman

Puritanism. The haunting fear that someone, somewhere,
may be happy.

H. L. Mencken 1880-1956 American journalist and literary
critic

It is now quite lawful for a Catholic woman to avoid pregnancy by a resort to mathematics, though she is still forbidden to resort to physics and chemistry.

H. L. Mencken 1880-1956 American journalist and literary critic

I celebrate everyone's religious holidays. If it's good enough for the righteous, it's good enough for the self-righteous I always say.

Bette Midler 1945- American actress

You are not an agnostic... You are just a fat slob who is too lazy to go to Mass.

Conor Cruise O'Brien 1917-2008 Irish politician, writer, and journalist

There's no reason to bring religion into it. I think we ought to have as great a regard for religion as we can, so as to keep it out of as many things as possible.

Sean O'Casey 1880-1964 Irish dramatist

No praying, it spoils business.

Thomas Otway 1652-85 English dramatist

on long sermons:

The mind cannot absorb what the backside cannot endure.

Prince Philip, Duke of Edinburgh 1921- British prince

I have wondered at times about what the Ten Commandments would have looked like if Moses had run them through the US Congress.

Ronald Reagan 1911-2004 American Republican statesman

The Chinese said they would...build a shrine to my memory. I have some slight regret that this did not happen as I might have become a god, which would have been very *chic* for an atheist.

    Bertrand Russell 1872–1970 British philosopher and mathematician

People may say what they like about the decay of Christianity; the religious system that produced green Chartreuse can never really die.

    Saki 1870–1916 Scottish writer

You can't expect the fatted calf to share the enthusiasm of the angels over the prodigal's return.

    Saki 1870–1916 Scottish writer

How can what an Englishman believes be heresy? It is a contradiction in terms.

    George Bernard Shaw 1856–1950 Irish dramatist

I'm a dyslexic Satanist; I worship the drivel.

    Linda Smith 1958–2006 British comedian

Deserves to be preached to death by wild curates.

    Sydney Smith 1771–1845 English clergyman and essayist

Protestant women may take the pill. Roman Catholic women must keep taking The Tablet.

    Irene Thomas 1919–2001 British writer and broadcaster

When the missionaries came to Africa, they had the Bible and we had the land. They said: 'Let us pray'. We closed our eyes. When we opened them we had the Bible and they had the land.

Desmond Tutu 1931- South African Anglican clergyman

Why do born-again people so often make you wish they'd never been born the first time?

Katharine Whitehorn 1928- English journalist

JAN STERLING: I don't go to church. Kneeling bags my nylons.

Billy Wilder 1906-2002 and **others** screenwriters, *in the film Ace in the Hole*

I'm a Protestant—Episcopal, Catholic-lite, same religion, half the guilt.

Robin Williams 1951-2014 American actor

Restaurants

WAITER WITH FISH ORDER: Are you smelt, sir?
JOHN BETJEMAN: Only by the discerning.

John Betjeman 1906-84 English poet

to diners, while being carried on a stretcher from his suite at the Savoy when dying of cancer:

It was the food. It was the food.

Richard Harris 1930-2002 Irish actor

'Can I have a table near the floor?'
'Certainly, I'll have the waiter saw the legs off.'

Groucho Marx 1890-1977 American film comedian

Avoid any restaurant where the waiter arrives with a handful of knives and forks just as you reach the punchline of your best story and says 'Which of you is having fish?'

John Mortimer 1923-2009 English writer and barrister

Someone at the table, whose order had not yet arrived, said, 'I think "waiter" is such a funny word. It is we who wait.'

Muriel Spark 1918-2006 British novelist

MARGARET THATCHER: This food is absolutely delicious.
DENIS THATCHER: So it should be. They're charging like the Light Brigade.

Denis Thatcher 1915-2003 English businessman, *eating in Harry's Bar*

I went to a restaurant that serves 'breakfast any time'. So I ordered French toast during the Renaissance.

Steven Wright 1955- American comedian

😄 Retirement

If anything could have pulled me out of retirement, it would have been an Indiana Jones film. But in the end, retirement is just too damned much fun.

Sean Connery 1930- Scottish actor

The transition from Who's Who to Who's He.

Eddie George 1938-2009 English banker, *view of the former Governor of the Bank of England on retirement*

I remember one of my staff asking me when I was going to retire. I said when I could no longer hear the sound of laughter. He said, 'That never stopped you before.'

Bob Hope 1903-2003 American comedian

Royalty 🦢

on her passion for horses:

When I appear in public people expect me to neigh, grind my teeth, paw the ground and swish my tail—none of which is easy.

Anne, Princess Royal 1950- British princess

How different, how very different from the home life of our own dear Queen!

Anonymous, *comment overheard at a performance of Cleopatra by Sarah Bernhardt*

I shall be an autocrat: that's my trade. And the good Lord will forgive me: that's his.

Catherine the Great 1729-96 Russian empress, *see Heine at* GOD

This is very true: for my words are my own, and my actions are my ministers'.

Charles II 1630-85 British king, *reply to Rochester at* ROYALTY *below*

Everyone likes flattery; and when you come to Royalty you should lay it on with a trowel.

Benjamin Disraeli 1804-81 British Tory statesman and novelist *on being asked if Queen Victoria would be happy in heaven:*

She will have to walk behind the angels—and she won't like that.

Edward VII 1841-1910 British king

I think everybody really will concede that on this, of all days, I should begin my speech with the words 'My husband and I'.

Elizabeth II 1926- British queen, *on her 25th wedding anniversary*

The whole world is in revolt. Soon there will be only five Kings left—the King of England, the King of Spades, the King of Clubs, the King of Hearts and the King of Diamonds.

Farouk 1920-65 Egyptian king

on H. G. Wells's comment on 'an alien and uninspiring court':

I may be uninspiring, but I'll be damned if I'm an alien!

George V 1865-1936 British king

I left England when I was four because I found out I could never be King.

Bob Hope 1903-2003 American comedian

notice on a playbill sent to her former lover, the Duke of Clarence, refusing his demand for repayment of her allowance:

Positively no money refunded after the curtain has risen.

Mrs Jordan 1761-1816 Irish-born actress

My children are not royal, they just happen to have the Queen as their aunt.

Princess Margaret 1930-2002 British princess

on the abdication of her son, Edward VIII:

Really, this might be Rumania.

    Queen Mary 1867-1953 British Queen Consort

Such an active lass. So outdoorsy. She loves nature in spite of what it did to her.

    Bette Midler 1945- American actress, *on Princess Anne*

I declare this thing open—whatever it is.

    Prince Philip, Duke of Edinburgh 1921- husband of Elizabeth II, *opening an annexe at Vancouver City Hall*

The Right Divine of Kings to govern wrong.

    Alexander Pope 1688-1744 English poet

on Charles, Prince of Wales:

He's so gay. He can't wait for his mother to die so he can be Queen.

    Joan Rivers 1933-2014 American comedienne

Here lies a great and mighty king
Whose promise none relies on;
He never said a foolish thing,
Nor ever did a wise one.

    Lord Rochester 1647-80 English poet, *proposed epitaph for Charles II; see Charles at* ROYALTY *above*

He speaks to Me as if I was a public meeting.

    Victoria 1819-1901 British queen, *of Gladstone*

to Edward IV whom she later married:

My liege, I know I am not good enough to be your queen, but I am far too good to become your mistress.

    Elizabeth Woodville c.1437-92 English queen of Edward IV

I'm doing pretty well considering. In the past, when anyone left the Royal family they had you beheaded.
Sarah, Duchess of York 1959-

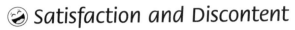

Satisfaction and Discontent

when asked what was the best day of her life:
It was a night.
Brigitte Bardot 1934- French actress

Clark Gable (as Rhett Butler):
Frankly, my dear, I don't give a damn.
Sidney Howard 1891-1939 American dramatist and screenwriter, *in the film* Gone with the Wind (*based on the novel by Margaret Mitchell*)

When fortune empties her chamberpot on your head, smile—and say 'we are going to have a summer shower'.
John A. Macdonald 1851-91 Scottish-born Canadian statesman

It's better to be looked over than overlooked.
Mae West 1892-1980 American film actress

Too much of a good thing can be wonderful.
Mae West 1892-1980 American film actress

If not actually disgruntled, he was far from being gruntled.
P. G. Wodehouse 1881-1975 English-born writer

 # Science

see also PROGRESS, TECHNOLOGY

Basic research is like shooting an arrow into the air and, where it lands, painting a target.

Homer Burton Adkins 1892–1949 American organic chemist

When I find myself in the company of scientists, I feel like a shabby curate who has strayed by mistake into a drawing room full of dukes.

W. H. Auden 1907–73 English poet

Basic research is what I am doing when I don't know what I am doing.

Wernher von Braun 1912–77 German-born American rocket engineer

If an elderly but distinguished scientist says that something is possible he is almost certainly right, but if he says that it is impossible he is very probably wrong.

Arthur C. Clarke 1917–2008 English science fiction writer

Someone told me that each equation I included in the book would halve the sales.

Stephen Hawking 1942–2018 English theoretical physicist

Cosmologists are often in error, but never in doubt.

Lev Landau 1908–68 Russian physicist

It was Einstein who made the real trouble. He announced in 1905 that there was no such thing as absolute rest. After that there never was.

Stephen Leacock 1869–1944 Canadian humorist

It is a good morning exercise for a research scientist to discard a pet hypothesis every day before breakfast.

Konrad Lorenz 1903–89 Austro-German zoologist

Her own mother lived the latter years of her life in the horrible suspicion that electricity was dripping invisibly all over the house.

James Thurber 1894-1961 American humorist

There is something fascinating about science. One gets such wholesale returns of conjecture out of such a trifling investment of fact.

Mark Twain 1835-1910 American writer

Scotland

There are few more impressive sights in the world than a Scotsman on the make.

J. M. Barrie 1860-1937 Scottish writer and dramatist

There are two seasons in Scotland: June and winter.

Billy Connolly 1942- Scottish comedian

Sir, let me tell you, the noblest prospect which a Scotchman ever sees, is the high road that leads him to England!

Samuel Johnson 1709-84 English poet, critic, and lexicographer

No McTavish
Was ever lavish.

Ogden Nash 1902-71 American humorist

That knuckle-end of England—that land of Calvin, oat-cakes, and sulphur.

Sydney Smith 1771-1845 English clergyman and essayist

It is never difficult to distinguish between a Scotsman with a grievance and a ray of sunshine.

P. G. Wodehouse 1881-1975 English writer

Secrecy

The best leaks always take place in the urinal.
John Cole 1927-2013 Northern Irish journalist and broadcaster

I know that's a secret, for it's whispered every where.
William Congreve 1670-1729 English dramatist

Once the toothpaste is out of the tube, it is awfully hard to get it back in.
H. R. Haldeman 1929-93 American Presidential assistant to Richard Nixon, *on Watergate*

Truth is suppressed, not to protect the country from enemy agents but to protect the Government of the day against the people.
Roy Hattersley 1932- British Labour politician

That's another of those irregular verbs, isn't it? I give confidential briefings; you leak; he has been charged under Section 2a of the Official Secrets Act.
Jonathan Lynn 1943- and **Antony Jay** 1930-2016 English writers

The most difficult secret for a man to keep is his own opinion of himself.
Marcel Pagnol 1895-1974 French dramatist and film-maker

Self-Knowledge and Self-Deception
see also CHARACTER

definition of an egotist:

A person of low taste, more interested in himself than in me.

Ambrose Bierce 1842–c.1914 American writer

The reward for conformity is that everyone likes you except yourself.

Rita Mae Brown 1944– American novelist and poet

They misunderestimated me.

George W. Bush 1946– American Republican statesman

I wouldn't say I was the best manager, but I was in the top one.

Brian Clough 1935–2004 English football manager

All my shows are great. Some of them are bad. But they are all great.

Lew Grade 1906–98 British television producer and executive

It's been my experience that people who make proclamations about themselves are usually the opposite of what they claim to be.

Chelsea Handler 1975– American comedienne and writer

The photograph is not quite true to my own notion of my gentleness and sweetness of nature, but neither perhaps is my external appearance.

A. E. Housman 1859–1936 English poet

I am not the type who wants to go back to the land; I am the type who wants to go back to the hotel.

Fran Lebowitz 1950– American writer

A journey of self-discovery starts with a single step ... But so does falling down a flight of stairs.

Kathy Lette 1958– Australian writer

Underneath this flabby exterior is an enormous lack of character.

Oscar Levant 1906-72 American pianist

A man always has two reasons for what he does—a good one and the real one.

John Pierpont Morgan 1837-1913 American financier and philanthropist

Every person is the star of their life story. No one goes through the world thinking: 'Well, I'm just a cameo'.

John C. Reilly 1965- American actor

You're so vain
You probably think this song is about you.

Carly Simon 1945- American singer and songwriter

I have often wished I had time to cultivate modesty...But I am too busy thinking about myself.

Edith Sitwell 1887-1964 English poet and critic

How awful to reflect that what people say of us is true!

Logan Pearsall Smith 1865-1946 American-born man of letters

Satire is a sort of glass, wherein beholders do generally discover everybody's face but their own.

Jonathan Swift 1667-1745 Irish poet and satirist

I am extraordinarily patient, provided I get my own way in the end.

Margaret Thatcher 1925-2013 British Conservative stateswoman

Pavarotti is not vain, but conscious of being unique.

Peter Ustinov 1921–2004 British actor, director, and writer

I'm the girl who lost her reputation and never missed it.

Mae West 1892–1980 American film actress

I don't at all like knowing what people say of me behind my back. It makes me far too conceited.

Oscar Wilde 1854–1900 Irish dramatist and poet

Early in life I had to choose between honest arrogance and hypocritical humility. I chose honest arrogance and have seen no occasion to change.

Frank Lloyd Wright 1867–1959 American architect

Sex

see also LOVE, MARRIAGE

WOODY ALLEN: Don't knock masturbation. It's sex with someone I love.

Woody Allen 1935– American film director, writer, and actor, in the film Annie Hall, written with **Marshall Brickman** (1941–)

WOODY ALLEN: That [sex] was the most fun I ever had without laughing.

Woody Allen 1935– American film director, writer, and actor, in the film Annie Hall, written with **Marshall Brickman** (1941–)

WOODY ALLEN: My love life is terrible. The last time I was inside a woman was when I visited the Statue of Liberty.

Woody Allen 1935– American film director, writer, and actor, *in the film* Crimes and Misdemeanors

Is sex dirty? Only if it's done right.

> **Woody Allen** 1935- American film director, writer, and actor, *in the film* Everything You Always Wanted to Know about Sex

A fast word about oral contraception. I asked a girl to go to bed with me and she said 'no'.

> **Woody Allen** 1935- American film director, writer, and actor

On bisexuality: It immediately doubles your chances for a date on Saturday night.

> **Woody Allen** 1935- American film director, writer, and actor

Give me chastity and continency—but not yet!

> **St Augustine** of Hippo AD 354-430 Roman Christian theologian

I'll come and make love to you at five o'clock. If I'm late start without me.

> **Tallulah Bankhead** 1903-68 American actress

at the age of ninety-seven, Blake was asked at what age the sex drive goes:

You'll have to ask somebody older than me.

> **Eubie Blake** 1883-1983 American ragtime pianist

On life's long road I have found the penis to be a most unreliable compass.

> **David L. Bloomer** 1912-96 Scottish badminton player

Sex has never been an obsession with me. It's just like eating a bag of crisps. Quite nice, but nothing marvellous.

> **Boy George** 1961- English pop singer and songwriter

If homosexuality were the normal way, God would have made Adam and Bruce.

Anita Bryant 1940- American singer

Sexual intercouse is kicking death in the ass while singing.

Charles Bukowski 1920-94 German-born American writer

He said it was artificial respiration, but now I find I am to have his child.

Anthony Burgess 1917-93 English novelist and critic

on homosexuality:

It doesn't matter what you do in the bedroom as long as you don't do it in the street and frighten the horses.

Mrs Patrick Campbell 1865-1940 English actress

I don't have a sex 'drive'. I have a sex 'just sit in the car and hope someone gets in.'

Louis C.K. 1967- American comedian

asked if he was superstitious:

Only about thirteen in a bed.

Noël Coward 1899-1973 English dramatist, actor, and composer

I became one of the stately homos of England.

Quentin Crisp 1908-99 English writer

Seduction is often difficult to distinguish from rape. In seduction, the rapist bothers to buy a bottle of wine.

Andrea Dworkin 1946-2005 American feminist and writer

When choosing sexual partners remember: Talent is not sexually transmittable.

Tina Fey 1970- American comedian and actress

He in a few minutes ravished this fair creature, or at least would have ravished her, if she had not, by a timely compliance, prevented him.

Henry Fielding 1707-54 English novelist and dramatist

on oral fixation:

Sometimes a cigar is just a cigar.

Sigmund Freud 1856-1939 Austrian psychiatrist

on her boyfriend Porfirio Rubirosa:

He may be the best lover in the world, but what do you do the other twenty-two hours of the day?

Zsa Zsa Gabor 1917-2016 Hungarian-born film actress

BILLY CRYSTAL: Women need a reason to have sex, men just need a place.

Lowell Ganz 1948- and **Babaloo Mandel** 1949- American screenwriters, *in the film* City Slickers

Masturbation is the thinking man's television.

Christopher Hampton 1946- English dramatist

Men don't realize that if we're sleeping with them on the first date, we're probably not interested in seeing them again either.

Chelsea Handler 1975- American comedienne and writer

I regret to say that we of the FBI are powerless to act in cases of oral-genital intimacy, unless it has in some way obstructed interstate commerce.

J. Edgar Hoover 1895-1972 American director of the FBI

There is no unhappier creature on earth than a fetishist who yearns to embrace a woman's shoe and has to embrace the whole woman.

Karl Kraus 1874-1936 Austrian satirist

He was into animal husbandry—until they caught him at it.

Tom Lehrer 1928- American humorist

All this male angst over size. It's *attitude* women are interested in. Women like a penis which says 'G'day! God am I glad to see *you*.'

Kathy Lette 1958- Australian writer

What's the worst thing about oral sex? The view.

Maureen Lipman 1946- English actress

on lesbianism:

I can understand two men. There is something to get hold of. But how do two insides make love?

Lydia Lopokova 1892-1981 Russian ballerina

Sex appeal is 50 per cent what you've got and 50 per cent what people think you've got.

Sophia Loren 1934- Italian actress

What's a promiscuous person? It's usually someone who is getting more sex than you are.

Victor Lownes 1928-2017 American businessman

Many years ago I chased a woman for almost two years, only to discover that her tastes were exactly like mine: we both were crazy about girls.

Groucho Marx 1890-1977 American film comedian

I've been around so long, I knew Doris Day before she was a virgin.

Groucho Marx 1890-1977 American film comedian

Contraceptives should be used on every conceivable occasion.

Spike Milligan 1918-2002 Irish comedian

Not tonight, Josephine.

Napoleon I 1769-1821 French emperor

Your idea of fidelity is not having more than one man in bed at the same time.

Frederic Raphael 1931- British novelist and screenwriter

My life has been one long descent into respectability.

Mandy Rice-Davies 1944-2014 English model and showgirl, *on life after the 'Profumo Affair' sex scandal*

It's so long since I've had sex I've forgotten who ties up whom.

Joan Rivers 1933-2014 American comedienne

Is it not strange that desire should so many years outlive performance?

William Shakespeare 1564-1616 English dramatist

There are times when a woman reading *Playboy* feels a little like a Jew reading a Nazi manual.

Gloria Steinem 1934- American journalist

I'm all for bringing back the birch, but only between consenting adults.

Gore Vidal 1925-2012 American novelist and critic

All this fuss about sleeping together. For physical pleasure I'd sooner go to my dentist any day.

Evelyn Waugh 1903-66 English novelist

Why don't you come up sometime, and see me?

Mae West 1892-1980 American film actress, *usually quoted as,* '*Why don't you come up and see me sometime?*'

It's not the men in my life that counts—it's the life in my men.

Mae West 1892-1980 American film actress

Sickness and Health

see also EXERCISE, MEDICINE

You know my father died of cancer when I was a teenager. He had it before it became popular.

Goodman Ace 1899-1982 American humorist

My Mum told us that only special people get cancer. I must be very special because I've had it in my lungs and my bladder as well.

Caroline Aherne 1963-2016 British comic actress and writer

I don't deserve this award, but I have arthritis, and I don't deserve that either.

Jack Benny 1894-1974 American comedian

In 1969 I gave up women and alcohol. It was the worst 20 minutes of my life.

George Best 1946-2005 Northern Irish footballer

Health ... what my friends are always drinking to before they fall down.

Phyllis Diller 1917-2012 American actress

The average, healthy, well-adjusted adult gets up at seven-thirty in the morning feeling just plain terrible.

Jean Kerr 1923-2003 American writer

Besides death, constipation is the big fear in hospitals.

Robert McCrum 1953- British writer

I think the worst time to have a heart attack is during a game of charades.

Demetri Martin 1973- American comedian

It's no longer a question of staying healthy. It's a question of finding a sickness you like.

Jackie Mason 1931- American comedian

on her replacement hips and knee:

I'm Dorothy's daughter up top and the Tin Man down below.

Liza Minelli 1946- American actress and singer

Varicose veins are the result of an improper selection of grandparents.

William Osler 1849-1919 Canadian-born physician

A man is as old as his arteries.

Thomas Sydenham 1624-89 English physician

on hearing that Peter Sellers had suffered a heart attack:

What do you mean, heart attack? You've got to have a heart before you can have an attack.

Billy Wilder 1906-2002 American screenwriter and director

 Singing

see SONGS *and Singing*

Sleep and Dreams

Sleep is when all the unsorted stuff comes flying out as from a dustbin upset in a high wind.
   William Golding 1911-93 English novelist

I love sleep because it is both pleasant and safe to use.
   Fran Lebowitz 1950-   American writer

Sometimes I lie awake at night and I ask, 'Where have I gone wrong?' Then a voice says to me, 'This is going to take more than one night.'
   Charles Monroe Schulz 1922-2000 American cartoonist

Many's the long night I've dreamed of cheese—toasted, mostly.
   Robert Louis Stevenson 1850-94 Scottish novelist

There ain't no way to find out why a snorer can't hear himself snore.
   Mark Twain 1835-1910 American writer

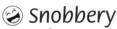 Snobbery

see also CLASS

Vulgarity has its uses. Vulgarity often cuts ice which refinement scrapes at vainly.
   Max Beerbohm 1872-1956 English critic, essayist, and caricaturist

From Poland to polo in one generation.
> **Arthur Caesar** 1892-1953 American screenwriter, *of Darryl Zanuck*

The trouble with Michael is that he had to buy all his furniture.
> **Michael Jopling** 1930- British Conservative politician, *of Michael Heseltine*

Thank goodness for Tesco. It keeps the riff-raff out of Waitrose.
> **Royce Mills** 1942- English actor

on being told that Clare Boothe Luce was always kind to her inferiors:
And where does she find them?
> **Dorothy Parker** 1893-1967 American critic and humorist

There is no stronger craving in the world than that of the rich for titles, except perhaps that of the titled for riches.
> **Hesketh Pearson** 1887-1964 English actor and biographer

You can be in the Horseguards and still be common, dear.
> **Terence Rattigan** 1911-77 English dramatist

Good God! I've never drunk a vintage that starts with the number two before.
> **Nicholas Soames** 1948- British Conservative politician

Whenever he met a great man he grovelled before him, and my-lorded him as only a free-born Briton can do.
> **William Makepeace Thackeray** 1811-63 English novelist

😀 Society and Social Life

see also PARTIES

It was a delightful visit;—perfect, in being much too short.
   Jane Austen 1775-1817 English novelist

I'm a man more dined against than dining.
   Maurice Bowra 1898-1971 English scholar and literary critic

In London, at the Café de Paris, I sang to café society; in
Las Vegas, at the Desert Inn, I sang to Nescafé society.
   Noël Coward 1899-1973 English dramatist, actor, and composer

PLEASE ACCEPT MY RESIGNATION. I DON'T WANT TO
BELONG TO ANY CLUB THAT WILL ACCEPT ME AS A
MEMBER.
   Groucho Marx 1890-1977 American film comedian

The truly free man is the one who will turn down an
invitation to dinner without giving an excuse.
   Jules Renard 1864-1910 French novelist and dramatist

All decent people live beyond their incomes nowadays,
and those who aren't respectable live beyond other
peoples'.
   Saki 1870-1916 Scottish writer

MENDOZA: I am a brigand: I live by robbing the rich.
TANNER: I am a gentleman: I live by robbing the poor.
   George Bernard Shaw 1856-1950 Irish dramatist

GERALD: I suppose society is wonderfully delightful!

LORD ILLINGWORTH: To be in it is merely a bore. But to be out of it simply a tragedy.

Oscar Wilde 1854–1900 Irish dramatist and poet

Songs and Singing

see also OPERA

Today if something is not worth saying, people sing it.

Pierre-Augustin Caron de Beaumarchais 1732–99 French dramatist

I love to sing. And I love to drink scotch. Most people would rather hear me drink scotch.

George Burns 1896–1996 American comedian

Swans sing before they die: 'twere no bad thing
Should certain persons die before they sing.

Samuel Taylor Coleridge 1772–1834 English poet, critic, and philosopher

People never talked about my music. They just counted how many knickers were on the stage.

Tom Jones 1940– Welsh pop singer

refusing to accept further changes to lyrics:

Call me Miss Birdseye. This show is frozen!

Ethel Merman 1909–84 American singer and actress

'Who wrote that song?'
'Rodgers and Hammerstein. If you can imagine it taking *two* men to write one song.'

Cole Porter 1891–1964 American songwriter, *of 'Some Enchanted Evening'*

Tenors are usually short, stout men (except when they are Wagnerian tenors, in which case they are large, stout men).

Harold Schonberg 1915-2003 American music critic

the president of CBS Records to Leonard Cohen:
Leonard, we know you're great, but we don't know if you're any good.

Walter Yetnikoff 1933- American businessman

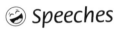 Speeches

I do not object to people looking at their watches when I am speaking. But I strongly object when they start shaking them to make certain they are still going.

Lord Birkett 1883-1962 English judge

If you don't say anything, you won't be called on to repeat it.

Calvin Coolidge 1872-1933 American Republican statesman

Strong message here.

Jeremy Corbyn 1949- British Labour politician, *reading out the autocue instruction*

I dreamt I was making a speech in the House. I woke up, and by Jove I was!

Duke of Devonshire 1833-1908 British Conservative politician

A sophistical rhetorician, inebriated with the exuberance of his own verbosity.

Benjamin Disraeli 1804-81 British Tory statesman and novelist, *of Gladstone*

Hubert Humphrey talks so fast that listening to him is like trying to read *Playboy* magazine with your wife turning the pages.

Barry Goldwater 1909-98 American Republican politician

Since I've become a central banker, I've learned to mumble with great incoherence. If I seem unduly clear to you, you must have misunderstood what I said.

Alan Greenspan 1926- American economist

The human brain starts working the moment you are born and never stops until you stand up to speak in public.

George Jessel 1898-1981 American comedian

I may not know much, but I know chicken shit from a chicken salad.

Lyndon Baines Johnson 1908-73 American Democratic statesman, *on a speech by Richard Nixon*

Did you ever think that making a speech on economics is a lot like pissing down your leg? It seems hot to you, but it never does to anyone else.

Lyndon Baines Johnson 1908-73 American Democratic statesman

I appreciate your welcome. As the cow said to the Maine farmer 'Thank you for a warm hand on a cold morning'.

John F. Kennedy 1917-63 American Democratic statesman

The most popular speaker is the one who sits down before he stands up.

John Pentland Mahaffy 1839-1919 Irish writer

A speech is like a love affair: any fool can start one but to end one requires considerable skill.

Lord Mancroft 1914-87 British Conservative politician

He has devoted the best years of his life to preparing his impromptu speeches.

F. E. Smith 1872-1930 British Conservative politician and lawyer, *on Winston Churchill*

I fear I cannot make an amusing speech. I have just been reading a book which says that 'all geniuses are devoid of humour'.

Stephen Spender 1909-95 English poet

Nixon's farm policy is vague, but he is going a long way toward solving the corn surplus by his speeches.

Adlai Stevenson 1900-65 American Democratic politician

Whales only get killed when they spout.

Denis Thatcher 1915-2003 British businessman, *declining a request to be interviewed*

To remain silent is the most useful service that a mediocre speaker can render to the public good.

Alexis de Tocqueville 1805-59 French historian and politician

I am here to propose a toast to the sports writers. It's up to you whether you stand or not.

Freddie Trueman 1931-2006 English cricketer

Better to keep your mouth shut and appear stupid than to open it and remove all doubt.

Mark Twain 1835-1910 American writer

Sports and Games

see also **BASEBALL, BOXING, CRICKET, FOOTBALL, GOLF, TENNIS**

Playing snooker gives you firm hands and helps to build up character. It is the ideal recreation for dedicated nuns.

Luigi Barbarito 1922-2017 Italian Roman Catholic clergyman

If you think squash is a competitive activity, try flower arrangement.

Alan Bennett 1934- English dramatist and actor

Rugby is a beastly game played by gentlemen.
Soccer is a gentleman's game played by beasts.
[American] Football is a beastly game played by beasts.

Henry Blaha American football player

I do not participate in any sport with ambulances at the bottom of the hill.

Erma Bombeck 1927-96 American humorist

A couple of weeks ago I knew nothing about the Olympics. Now I can't wait for next year's.

Frankie Boyle 1972- British comedian

on running the London Marathon:

I've set myself a target. I'm going for less than eleven-and-a-half days.

Jo Brand 1957- English comedian

Life's too short for chess.

H. J. Byron 1835-84 English dramatist

319

The trouble with referees is that they just don't care which side wins.

    Tom Canterbury American basketball player

As elaborate a waste of human intelligence as you could find anywhere outside an advertising agency.

    Raymond Chandler 1888-1959 American writer, *on chess*

If you lived in Sheffield and were called Sebastian, you had to learn to run fast at a very early stage.

    Sebastian Coe 1956- English athlete

I went to a fight the other night and an ice hockey game broke out.

    Rodney Dangerfield 1921-2004 American comedian

The thing about sport, any sport, is that swearing is very much part of it.

    Jimmy Greaves 1940- English footballer, commenting on a football match

Get your retaliation in first.

    Carwyn James 1929-83 Welsh rugby football coach

The only athletic sport I ever mastered was backgammon.

    Douglas Jerrold 1803-57 English dramatist and journalist

We break bones and we lose teeth. We play rugby.

    Martin Johnson 1970- English rugby player

If you play bridge badly you make your partner suffer, but if you play poker badly you make everybody happy.

    Joe Laurie Jr. 1892-1954 American comedian

If you don't have confidence, you'll always find a way not to win.

Carl Lewis 1961- American athlete

Rodeoing is about the only sport you can't fix. You'd have to talk to the bulls and the horses, and they wouldn't understand you.

Bill Linderman 1920-65 American rodeo cowboy

Athletic sports, save in the case of young boys, are designed for idiots.

George Jean Nathan 1882-1958 American critic and writer

The atmosphere here is a cross between the Munich Beer Festival and the Coliseum at Rome when the Christians were on the menu.

Sid Waddell 1940-2012 English sports commentator, *at a darts match*

The English country gentleman galloping after a fox—the unspeakable in full pursuit of the uneatable.

Oscar Wilde 1854-1900 Irish dramatist and poet, *see Zobel at* LAW

on American football:

Football combines the two worst features of modern American life: it's violence punctuated by committee meetings.

George F. Will 1941- American columnist

The fascination of shooting as a sport depends almost wholly on whether you are at the right or wrong end of a gun.

P. G. Wodehouse 1881-1975 English writer

Jogging is for people who aren't intelligent enough to watch television.
  Victoria Wood 1953-2016 British writer and comedienne

 Statistics

[The War Office kept three sets of figures:] one to mislead the public, another to mislead the Cabinet, and the third to mislead itself.
  Herbert Asquith 1852-1928 British Liberal statesman

There are three kinds of lies: lies, damned lies and statistics.
  Benjamin Disraeli 1804-81 British Tory statesman and novelist

He uses statistics as a drunken man uses lamp posts—for support rather than illumination.
  Andrew Lang 1844-1912 Scottish man of letters

Statistics are like a bikini. What they reveal is suggestive, but what they conceal is vital.
  Aaron Levenstein 1911-86 American academic

Success

see also FAILURE

Eighty per cent of success is showing up.
  Woody Allen 1935- American film director, writer, and actor

The road to success is always under construction.
  Anonymous, *traditional saying, today associated with Lily Tomlin*

Behind every successful man you'll find a woman who has nothing to wear.

Harold Coffin d. 1981 American columnist

Whom the gods wish to destroy they first call promising.

Cyril Connolly 1903-74 English writer

Nothing succeeds, they say, like success. And certainly nothing fails like failure.

Margaret Drabble 1939- English novelist

Success is a lousy teacher. It seduces smart people into thinking they can't lose.

Bill Gates 1955- American computer entrepreneur

formula for success:

Rise early. Work late. Strike oil.

John Paul Getty 1892-1976 American industrialist

Behind every man's achievement is a proud wife and a surprised mother-in-law.

Brooks Hays 1898-1981 American Democratic politician

Well, we knocked the bastard off!

Edmund Hillary 1919-2008 New Zealand mountaineer, *on conquering Mount Everest, 1953*

Luck, like a Russian car, generally only works if you push it.

Tom Holt 1961- English novelist

Success didn't spoil me. I've always been insufferable.

Fran Lebowitz 1950- American writer

It is sobering to consider that when Mozart was my age he had already been dead for a year.

Tom Lehrer 1928- American humorist

Be nice to people on your way up because you'll meet 'em on your way down.

Wilson Mizner 1876-1933 American dramatist

On the highest throne in the world, we still sit only on our bottom.

Montaigne 1533-92 French moralist and essayist

The world is divided into people who do things and people who get the credit. Try, if you can, to belong to the first class. There's far less competition.

Dwight Morrow 1873-1931 American lawyer, banker, and diplomat

David Frost has risen without trace.

Kitty Muggeridge 1903-94 English writer

I never climbed any ladder: I have achieved eminence by sheer gravitation.

George Bernard Shaw 1856-1950 Irish dramatist

Our business in this world is not to succeed, but to continue to fail, in good spirits.

Robert Louis Stevenson 1850-94 Scottish novelist

President George W. Bush overcame an incredible lack of obstacles to achieve his success.

Jon Stewart 1962- American satirist

There's no deodorant like success.
Elizabeth Taylor 1932–2011 English-born American actress

Whenever a friend succeeds, a little something in me dies.
Gore Vidal 1925–2012 American novelist and critic

It matters not whether you win or lose: what matters is whether I win or lose.
Darin Weinberg

Moderation is a fatal thing, Lady Hunstanton. Nothing succeeds like excess.
Oscar Wilde 1854–1900 Irish dramatist and poet

Success is a science; if you have the conditions, you get the result.
Oscar Wilde 1854–1900 Irish dramatist and poet

Taxes

Why does a slight tax increase cost you two hundred dollars and a substantial tax cut save you thirty cents?
Peg Bracken 1918–2007 American writer

Mansions can't run away to Switzerland.
Vince Cable 1943– British Liberal Democrat politician, *on taxing the homes of the wealthy*

It was as true … as taxes is. And nothing's truer than them.
Charles Dickens 1812–70 English novelist

Why sir, there is every possibility that you will soon be able to tax it!

Michael Faraday 1791-1867 English physicist and chemist, *to Gladstone, when asked about the usefulness of electricity*

Excise. A hateful tax levied upon commodities.

Samuel Johnson 1709-84 English poet, critic, and lexicographer

Taxation, gentlemen, is very much like dairy farming. The task is to extract the maximum amount of milk with the minimum of moo.

Terry Pratchett 1948-2015 English fantasy writer

Income Tax has made more Liars out of the American people than Golf.

Will Rogers 1879-1935 American actor and humorist

What is the difference between a taxidermist and a tax collector? The taxidermist takes only your skin.

Mark Twain 1835-1910 American writer

😄 Technology

see also PROGRESS, SCIENCE

When man wanted to make a machine that would walk he created the wheel, which does not resemble a leg.

Guillaume Apollinaire 1880-1918 French poet

Inanimate objects are classified scientifically into three major categories—those that don't work, those that break down, and those that get lost.

Russell Baker 1925- American journalist and columnist

The first rule of intelligent tinkering is to save all the parts.
  Paul Ralph Ehrlich 1932- American biologist

Technology . . . the knack of so arranging the world that we need not experience it.
  Max Frisch 1911-91 Swiss novelist and dramatist

If it weren't for electricity, we'd all be watching television by candlelight.
  George Gobel 1919-91 American comedian

The itemised phone bill ranks up there with suspender belts, Sky Sports Channels and Loaded magazine as inventions women could do without.
  Maeve Haran 1932- British writer

The thing with high-tech is that you always end up using scissors.
  David Hockney 1937- British artist

Our toaster works on either AC or DC but not on bread. It has two settings—too soon or too late.
  Sam Levenson 1911-80 American humorist

Xerox: a trademark for a photocopying device that can make rapid reproductions of human error, perfectly.
  Merle L. Meacham

No man can hear his telephone ring without wishing heartily that Alexander Graham Bell had been run over by an ice wagon at the age of four.
  H. L. Mencken 1880-1956 American journalist and literary critic

When the inventor of the drawing board messed things up, what did he go back to?

Bob Monkhouse 1928–2003 English entertainer

Telegrams

telegraph message on arriving in Venice:

STREETS FLOODED. PLEASE ADVISE.

Robert Benchley 1889–1945 American humorist

appeal to his wife:

AM IN MARKET HARBOROUGH. WHERE OUGHT I TO BE?

G. K. Chesterton 1874–1936 English essayist, novelist, and poet

HAVE MOVED HOTEL EXCELSIOR COUGHING MYSELF INTO A FIRENZE.

Noël Coward 1899–1973 English dramatist, actor, and composer, *telegram from Florence*

sent by W. G. Grace's elder brother, a cricket-playing coroner, to postpone an inquest:

PUT CORPSE ON ICE TILL CLOSE OF PLAY.

E. M. Grace 1841–1911 English cricketer

response to a telegraphic enquiry, HOW OLD CARY GRANT?:

OLD CARY GRANT FINE. HOW YOU?

Cary Grant 1904–86 British-born American actor

an estate agent in Bermuda told her that the house she was considering came with a maid, a secretary, and a chauffeur:

AIRMAIL PHOTOGRAPH OF CHAUFFEUR.

Beatrice Lillie 1894–1989 Canadian-born comedienne

telegram to Mrs Sherwood on the arrival of her baby:

GOOD WORK, MARY. WE ALL KNEW YOU HAD IT IN YOU.

Dorothy Parker 1893-1967 American critic and humorist

cables were soon arriving … 'Require earliest name life story photograph American nurse upblown Adowa.' We replied:

NURSE UNUPBLOWN.

Evelyn Waugh 1903-66 English novelist

FEAR I MAY NOT BE ABLE TO REACH YOU IN TIME FOR THE CEREMONY. DON'T WAIT.

James McNeill Whistler 1834-1903 American-born painter, *telegram of apology for missing Oscar Wilde's wedding*

his wife had requested him, when in Paris, to buy and send her a bidet:

UNABLE OBTAIN BIDET. SUGGEST HANDSTAND IN SHOWER.

Billy Wilder 1906-2002 American screenwriter and director

Television

The best that can be said for Norwegian television is that it gives you the sensation of a coma without the worry and inconvenience.

Bill Bryson 1951- American travel writer

Theatre actors look down on film actors, who look down on TV actors. Thank God for reality shows or we wouldn't have anybody to look down on.

George Clooney 1961- American actor and director

Television is more interesting than people. If it were not, we should have people standing in the corners of our rooms.

Alan Coren 1938-2007 English humorist

Television is for appearing on, not looking at.

Noël Coward 1899-1973 English dramatist, actor, and composer

Television is an invention that permits you to be entertained in your living room by people you wouldn't have in your home.

David Frost 1939-2013 English broadcaster and writer

IAN ST JOHN: Is he speaking to you yet?
JIMMY GREAVES: Not yet, but I hope to be incommunicado with him in a very short space of time.

Jimmy Greaves 1940- English footballer

Television is simultaneously blamed, often by the same people, for worsening the world and for being powerless to change it.

Clive James 1939- Australian critic and writer

Television has proved that people will look at anything rather than each other.

Ann Landers 1918-2002 American advice columnist

I find television very educational. Every time someone switches it on I go into another room and read a good book.

Groucho Marx 1890-1977 American film comedian

Television? The word is half Greek, half Latin. No good can come of it.

C. P. Scott 1846-1932 British journalist

The media. It sounds like a convention of spiritualists.

Tom Stoppard 1937- British dramatist

Never miss a chance to have sex or appear on television.

Gore Vidal 1925-2012 American novelist and critic

of television:

It used to be that we in films were the lowest form of art. Now we have something to look down on.

Billy Wilder 1906-2002 American screenwriter and director

Tennis ✍

I call tennis the McDonald's of sport—you go in, they make a quick buck out of you, and you're out.

Pat Cash 1965- Australian tennis player

New Yorkers love it when you spill your guts out there. Spill your guts at Wimbledon and they make you stop and clean it up.

Jimmy Connors 1952- American tennis player

The depressing thing about tennis is that no matter how good I get, I'll never be as good as a wall.

Mitch Hedberg 1968-2005 American comedian

You cannot be serious!

John McEnroe 1959- American tennis player

I threw the kitchen sink at him, but he went to the bathroom and got his tub.

Andy Roddick 1982- American tennis player, *defeated by Roger Federer in the Wimbledon Final, 2004*

 The Theatre

see also ACTING, AUDIENCES

Shaw's plays are the price we pay for Shaw's prefaces.
  James Agate 1877-1947 British drama critic and novelist

YOUNG ACTOR: Did Hamlet actually sleep with Ophelia?
OLD ACTOR: I don't know about the West End, laddie, but
we always did on tour.
  Anonymous

God, send me some good actors. Cheap.
  Lilian Baylis 1874-1937 English theatre manager

*on being asked 'What was the message of your play' after a
performance of* The Hostage:

Message? Message? What the hell do you think I am, a
bloody postman?
  Brendan Behan 1923-64 Irish dramatist

I go to the theatre to be entertained, I want to be taken out
of myself, I don't want to see lust and rape and incest and
sodomy and so on, I can get all that at home.
  Alan Bennett 1934- English dramatist and actor and **others**

Anyone can do theatre. Even actors. And theatre can be
done everywhere. Even in a theatre.
  Augusto Boal 1931-2009 Brazilian theatre director

Shut up, Arnold, or I'll direct this play the way you
wrote it!
  John Dexter 1925-90 English director, *to the playwright Arnold
  Wesker*

after a play about Napoleon had failed:

Never, never, will I do another play where a guy writes with a feather.

Max Gordon 1892–1978 American Broadway producer

The difficulty about a theatre job is that it interferes with party-going.

Barry Humphries 1934– Australian actor and writer

Satire is what closes Saturday night.

George S. Kaufman 1889–1961 American dramatist

stage direction to any new cast he worked with:

Stand upstage of me and do your worst.

Edmund Kean c.1787–1833 English actor

A play in which nothing happens, twice.

Vivian Mercier 1919–89 Irish literary historian, *reviewing* Waiting for Godot

Don't clap too hard—it's a very old building.

John Osborne 1929–94 English dramatist

It is better to have written a damned play, than no play at all—it snatches a man from obscurity.

Frederic Reynolds 1764–1841 English dramatist

You've got to perform in a role hundreds of times. In keeping it fresh one can become a large, madly humming, demented refrigerator.

Ralph Richardson 1902–83 English actor

In the old days, you went from ingénue to old bag with a long stretch of unemployment in between.

    Julie Walters 1950- British actress

Musical comedy is the Irish stew of drama. Anything may be put into it, with the certainty that it will improve the general effect.

    P. G. Wodehouse 1881–1975 English-born writer

😄 Time

This must be Thursday. I never could get the hang of Thursdays.

    Douglas Adams 1952–2001 English science fiction writer

Time is an illusion. Lunchtime doubly so.

    Douglas Adams 1952–2001 English science fiction writer

I do love deadlines. I love the whooshing sound they make as they go past.

    Douglas Adams 1952–2001 English science fiction writer

And meanwhile time goes about its immemorial work of making everyone look and feel like shit.

    Martin Amis 1949- English novelist

on receiving an invitation for 9 a.m.:

Oh, are there two nine o'clocks in the day?

    Tallulah Bankhead 1903-68 American actress

to an effusive greeting 'I haven't seen you for 41 years':

I thought I told you to wait in the car.

    Tallulah Bankhead 1903-68 American actress

VLADIMIR: That passed the time.
ESTRAGON: It would have passed in any case.
VLADIMIR: Yes, but not so rapidly.

Samuel Beckett 1906-89 Irish dramatist, novelist, and poet

Life is too short to stuff a mushroom.

Shirley Conran 1932- English writer

An hour sitting with a pretty girl on a park bench passes like a minute, but a minute sitting on a hot stove seems like an hour.

Albert Einstein 1879-1955 German-born theoretical physicist, *explaining relativity*

We have passed a lot of water since then.

Sam Goldwyn 1882-1974 American film producer

Morning comes whether you set the alarm or not.

Ursula K. Le Guin 1929-2018 American writer

Time spent on any item of the agenda will be in inverse proportion to the sum involved.

C. Northcote Parkinson 1909-93 English writer

Three o'clock is always too late or too early for anything you want to do.

Jean-Paul Sartre 1905-80 French philosopher

Eternity's a terrible thought. I mean, where's it all going to end?

Tom Stoppard 1937- British dramatist

to a man in the street, carrying a grandfather clock:
My poor fellow, why not carry a watch?
   Herbert Beerbohm Tree 1852–1917 English actor-manager

😄 Towns and Cities

I passed through Glasgow on my way here and couldn't help noticing how different it was from Venice.
   Raymond Asquith 1878–1916 English lawyer

One has no great hopes from Birmingham. I always say there is something direful in the sound.
   Jane Austen 1775–1817 English novelist

Come, friendly bombs, and fall on Slough!
It isn't fit for humans now.
   John Betjeman 1906–84 English poet

Venice is like eating an entire box of chocolate liqueurs in one go.
   Truman Capote 1924–84 American writer

A big hard-boiled city with no more personality than a paper cup.
   Raymond Chandler 1888–1959 American writer, *of Los Angeles*

This is Soho, where anything goes, just make sure it's not your wallet.
   Len Deighton 1929– English writer

Last week, I went to Philadelphia, but it was closed.
   W. C. Fields 1880–1946 American humorist

They used to say that Cambridge was the first stopping place for the wind that swept down from the Urals: in the thirties that was as true of the politics as the weather.

Stephen Fry 1957- English comedian, actor, and writer

The people of Berlin are doing very exciting things with their city at the moment. Basically they had this idea of just knocking it through.

Stephen Fry 1957- and **Hugh Laurie** 1959-

Liverpool, though not very delightful as a place of residence, is a most convenient and admirable point to get away from.

Nathaniel Hawthorne 1804-64 American novelist

Taunton is no longer a one-horse town; these days, they have a bicycle as well.

Tom Holt 1961- English novelist

When a man is tired of London, he is tired of life; for there is in London all that life can afford.

Samuel Johnson 1709-84 English lexicographer

According to legend, Telford is so dull that the bypass was built before the town.

Victor Lewis-Smith British television producer

A car is useless in New York, essential everywhere else. The same with good manners.

Mignon McLaughlin 1913-83 American writer

sitting in a New York bar in the 1940s:

Oh, to be back in Hollywood, wishing I was back in New York.

Herman J. Mankiewicz 1897-1953 American screenwriter

When it's three o'clock in New York, it's still 1938 in London.

Bette Midler 1945- American actress

Saigon is like all the other great modern cities of the world. It's the mess left over from people getting rich.

P. J. O'Rourke 1947- American humorous writer

City of perspiring dreams.

Frederic Raphael 1931- British novelist, *of Cambridge*

Toronto is a kind of New York operated by the Swiss.

Peter Ustinov 1921-2004 British actor

☺ Transport

Railways and the Church have their critics, but both are the best ways of getting a man to his ultimate destination.

Revd W. Awdry 1911-97 English writer of children's books

Q: If Mrs Thatcher were run over by a bus...?
LORD CARRINGTON: It wouldn't dare.

Lord Carrington 1919- British Conservative politician

The only way of catching a train I ever discovered is to miss the train before.

G. K. Chesterton 1874-1936 English essayist, novelist, and poet

I prefer to travel on French ships because there is none of that 'women and children first' nonsense.

Noël Coward 1899-1973 English dramatist, actor, and composer

Sir, Saturday morning, although recurring at regular and well-foreseen intervals, always seems to take this railway by surprise.

W. S. Gilbert 1836-1911 English writer

There is *nothing*—absolutely nothing—half so much worth doing as simply messing about in boats.

Kenneth Grahame 1859-1932 Scottish-born writer

seeing the Morris Minor prototype in 1945:

It looks like a poached egg—we can't make that.

Lord Nuffield 1877-1963 British motor manufacturer and philanthropist

What is better than presence of mind in a railway accident? Absence of body.

Punch 1841-1992 English humorous weekly periodical

I don't even like *old* cars. I mean they don't even interest me. I'd rather have a goddam horse. A horse is at least *human*, for God's sake.

J. D. Salinger 1919-2010 American novelist and short-story writer

Walk! Not bloody likely. I am going in a taxi.

George Bernard Shaw 1856-1950 Irish dramatist

😃 Travel

A trip is what you take when you can't take any more of what you've been taking.
  Adeline Ainsworth

In America there are two classes of travel—first class, and with children.
  Robert Benchley 1889-1945 American humorist

The longer the cruise, the older the passengers.
  Peg Bracken 1918-2007 American writer

Polar exploration is at once the cleanest and most isolated way of having a bad time which has been devised.
  Apsley Cherry-Garrard 1882-1959 English polar explorer

They say travel broadens the mind; but you must have the mind.
  G. K. Chesterton 1874-1936 English essayist, novelist, and poet

on his arrival in Turkey:
I am of course known here as English Delight.
  Noël Coward 1899-1973 English dramatist, actor, and composer

Like all great travellers, I have seen more than I remember, and remember more than I have seen.
  Benjamin Disraeli 1804-81 British Tory statesman and novelist

At my age travel broadens the behind.
  Stephen Fry 1957- English comedian, actor, and writer

Abroad is bloody.
  George VI 1895-1952 British king

on the Giant's Causeway:

Worth seeing, yes; but not worth going to see.

Samuel Johnson 1709-84 English lexicographer

If you look like your passport photo, you're too ill to travel.

Will Kommen

What good is speed if the brain has oozed out on the way?

Karl Kraus 1874-1936 Austrian satirist

Thanks to the interstate highway system, it is now possible to travel from coast to coast without seeing anything.

Charles Kuralt 1934-97 American journalist and broadcaster

I wouldn't mind seeing China if I could come back the same day.

Philip Larkin 1922-85 English poet

on seasickness:

At first, you fear you will die; then, after it has a good hold on you, you fear you won't die.

Jack London 1876-1916 American novelist

A sure cure for seasickness is to sit under a tree.

Spike Milligan 1918-2002 Irish comedian

She said that all the sights in Rome were called after London cinemas.

Nancy Mitford 1904-73 English writer

The Devil himself had probably re-designed Hell in the light of information he had gained from observing airport layouts.

Anthony Price 1928- English writer and editor

All my wife has ever taken from the Mediterranean—from that whole vast intuitive culture—are four bottles of Chianti to make into lamps.

Peter Shaffer 1926-2016 English dramatist

If it's Tuesday, this must be Belgium.

David Shaw

asked why he had come to America:

In pursuit of my life-long quest for naked women in wet mackintoshes.

Dylan Thomas 1914-53 Welsh poet

J. M. BARRIE: What was your most dangerous journey?
THOMSON: Crossing Piccadilly Circus.

Joseph Thomson 1858-94 Scottish explorer

It is not worthwhile to go around the world to count the cats in Zanzibar.

Henry David Thoreau 1817-62 American writer

It used to be a good hotel, but that proves nothing—I used to be a good boy.

Mark Twain 1835-1910 American writer

😀 Trust and Treachery

The only recorded instance in history of a rat swimming *towards* a sinking ship.

Winston Churchill 1874-1965 British Conservative statesman, *of a former Conservative who proposed to stand as a Liberal*

Pension. Pay given to a state hireling for treason to his country.
   Samuel Johnson 1709-84 English poet, critic, and lexicographer

Defectors are like grapes. The first pressings from them are the best. The third and fourth lack body.
   Maurice Oldfield 1915-81 English intelligence officer

Never take a reference from a clergyman. They always want to give someone a second chance.
   Lady Selborne 1858-1950 English suffragist

[Treason], Sire, is a question of dates.
   Charles-Maurice de Talleyrand 1754-1838 French statesman

Truth
see also LIES

'Tis strange—but true; for truth is always strange;
Stranger than fiction.
   Lord Byron 1788-1824 English poet

Our old friend...economical with the *actualité*.
   Alan Clark 1928-99 British Conservative politician

It is always the best policy to speak the truth—unless, of course, you are an exceptionally good liar.
   Jerome K. Jerome 1859-1927 English writer

I never give them [the public] hell. I just tell the truth, and they think it is hell.
   Harry S. Truman 1884-1972 American Democratic statesman

Get your facts first, and then you can distort 'em as much as you please.
Mark Twain 1835-1910 American writer

The truth is rarely pure, and never simple.
Oscar Wilde 1854-1900 Irish dramatist and poet

😄 Unintended Humour

I am the Jesus Christ of politics...I sacrifice myself for everyone.
Silvio Berlusconi 1936- Italian statesman

When I have my photo taken, I don't say 'cheese'. I say 'sex'.
Carla Bruni 1967- Italian-French singer and model

talking about Ronald Reagan:
I'm proud to be his partner. We've had triumphs, we've made mistakes, we've had sex.
George Bush 1924- American Republican statesman, *quickly corrected to 'setbacks, we've had setbacks'*

I know the human being and fish can coexist peacefully.
George W. Bush 1946- American Republican statesman

Our enemies are innovative and resourceful, and so are we. They never stop thinking about new ways to harm our country and our people, and neither do we.
George W. Bush 1946- American Republican statesman

That's the fastest time ever run—but it's not as fast as the world record.

David Coleman 1926-2013 British sports commentator

All my concerts had no sounds in them: they were completely silent…People had to make their own music in their minds.

Yoko Ono 1933- Japanese poet and songwriter

Having committed political suicide, the Conservative Party is now living to regret it.

Chris Patten 1944- British Conservative politician

I think that gay marriage is something that should be between a man and a woman.

Arnold Schwarzenegger 1947- Austrian-born American actor and Republican politician

I can't see who's in the lead but it's either Oxford or Cambridge.

John Snagge 1904-96 English sports commentator, *on the Boat Race*

I don't have time to sit down and write. When I think of a melody, I call my answering machine and sing it.

Britney Spears 1981- American pop singer

We have become a grandmother.

Margaret Thatcher 1925-2013 British Conservative stateswoman

I think I'm much more humble than you would understand.

Donald Trump 1946- American businessman and Republican statesman

☺ The Universe

Had I been present at the Creation, I would have given some useful hints for the better ordering of the universe.

Alfonso, King of Castile 1221-84

After one look at this planet any visitor from outer space would say 'I WANT TO SEE THE MANAGER'.

William S. Burroughs 1914-97 American novelist

Now, my own suspicion is that the universe is not only queerer than we suppose, but queerer than we *can* suppose.

J. B. S. Haldane 1892-1964 Scottish mathematical biologist

Space isn't remote at all. It's only an hour's drive away if your car could go straight upwards.

Fred Hoyle 1915-2001 English astrophysicist

I don't think there's intelligent life on other planets. Why should other planets be any different from this one?

Bob Monkhouse 1928-2003 English entertainer

Space is almost infinite. As a matter of fact, we think it is infinite.

Dan Quayle 1947- American Republican politician

Sometimes I think the surest sign that intelligent life exists elsewhere in the universe is that none of it has tried to contact us.

Bill Watterson 1958- American cartoonist

Virtue and Vice

see also **MORALITY**

Most plain girls are virtuous because of the scarcity of opportunity to be otherwise.

Maya Angelou 1928-2014 American writer

I'm as pure as the driven slush.

Tallulah Bankhead 1903-68 American actress

Lead me not into temptation; I can find the way myself.

Rita Mae Brown 1944- American novelist and poet

The louder he talked of his honour, the faster we counted our spoons.

Ralph Waldo Emerson 1803-82 American philosopher and poet

Of the seven deadly sins, only envy is no fun at all.

Joseph Epstein 1937- American writer

If you resolve to give up smoking, drinking and loving, you don't actually live longer, it just seems longer.

Clement Freud 1924-2009 English politician, broadcaster, and writer

But if he does really think that there is no distinction between virtue and vice, why, Sir, when he leaves our houses, let us count our spoons.

Samuel Johnson 1709-84 English poet, critic, and lexicographer

Virtue and Vice

He that but looketh on a plate of ham and eggs to lust after it, hath already committed breakfast with it in his heart.

C. S. Lewis 1898-1963 English literary scholar and writer

The problem with people who have no vices is that generally you can be pretty sure they're going to have some pretty annoying virtues.

Elizabeth Taylor 1932-2011 English-born American actress

When I'm good, I'm very, very good, but when I'm bad, I'm better.

Mae West 1892-1980 American film actress

I used to be Snow White...but I drifted.

Mae West 1892-1980 American film actress

Between two evils, I always pick the one I never tried before.

Mae West 1892-1980 American film actress

To err is human—but it feels divine.

Mae West 1892-1980 American film actress

Charity, dear Miss Prism, charity! None of us are perfect. I myself am peculiarly susceptible to draughts.

Oscar Wilde 1854-1900 Irish dramatist and poet

I can resist everything except temptation.

Oscar Wilde 1854-1900 Irish dramatist and poet

A little sincerity is a dangerous thing, and a great deal of it is absolutely fatal.

Oscar Wilde 1854-1900 Irish dramatist and poet

Wales

It profits a man nothing to give his soul for the whole world . . . But for Wales—!

Robert Bolt 1924–95 English dramatist

I am Anglo Welsh. My grandparents were Anglo Welsh. My parents were Anglo Welsh; indeed my parents burned down their own cottage.

Gyles Brandreth 1948– English writer and broadcaster

The land of my fathers. My fathers can have it.

Dylan Thomas 1914–53 Welsh poet

'I often think,' he continued, 'that we can trace almost all the disasters of English history to the influence of Wales!'

Evelyn Waugh 1903–66 English novelist

War

see also ARMED FORCES

DAVID MITCHELL: War is never a picnic. Although obviously soldiers do end up eating outdoors a lot.

Jesse Armstrong and **Sam Bain** 1971– British screenwriters, *in* Peep Show

Well, if you knows of a better 'ole, go to it.

Bruce Bairnsfather 1888–1959 British cartoonist

We need a futile gesture at this stage. It will raise the whole tone of the war.

Peter Cook 1937–95 English comedian and actor

There never was a good war, or a bad peace.

Benjamin Franklin 1706-90 American politician, inventor, and scientist

I'd like to see the government get out of war altogether and leave the whole field to private industry.

Joseph Heller 1923-99 American novelist

to George VI, summer 1940:

All the same, sir, I would put some of the colonies in your wife's name.

Joseph Herman Hertz 1872-1946 Slovakian-born British chief rabbi

of war in Iraq:

Vietnam without the mosquitoes.

Carl Hiaasen 1953- American writer

I think from now on they're shooting without a script.

George S. Kaufman 1889-1961 American dramatist, *on the German invasion of Russia*

All castles had one major weakness. The enemy used to get in through the gift shop.

Peter Kay 1973- British comedian

If we'd had as many soldiers as that, we'd have won the war!

Margaret Mitchell 1900-49 American novelist, *on seeing the number of Confederate troops in* Gone with the Wind

The quickest way of ending a war is to lose it.

George Orwell 1903-50 English novelist

Sometime they'll give a war and nobody will come.
Carl Sandburg 1878-1967 American poet

Retreat, hell! We're only attacking in another direction.
Oliver P. Smith 1893-1977 American general

asked his impression of his first battle:
Like German opera, too long and too loud.
Evelyn Waugh 1903-66 English novelist

As Lord Chesterfield said of the generals of his day, 'I only hope that when the enemy reads the list of their names, he trembles as I do.'
Duke of Wellington 1769-1852 British soldier and statesman, *usually quoted 'I don't know what effect these men will have upon the enemy, but, by God, they frighten me'*

Wealth

see also MONEY, POVERTY

If you would know what the Lord God thinks of money, you have only to look at those to whom he gives it.
Maurice Baring 1874-1945 British writer

People say I wasted my money. I say 90 per cent went on women, fast cars and booze. The rest I wasted.
George Best 1946-2005 Northern Irish footballer

A very rich person should leave his kids enough to do anything but not enough to do nothing.
Warren Buffett 1930- American businessman

I really love having money, because it lets me be lazy.
Work's really overrated.
Charlotte Church 1986- Welsh soprano

£40,000 a year [is] a moderate income—such a one as a
man might jog on with.
Lord Durham 1792-1840 English Whig politician

A rich man is nothing but a poor man with money.
W. C. Fields 1880-1946 American humorist

The meek shall inherit the earth, but not the mineral
rights.
John Paul Getty 1892-1976 American industrialist

Wealth—any income that is at least $100 more a year than
the income of one's wife's sister's husband.
H. L. Mencken 1880-1956 American journalist and literary critic

The average millionaire is only the average dishwasher
dressed in a new suit.
George Orwell 1903-50 English novelist

I am a Millionaire. That is my religion.
George Bernard Shaw 1856-1950 Irish dramatist

It is the wretchedness of being rich that you have to live
with rich people.
Logan Pearsall Smith 1865-1946 American-born man of letters

I've been poor and I've been rich—rich is better.
Sophie Tucker 1884-1966 Russian-born American vaudeville
artist

MARILYN MONROE: Real diamonds! They must be worth their weight in gold.

Billy Wilder 1906–2002 and **I. A. L. Diamond** 1915–88 screenwriters, *in the film* Some Like it Hot

I am grateful for the blessings of wealth, but it hasn't changed who I am. My feet are still on the ground. I'm just wearing better shoes.

Oprah Winfrey 1954– American talk-show host

The Weather

The English winter—ending in July,
To recommence in August.

Lord Byron 1788–1824 English poet

Summer has set in with its usual severity.

Samuel Taylor Coleridge 1772–1834 English poet, critic, and philosopher

to his cat, who disliked rain:

I know what's wrong, my dear, but I really do not know how to turn it off.

Albert Einstein 1879–1955 German-born theoretical physicist

There is no such thing as bad weather, only inappropriate clothing.

Ranulph Fiennes 1944– English explorer

A woman rang to say she heard there was a hurricane on the way. Well don't worry, there isn't.

Michael Fish 1944– British weather forecaster, *weather forecast on the night before catastrophic gales in southern England*

The weather is like the Government, always in the wrong.
Jerome K. Jerome 1859-1927 English writer

When two Englishmen meet, their first talk is of the weather.
Samuel Johnson 1709-84 English poet, critic, and lexicographer

The most serious charge which can be brought against New England is not Puritanism but February.
Joseph Wood Krutch 1893-1970 American critic and naturalist

It was such a lovely day I thought it was a pity to get up.
W. Somerset Maugham 1874-1965 English novelist

Thank heavens, the sun has gone in, and I don't have to go out and enjoy it.
Logan Pearsall Smith 1865-1946 American-born man of letters

It was the wrong kind of snow.
Terry Worrall British spokesman for British Rail, *explaining disruption on British Rail*

Weddings
see also MARRIAGE

If it were not for the presents, an elopement would be preferable.
George Ade 1866-1944 American humorist and dramatist

Egghead weds hourglass.
Anonymous, *on the marriage of Arthur Miller and Marilyn Monroe*

to guests as they arrived at the reception given for a smart society wedding:

Don't go upstairs. The bride's hideous.

Margot Asquith 1864–1945 British political hostess

It's pretty easy. Just say 'I do' whenever anyone asks you a question.

Richard Curtis 1956– British comedy scriptwriter, *advice to a prospective bridegroom, in the film* Four Weddings and a Funeral

We had a civil ceremony—his mother couldn't come.

Phyllis Diller 1917–2012 American actress, *on her wedding*

A bride's attitude towards her betrothed can be summed up in three words: Aisle. Altar. Hymn.

Frank Muir 1920–98 English writer and broadcaster

In olden times sacrifices were made at the altar—a custom which is still continued.

Helen Rowland 1875–1950 American writer

You can always surprise your husband on your anniversary just by mentioning it.

Al Schock 1920–2009 American businessman

Wine

see also CHAMPAGNE, DRINK

of claret:

It would be port if it could.

Richard Bentley 1662–1742 English classical scholar

when the Queen accepted a second glass of wine at lunch:
Do you think it's wise, darling? You know you've got to rule this afternoon.

Queen Elizabeth, the Queen Mother 1900-2002

I cook with wine, sometimes I even add it to food.

W. C. Fields 1880-1946 American humorist

A good general rule is to state that the bouquet is better than the taste, and vice versa.

Stephen Potter 1900-69 British writer, *on wine-tasting*

It's the old wine ramp, vicar! Cheapish, reddish and Spanish.

Tom Stoppard 1937- British dramatist

It's a naïve domestic Burgundy without any breeding, but I think you'll be amused by its presumption.

James Thurber 1894-1961 American humorist

Poor wine at the table of a rich host is an insult without an apology.

Johann Georg Zimmerman 1728-95 Swiss physician and writer

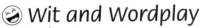 Wit and Wordplay
see also HUMOUR, PUNS

review of the film musical You Were Meant For Me:
That's what you think.

James Agee 1909-55 American writer

version of an old joke:

VICTOR LEWIS SMITH: You clearly don't know the difference between a Joist and a Girder.
IRISH BUILDER: Yes I do. Joist wrote Ulysses and Girder wrote Faust.

Anonymous

My problem was that I was always missing. Miss World, Miss England, Miss UK...

George Best 1946-2005 Northern Irish footballer

I'm a trisexual. I'll try anything once.

Jenny Bicks

on being told he should not marry anyone as plain as his fiancée:
My dear fellow, buggers can't be choosers.

Maurice Bowra 1898-1971 English scholar and literary critic

Wit ought to be a glorious treat, like caviar. It should be served in small elegant portions; never spread it about like marmalade.

Noël Coward 1899-1973 English dramatist, actor, and composer

to an author who had presented him with an unwelcome book:
Many thanks. I shall lose no time in reading it.

Benjamin Disraeli 1804-81 British Tory statesman and novelist

to a footman who had accidentally spilt cream over him:
My good man, I'm not a strawberry!

Edward VII 1841-1910 British king

I can answer you in two words, im-possible.

Sam Goldwyn 1882-1974 American film producer

cannibal Hannibal Lecter:

ANTHONY HOPKINS: I do wish we could chat longer, but I'm having an old friend for dinner.

Thomas Harris 1940- and **Ted Tally** 1952- screenwriters, *in the film* The Silence of the Lambs

Dentist fills wrong cavity.

Ben Hecht 1894-1964 American screenwriter, *report of a dentist convicted of interfering with a patient*

Lisp: to call a spade a thpade.

Oliver Herford 1863-1935 American humorist

I am trisexual. The Army, the Navy, and the Household Cavalry.

Brian Desmond Hurst 1895-1986 Irish film director

'*Succès d'estime*' translates as 'a success that ran out of steam'.

George S. Kaufman 1889-1961 American dramatist

MARGARET IRVING: That's bigamy.
GROUCHO MARX: Yes, and it's big of me, too.

George S. Kaufman 1889-1961 and **Morrie Ryskind** 1895-1985 screenwriters, *in the film* Animal Crackers

The first thing I do in the morning is brush my teeth and sharpen my tongue.

Oscar Levant 1906-72 American pianist

DANNY KAYE: The pellet with the poison's in the vessel with the pestle. The chalice from the palace has the brew that is true.

Norman Panama 1914-2003 and **Melvin Frank** 1913-88 American screenwriters, *in the film* The Court Jester

*to the British actor Herbert Marshall who annoyed her by repeated
references to his busy 'shedule':*

I think you're full of skit.

Dorothy Parker 1893-1967 American critic and humorist

You beat your pate, and fancy wit will come:
Knock as you please, there's nobody at home.

Alexander Pope 1688-1744 English poet

Comparisons are odorous.

William Shakespeare 1564-1616 English dramatist

MRS MALAPROP: He is the very pineapple of politeness!

Richard Brinsley Sheridan 1751-1816 Irish dramatist and
Whig politician

MRS MALAPROP: No caparisons, Miss, if you please!—
Caparisons don't become a young woman.

Richard Brinsley Sheridan 1751-1816 Irish dramatist and Whig
politician

MRS MALAPROP: She's as headstrong as an allegory on the
banks of the Nile.

Richard Brinsley Sheridan 1751-1816 Irish dramatist and Whig
politician

LADY SNEERWELL: There's no possibility of being witty
without a little ill-nature; the malice of a good thing is the
barb that makes it stick.

Richard Brinsley Sheridan 1751-1816 Irish dramatist and Whig
politician

Wit and Wordplay

on seeing Mrs Grote in a huge rose-coloured turban:

Now I know the meaning of the word 'grotesque'.

Sydney Smith 1771-1845 English clergyman and essayist

a toast:

To our queer old dean.

William Archibald Spooner 1844-1930 English academic

to an undergraduate:

You have tasted your worm, you have hissed my mystery
lectures, and you must leave by the first town drain.

William Archibald Spooner 1844-1930 English academic

To those waiting with bated breath for that favourite
media catchphrase, the U-turn, I have only this to say.
'You turn if you want to; the lady's not for turning.'

Margaret Thatcher 1925-2013 British Conservative
stateswoman

When you see the sign 'African Primates Meeting' you
expect someone to produce bananas.

Desmond Tutu 1931- South African Anglican clergyman

I'm on the horns of a Dalai Lama.

Dick Vosburgh 1929-2007 American writer

OSCAR WILDE: How I wish I had said that.
WHISTLER: You will, Oscar, you will.

James McNeill Whistler 1834-1903 American-born painter

I thought coq au vin was love in a lorry.

Victoria Wood 1953-2016 British writer and comedienne

Wives

see also MARRIAGE

Many a man owes his success to his first wife and his
second wife to his success.

Jim Backus 1913-89 American actor

Here lies my wife; here let her lie!
Now she's at peace and so am I.

John Dryden 1631-1700 English poet, critic, and dramatist

The comfortable estate of widowhood, is the only hope
that keeps up a wife's spirits.

John Gay 1685-1732 English poet and dramatist

When you marry your mistress you create a job vacancy.

James Goldsmith 1933-97 British financier and politician

Only two things are necessary to keep one's wife happy.
One is to let her think she is having her own way, and the
other, to let her have it.

Lyndon Baines Johnson 1908-73 American Democratic
statesman

There's nothing like a good dose of another woman to
make a man appreciate his wife.

Clare Booth Luce 1903-87 American diplomat, politician,
and writer

Who was that lady I saw you with last night?
She ain't no lady; she's my wife.

Joe Weber 1867-1942 and **Lew Fields** 1867-1941 American
comedians

Twenty years of romance make a woman look like a ruin; but twenty years of marriage make her something like a public building.

Oscar Wilde 1854-1900 Irish dramatist and poet

Marriage is a bribe to make a housekeeper think she's a householder.

Thornton Wilder 1897-1975 American novelist and dramatist

There are men who fear repartee in a wife more keenly than a sword.

P. G. Wodehouse 1881-1975 English writer

 # Women and Woman's Role

see also FEMINISM, MEN AND WOMEN

We women do talk too much, but even then we don't tell half we know.

Nancy Astor 1879-1964 American-born British Conservative politician

I believe a woman's place is in the home—or anyway in some cosy nightclub.

Lucille Ball 1911-89 American actress

Women complain about premenstrual syndrome, but I think of it as the only time of the month I can be myself.

Roseanne Barr 1952- American comedienne and actress

A woman who looks like a girl and thinks like a man is the best sort, the most enjoyable to be and the most pleasurable to have and to hold.

Julie Burchill 1960- English journalist and writer

The trouble with some women is that they get all excited about nothing—and then marry him.

Cher 1946- American singer and actress

A woman needs a man like a fish needs a bicycle.

Irina Dunn 1948- Australian writer and politician

Women are like elephants to me; I like to look at them, but I wouldn't want to own one.

W. C. Fields 1880-1946 American humorist

She had the loaded handbag of someone who camps out and seldom goes home.

Mavis Gallant 1922-2014 Canadian writer

Nothing is ever so wrong in this world that a sensible woman can't set it right in the course of an afternoon.

Jean Giraudoux 1882-1944 French dramatist

The Conservative Establishment has always treated women as nannies, grannies and fannies.

Teresa Gorman 1931-2015 British Conservative politician

Every woman should have four pets in her life: a mink in her closet, a Jaguar in her garage, a tiger in her bed and a jackass who pays for everything.

Paris Hilton 1981- American heiress

A woman's preaching is like a dog's walking on his hinder legs. It is not done well; but you are surprised to find it done at all.

Samuel Johnson 1709-84 English poet, critic, and lexicographer

GROUCHO MARX: Remember, you're fighting for this woman's honour…which is probably more than she ever did.

Bert Kalmar 1884-1947 and **others** screenwriters, *in the film* Duck Soup

Being a woman is of special interest only to aspiring male transsexuals. To actual women, it is merely a good excuse not to play football.

Fran Lebowitz 1950- American writer

You know that look women get when they want to have sex? Me neither.

Steve Martin 1945- American comedian

The lady doth protest too much, methinks.

William Shakespeare 1564-1616 English dramatist

The fickleness of the women I love is only equalled by the infernal constancy of the women who love me.

George Bernard Shaw 1856-1950 Irish dramatist

A woman seldom writes her mind but in her postscript.

Richard Steele 1672-1729 Irish-born essayist and dramatist

We are becoming the men we wanted to marry.

Gloria Steinem 1934- American journalist

There are worse occupations in this world than feeling a woman's pulse.

Laurence Sterne 1713-68 English novelist

She was a blonde—with a brunette past.

Gwyn Thomas 1913-81 Welsh novelist and dramatist

When once a woman has given you her heart, you can never get rid of the rest of her body.

John Vanbrugh 1664-1726 English architect and dramatist

You may admire a girl's curves on first introduction, but the second meeting shows up new angles.

Mae West 1892-1980 American film actress

Many a woman has a past, but I am told that she has at least a dozen, and that they all fit.

Oscar Wilde 1854-1900 Irish dramatist and poet

Wordplay
see WIT *and Wordplay*

Words
see also LANGUAGE

WOODY ALLEN: The most beautiful words in the English language are not 'I love you' but 'It's benign'.

Woody Allen 1935- American film director, writer, and actor, *in the film* Deconstructing Harry

It depends on what the meaning of 'is' is.

Bill Clinton 1946- American Democratic statesman, *evidence to the grand jury, when questioned in relation to Monica Lewinsky*

Euphemisms are unpleasant truths wearing diplomatic cologne.

Quentin Crisp 1908-99 English writer

Some word that teems with hidden meaning—like Basingstoke.

W. S. Gilbert 1836-1911 English writer

I had always assumed that Cliché was a suburb of Paris, until I discovered it to be a street in Oxford.

Philip Guedalla 1889-1944 British historian and biographer

It's a damn poor mind, indeed, which can't think of at least two ways to spell any word.

Andrew Jackson 1767-1845 American Democratic statesman

I understand your new play is full of single entendre.

George S. Kaufman 1889-1961 American dramatist

Avant-garde? That's the French for bullshit.

John Lennon 1940-80 English pop singer and songwriter

Hypochondria is Greek for 'men'.

Kathy Lette 1958- Australian writer

They say the definition of ambivalence is watching your mother-in-law drive over a cliff in your new Cadillac.

David Mamet 1947- American dramatist and director

The trouble with words is that you never know whose mouth they've been in.

Dennis Potter 1935-94 English television dramatist

Man does not live by words alone, despite the fact that he sometimes has to eat them.

Adlai Stevenson 1900-65 American Democratic politician

Work

see also HOLIDAYS

A professional is a man who can do his job when he doesn't feel like it. An amateur is a man who can't do his job when he does feel like it.

James Agate 1877–1947 British drama critic and novelist

Nothing is really work unless you would rather be doing something else.

J. M. Barrie 1860–1937 Scottish writer and dramatist

Oh you hate your job? Why didn't you say so? There's a support group for that. It's called EVERYBODY and they meet at the bar.

Drew Carey 1958– American comedian and actor

when criticized for continually arriving late for work:

But think how early I go.

Lord Castlerosse 1891–1943

Work is always so much more fun than fun.

Noël Coward 1899–1973 English dramatist, actor, and composer

I never work. Work does age you so.

Quentin Crisp 1908–99 English writer

By working faithfully eight hours a day, you may eventually get to be a boss and work twelve hours a day.

Robert Frost 1874–1963 American poet

I have long been of the opinion that if work were such a splendid thing the rich would have kept more of it for themselves.

Bruce Grocott 1940- British Labour politician

I like work: it fascinates me. I can sit and look at it for hours.

Jerome K. Jerome 1859-1927 English writer

There are so many things that we wish we had done yesterday, so few that we feel like doing today.

Mignon McLaughlin 1913-83 American writer

Work expands so as to fill the time available for its completion.

C. Northcote Parkinson 1909-93 English writer

It's true hard work never killed anybody, but I figure why take the chance?

Ronald Reagan 1911-2004 American Republican statesman

I have yet to hear a man ask for advice on how to combine marriage and a career.

Gloria Steinem 1934- American journalist

You learn a lot about yourself, doing physical work. And what I learned about myself was that I didn't like doing physical work.

Rod Stewart 1945- British pop singer and songwriter

Work is the curse of the drinking classes.

Oscar Wilde 1854-1900 Irish dramatist and poet

Writers

see also LITERATURE, POETS

Wanting to know an author because you like his work is like wanting to know a duck because you like pâté.

Margaret Atwood 1939- Canadian novelist

He's always backing into the limelight.

Lord Berners 1883-1950 English composer, artist, and writer, *of T. E. Lawrence*

of the vegetarian George Bernard Shaw:

If you give him meat no woman in London will be safe.

Mrs Patrick Campbell 1865-1940 English actress

Oh, Jack Kerouac—that isn't writing, it's typing.

Truman Capote 1924-84 American writer

A good storyteller is a person who has a good memory and hopes other people haven't.

Irvin S. Cobb 1876-1944 American writer

I love being a writer. What I can't stand is the paperwork.

Peter De Vries 1910-93 American novelist

An author who speaks about his own books is almost as bad as a mother who talks about her own children.

Benjamin Disraeli 1804-81 British Tory statesman and novelist

on Henry James:

He had a mind so fine no idea could violate it.

T. S. Eliot 1888-1965 American-born British poet, critic, and dramatist

The mama of dada.

    Clifton Fadiman 1904–99 American critic, *of Gertrude Stein*

The nicest old lady I ever met.

    William Faulkner 1897–1962 American novelist, *of Henry James*

The book of my enemy has been remaindered
And I rejoice.

    Clive James 1939– Australian critic and writer

Whatever Wells writes is not only alive, but kicking.

    Henry James 1843–1916 American novelist, *on H. G. Wells*

a young admirer had asked if he might kiss the hand that wrote Ulysses:
No, it did lots of other things too.

    James Joyce 1882–1941 Irish novelist

E. M. Forster never gets any further than warming the
teapot. He's a rare fine hand at that. Feel this teapot. Is it
not beautifully warm? Yes, but there ain't going to be
no tea.

    Katherine Mansfield 1888–1923 New Zealand-born short-story
    writer

The triumph of sugar over diabetes.

    George Jean Nathan 1882–1958 American critic, *of J. M. Barrie,*
    author of Peter Pan

Every author, however modest, keeps a most outrageous
vanity chained like a madman in the padded cell of his
breast.

    Logan Pearsall Smith 1865–1946 American-born man of letters

The shelf life of the modern hardback writer is somewhere between the milk and the yoghurt.

Calvin Trillin 1935- American journalist and writer

Truman made lying an art form—a minor art form.

Gore Vidal 1925-2012 American novelist and critic, *on Truman Capote*

What other culture could have produced someone like Hemingway and *not* seen the joke?

Gore Vidal 1925-2012 American novelist and critic

A magnificent but painful hippopotamus resolved at any cost, even at the cost of its dignity, upon picking up a pea which has got into a corner of its den.

H. G. Wells 1866-1946 English novelist, *of Henry James*

She is so odd a blend of Little Nell and Lady Macbeth.

Alexander Woollcott 1887-1943 American writer, *of Dorothy Parker*

Writing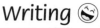

see also **BOOKS, LITERATURE, POETRY**

After being turned down by numerous publishers, he had decided to write for posterity.

George Ade 1866-1944 American humorist and dramatist

He writes so well, he makes me feel like putting my quill back in my goose.

Fred Allen 1894-1956 American humorist

If you can't annoy somebody with what you write, I think there's little point in writing.

Kingsley Amis 1922-95 English novelist and poet

A good novel tells us the truth about its hero; but a bad novel tells us the truth about its author.

G. K. Chesterton 1874-1936 English essayist, novelist, and poet

Writing a novel is like driving a car at night. You can see only as far as your headlights, but you can make the whole trip that way.

E. L. Doctorow 1931-2015 American novelist

I suppose most editors are failed writers—but so are most writers.

T. S. Eliot 1888-1965 Anglo-American poet, critic, and dramatist

to Edward Gibbon, author of The Decline and Fall of the Roman Empire:

Another damned, thick, square book! Always scribble, scribble, scribble! Eh! Mr Gibbon?

Duke of Gloucester 1743-1805

No man but a blockhead ever wrote, except for money.

Samuel Johnson 1709-84 English poet, critic, and lexicographer

'The cat sat on the mat' is not a story. 'The cat sat on the dog's mat' is a story.

John le Carré 1931- English thriller writer

Try to leave out the part that readers tend to skip.

Elmore Leonard 1925-2013 American thriller writer

If you steal from one author, it's plagiarism; if you steal from many, it's research.

Wilson Mizner 1876-1933 American dramatist

I'm glad you'll write,
You'll furnish paper when I shite.

Lady Mary Wortley Montagu 1689-1762 English writer

It is our national joy to mistake for the first-rate, the fecund rate.

Dorothy Parker 1893-1967 American critic and humorist

As to the Adjective: when in doubt, strike it out.

Mark Twain 1835-1910 American writer

Youth

see also **CHILDREN**

It is better to waste one's youth than to do nothing with it at all.

Georges Courteline 1858-1929 French writer and dramatist

Remember that as a teenager you are at the last stage in your life when you will be happy to hear that the phone is for you.

Fran Lebowitz 1950- American writer

It's all that the young can do for the old, to shock them and keep them up to date.

George Bernard Shaw 1856-1950 Irish dramatist

What music is more enchanting than the voices of young people, when you can't hear what they say?

Logan Pearsall Smith 1865-1946 American-born man of letters

The only way to stay young is to avoid old people.

James D. Watson 1928- American biologist

Being young is not having any money; being young is not minding not having any money.

Katharine Whitehorn 1928- English journalist

MORRIS AUTOMATED INFORMATION NETWORK

0 1004 0344543 8

For Reference

Not to be taken

from this library

MAY - - 2019